WARNING!
POISON MOONSHINE

... U. S. Government Laboratory tests disclose that Moonshine Whiskey often contains Poisonous lead salts. Continued drinking of Moonshine Whiskey may result in disability or death ...

U.S. TREASURY DEPARTMENT Internal Revenue Service

Document No. 5304 (12-60)
GPO: 1960 O - 576647

MOONSHINERS BOOTLEGGERS & RUMRUNNERS

Derek Nelson

Motorbooks International
Publishers & Wholesalers ®

First published in 1995 by Motorbooks International Publishers & Wholesalers, PO Box 2, 729 Prospect Avenue, Osceola, WI 54020 USA

We recognize that some words, model names and designations, for example, mentioned herein are the property of the trademark holder. We use them for identification purposes only. This is not an official publication

Motorbooks International books are also available at discounts in bulk quantity for industrial or sales-promotional use. For details write to Special Sales Manager at the Publisher's address

Library of Congress Cataloging-in-Publication Data
Nelson, Derek.
    Moonshiners, bootleggers, and rumrunners/ Derek Nelson.
        p. cm.
    Includes index.
    ISBN 0-87938-956-7 (pbk.)
    1. Distilling, Illicit—United States. 2. Liquors—Taxation—United States. I. Title.
    HJ5021.N44   1995
    364.1'33—dc20   95-5913

On the front cover: 1920s-era revenue agents with booty from a seized still. *Courtesy Georgia Department of Archives and History*

On the frontispiece: A government warning, circa 1960, to those who imbibed . . .

On the title page: Revenuers seizing a very large still in the early 1950s. *C. W. Herndon, Courtesy Georgia Department of Archives and History*

On the back cover: Top: Moonshiners sample the fruits of their labors. *Photographic Archives, Alice Lloyd College* Bottom: A rumrunner's booty goes overboard. *Sargent Memorial Room, Kirn Library, Norfolk*

Printed and bound in Hong Kong

Contents

Acknowledgments

Among the Nelson clan, foremost (as always) is my wife Mary, info sleuth extraordinaire, for her encouragement and advice, and for being the flawless parental backup system when I was on the road or plugged into the keyboard. My son, Nate, for his interest, enthusiasm, and sense of humor. My father, Glenn, for rooting out and sharing arcana, tidbits, and leads, and my mother, Donna, for pottery and support. My brother Kent (who, as biologist and sportsman, has delved deep into the Carolina woods) for his cronies and connections. Also to Bill Tetterton, former agent for the Bureau of Alcohol, Tobacco and Firearms in Norfolk. If everyone were as helpful as him, I could write fifty books a year.

Derek Nelson

Thanks to my editors at Motorbooks, Greg Field (who launched the project), and Zack Miller (who inherited it). Zack did a great job at weeding out the extraneous and controlling the almost overpowering sprawl of the draft. Katie Finney gets the credit for this book's excellent design.

Thanks also to the following fine folks, listed not by magnitude of helpfulness, but in alphabetic order:

Brooks Blevins, Ozark Oral Historian, The Ozark Folk Center Mountain View, Arkansas; Matt Brletich, Burnsville, Minnesota; Al Clark, editor of *The Daily Reflector*, Greenville, North Carolina, and staff photographer Cliff Hollis; Jim Clark of "The Andy Griffith Show" Rerun Watchers Club in Nashville, Tenn. If Sheriff Andy had to describe Jim's help, his verdict would be, "Outstandin'!" Tom Cotter, Cotter Communications, Charlotte, North Carolina; Tom Crew, curator of the Mariner's Museum, along with librarian Ben Trask and the staff of the library, Newport News, Virginia; Bryan Davis, Coinhog emeritus and magazine sleuth, Chesapeake, Virginia; Gail Deloach, prints archivist, Georgia Department of Archives and History, Atlanta, Georgia; and Judge Frank Eppes, Greenville, South Carolina.

Alex Gabbard, author and *Thunder Road* expert, Lenoir City, Tennessee; Allan Girdler, Rainbow, California, author of books and amusing correspondence; Eddie Gossage, Public Relations, Charlotte Motor Speedway; Fred Goswick, Marietta, Georgia; Tom Graham, Oral History Project, Alice Lloyd College, Pippa Passes, Kentucky; Howard L. Green, research director, New Jersey Historical Commission; Jess Grider, U.S. Marshall Service, Louisville, Kentucky; Carl Griffler and Sue Balwin, Interlibrary Loans, Kirn Library, Norfolk, Virginia; Peggy Haile, Sargeant Memorial Room, Kirn Library, Norfolk, Virginia; Dr. Bob Hart, Hickory, North Carolina; Dr. Keith Heim, Special Collections, Murray State University, Kentucky; Billy Henson, potter, South Carolina; special thanks also to Vicki Herrmann, librarian at ATF headquarters in Washington, D.C., a rare combination of cheerfulness and efficiency; Dawn Hugh, Curatorial Assistant, Research Center, The Historical Museum Metro-Dade Cultural Center, Miami, Florida; Jay Keehn, antique-auto ace, Norfolk, Virginia; Mary Jean Kinsman, Filson Club, Louisville, Kentucky; Ron Main, Canoga, California; Steve Massengill, North Carolina State Archives, Raleigh, North Carolina; W.K. McNeil, Folklorist, Ozark Folk Center, Mountain View, Arkansas; Peter Mersky, naval historian cum laude, Norfolk, Virginia; Connie Mills, Kentucky Library Coordinator, Western Kentucky University, Bowling Green, Kentucky; Jim and Kay Pice, Norfolk, Virginia; Diane Powers, Picture Collection, Mid-Manhattan Library, New York, New York; Bob Rihel, high-performance engine consultant, Norfolk, Virginia; Ginger Rives and her parents, Olen and Mary Williams of Bedford County, Virginia; Traci Scates, Executive Director, Dawson County Chamber of Commerce, Dawsonville, Georgia; Richard Schutz, records officer, Internal Revenue Service, Washington, D.C.; Bill Sherman, National Archives, Washington, D.C.; Peggy Simmons, News Research Department Library, *News and Observer Publishing Co.*, Raleigh, North Carolina; Edward D. Sloan, Jr., President, Greenville County Historical Society, Inc., Greenville, South Carolina; Gary Thompson, pottery collector, Greenville, South Carolina; Jim Ward, Greenville, North Carolina (happy birthday, Jim!); Charlie Weems, Luttrell, Tennessee; Lloyd Westlund, St. Croix Falls, Minnesota; Ronald Westphal, Program Coordinator, The Homeplace-1850, Golden Pond, Kentucky; Shannon Wilson, Special Collections, and Priscilla Tipton, public relations office manager, Berea College, Berea, Kentucky; and Phil Wingard, Clover, South Carolina.

Introduction

> When Gabriel blows his trumpet, there'll probably be men in Rockcastle County who can't come because they have to finish straining the mash.
> —William Bernard "Big Six" Henderson, as told to author Esther Kellner

This lithograph, produced by Strobridge & Company of Cincinnati, appears to be the label from legal whiskey (the brand name, "Old 76," is listed three times). The buckskinned hunter looks troubled, hardly what you'd suspect when surrounded by such an idyllic scene. The mash tubs are at the rear center; note the water pouring into the large condensing barrel at the far right, with the finished liquor going straight into the smaller, horizontal barrel that says "Old 76 Pure Fire Copper." *Library of Congress*

Of the first dozen people I told about this book, nine had stories about moonshine. This fact isn't a slur on my family, friends, and coworkers, who all seem to be law-abiding, prosperous citizens. Instead, it reflects the universality of America's love-hate relationship with Demon Rum and the Balm of Gilead.

My parents once sampled some moonshine at a relative's home in southwestern Pennsylvania. The host was a grocer who sold large amounts of sugar to the moonshiners, getting samples in return for this semi-legal courtesy. The liquor had been flavored with anisette. My dad said it was awful; my mom said it was okay if you liked licorice.

My brother, a regional biologist in North Carolina, got a jar of moonshine one Christmas from a hunting crony. It was smooth, clear, and strong—palatable, but nothing you'd risk getting arrested for.

One of my running partners, now a Navy flight surgeon, remembers coming across stills during Boy Scout hikes in Georgia. One still appeared defunct, the other seemed serviceable. In both cases, the leader rapidly shooed the Scouts away.

Several coworkers had anecdotes to tell. My secretary's parents live in Bedford County, Virginia, "the moonshine capital of the state," she said. When she lived at home and the topic of moonshine came up, her father refused to discuss it, though he seemed to know something about it. He insisted that he wasn't going to catch a bullet for blabbing. When she told him about my project, he had one question: "Does that boy want to get shot?"

A former boss has an uncle who bought a piece of property in the boondocks of Virginia. The first time they visited the property, a truck abruptly pulled out of the woods and blocked the access road ahead, and another truck pulled in behind. The truck drivers demanded to know the uncle's business; when they found out he owned the property, they told him they'd "keep an eye" on the place for him, and whenever he wanted to come visit, he'd best give them a call first.

Another coworker, born near Fairmont, West Virginia, remembered his grandfather telling him about his own distant moonshining days. Nobody had a car, so they'd have to walk into town with the product. To avoid getting caught, they rigged up a series of locust fence posts that were hollow so they could lift them up and hide a jar underneath, if they saw a revenuer or a sheriff.

This seizure, on January 28, 1931, was touted as the largest ever in New York State. It took place at the Hoffman Brewery in Kingston, New York, and featured a 10,000 gallon still. Including mash, liquor, and other equipment, authorities valued the seizure at $500,000. Four men were captured at the huge distillery. *National Archives*

These anecdotes and snippets reflect the fact that I've lived in Virginia for the past three decades; I'm sure that if I lived up north, I'd have equal numbers about bootleggers and rumrunners. They offer mere glimpses of a great American saga that began before the American revolution, reached a crescendo during the Prohibition era, and continues today.

The cast of characters includes Scotch-Irish immigrants, Revolutionary War heroes, blockade-runners, pirates, and hard-drinking pioneers; wealthy and vicious gangsters rub shoulders with devil-may-care adventurers and ludicrously incompetent amateurs.

The story winds through obscure places and famous cities, from the gray Atlantic seas of Rum Row to smoky Appalachian hollows, from pitch-dark dirt roads in Carolina to the blaring speakeasies of New York in the 1930s. What ties it all together is illicit liquor—cases, bags, bottles, and barrels of it—all aimed at fulfilling humanity's ancient quest for the easy buck and the rapid buzz.

The liquor—premium or rotgut, pure, watered, or "cut,"—flooded into, across, and around America. In 1924, two-thirds of the imported liquor came across the border from Canada, one-third from Rum Row (the nautical liquor bazaar that anchored just outside territorial limits during Prohibition). But in spite of the best efforts of our Canadian, British, French, and German allies, most of the illicit liquor swilled in speakeasies during Prohibition was distilled in the good old U.S.A. "Domestic production exceeded by a large percentage the amount available from outside the country—whether by land or sea routes," wrote Donald L. Canney in *Rum War: The U.S. Coast Guard and Prohibition*.

Unpopular laws didn't start with Prohibition, after all, and the response to them by large numbers of citizens has always been unanimous: to ignore them and circumvent them. At the end of the seventeenth century, the public's feelings toward pirates alternated between public approval and condemnation based on with whom the country was officially at war. With hostilities declared, as long as pirates confined their attention to the enemy, they were heroic privateers, officially sanctioned and rewarded. In peacetime, when they showed the same attention to domestic shipping, they reverted to being criminals and risked beheading.

Before and during the American Revolution, and during the War of 1812, getting contraband past the British blockades was a valuable public service. Bill McCoy, putative founder of Rum Row, cited John Hancock himself as the owner of a fleet of smuggling ships that brought tax-free Madeira wine into Boston.

During the Civil War, confederate blockade-runners were local heroes; moonshine transporters in the South were called "blockaders" for generations. In each case, the smugglers broke unpopular (and, to some people, unjustified) laws for the benefit of the oppressed. Even before the War Between the States, the 100-proof civil disobedience of moonshine was thoroughly enmeshed with the concepts of states rights and personal freedom, and the questions of who could levy taxes and why.

As a result, there is ample precedent for confusion between the usual definitions of hero and villain. As we trace the intertwining tales of moonshining, bootlegging, and rumrunning through the decades, we meet folks who blend inventiveness, optimism, greed, and persistence. The topic has spawned myths and legends that glorify scofflaws and enforcement agents alike. Classic anecdotes have dubious origins. Partly as a result, mystery and conundrum abound.

We Americans seem irresistibly drawn to outlaws. In our tales of the old West, the Dalton Gang and Jesse James command as much of the spotlight as the sheriffs and marshals, just as flashy mobsters would in the 1920s and 1930s. We can't seem to define "exploit,"

that fascinating blend of the daring, audacious, and illegal. When does it lose its allure and simply become a crime?

In April 1936, a reporter for the New Bedford *Standard-Times* interviewed some former rumrunners. He wrote, "Tales of danger, excitement and thrills roll off their tongues as easily as the latest weather discussion . . . Daredeviltry, nerve, seamanship—it was all a game with good pay for the successful." wrote Everett Allen in *The Black Ships: Rumrunners of Prohibition.* "To this day, America has not really decided whether the seagoing principals of this period were heroes, villains, or simply pawns of the larger circumstance, as are we all, to varying degrees."

You will decide for yourself. Along the way you'll find that this topic has generated a wealth of colorful jargon, so vivid and enjoyable that I've attached a small glossary. Word fanciers can browse the section at will, but because some crucial terms overlap, I'll define a few of the key ones here.

"Moonshine" is unlawfully distilled whiskey. American folklore pictures the moonshiner as a barefoot hillbilly wearing overalls and sporting a scraggly beard. That cartoon is inaccurate, although in general, the term does refer to small-scale distillers, working alone or in small crews,

both rural and urban. During Prohibition (and at other times), given the ambition, resources, and market of the people involved, makers of illegal whiskey have constructed huge operations that rival the size of commercial distilleries. At that end of the spectrum, the term "moonshiner" seems inappropriate.

Although dictionaries define a "bootlegger" as someone who "makes, carries, or sells" illegal whiskey, I restrict the term to mean those who smuggle it to customers. Bootleggers hauled Canadian whiskey to America during Prohibition; they also carried moonshine anywhere, anytime. Other sources cited in this book refer to them by the more modern term "transporter," or the older term "blockader."

The clever or lucky people who lived in the houses built on the American-Canadian border were not bootleggers, even though in some rare instances the boundary ran through a living room, and all that the residents had to do to flummox American cops during a raid was to hustle across the floor to be in another country. Some of these houses were eventually padlocked, and construction of others banned. Sprinting across a piece of carpet does not constitute bootlegging in the truest sense of the word.

an ocean-going schooner to land wooden cases or burlap bags of Dewars, Bisquit brandy, or Golden Wedding. According to author Everett Allen, "in the dark of the moon, the rumrunner was more comfortable and more active."

Rumrunners and moonshiners alike tend to be nocturnal. In *Moonshine: A Life in Pursuit of White Liquor*, Alec Wilkinson wrote that moonshine, as a rule, "is sold only at night and on Sundays after hours, when it can command a higher price. A bootlegger meeting a man who wants to buy at any other time—that is, a man who appears to prefer rotgut and a virulent hangover—assumes he is dealing with a fool or a liquor agent."

The heyday of the rumrunners was in the early 1920s, before the United States Coast Guard got the tools to do its job effectively. Then the major criminal syndicates built illegal distilleries and bottling plants, often counterfeiting labels, too. Moonshiners, mostly in the South and oblivious to nautical affairs, had plenty of business either way. It had been a small-scale, local affair until Prohibition; then it exploded, with syndicates taking more and more control.

"Revenuer" is the usual term for the law-enforcement agents who play cat to the moonshiner's mouse. The term derives from the revenue agents of the Treasury Department (in modern times from the Bureau of Alcohol, Tobacco, and Firearms, or ATF, of the Internal Revenue Service). People from numerous other military and civilian agencies were involved in the war against illegal liquor, however, including customs agents, Coast Guard personnel, soldiers, sailors, and local and state sheriffs and marshals. One thing about the photographic record of their activities is constant through the centuries: they posed with the stills they seized, like fishermen with big fish on a dock.

In this book, you will meet some unusual and memorable folks on both sides of the law:

In *Rum Across the Border*, Allan S. Everest quoted a United States Customs Service patrol officer who worked on the border between New York and Quebec: "Some of the strongest breaths the world has known pass through here," he said. "I am often glad that we use an electric torch instead of an oil lamp in making our night searches, because there might be serious explosions if a naked flame ran afoul of the exhalations of the tourists." Carrying a snootful doesn't qualify as bootlegging, either. And since the Volstead Act (the enforcing legislation for the Eighteenth Amendment, popularly called "Prohibition") didn't forbid buying or drinking liquor, they weren't even breaking the law.

A "rumrunner" is a nautical bootlegger, using anything from a wooden dory to

This captured contact boat's name proved portentous, as white lightning gushes into the harbor in downtown Norfolk, 1922. It was tied up at the pier at Boush Street and City Hall Avenue, near what is now the site of the city's Nauticus marine attraction. The 5 gallon glass jug was an unusual container, especially in boats, since it was both heavy and breakable. *Sargent Memorial Room, Kirn Library, Norfolk*

• Garland Bunting of Halifax County, North Carolina, perhaps the most successful revenue agent in the history of a state that has been a perennial leader in moonshine output.

• Prohibition agent Isadore "Izzy" Einstein, a corpulent chameleon, who was fired for being too successful.

• William "Big Six" Henderson, who arrested more than 5,000 violators in his career as a federal treasury agent.

• Rumrunner Bill McCoy, who many erroneously credit with inspiring the phrase "the real McCoy."

• Moonshine runner Jaybird Philpot of Manchester, Kentucky, who "handled his tanker-car like a jet-propelled demon."

• Lewis Redmond, a moonshiner who in the 1870s was "regarded as the most notorious character in America."

New Year's Eve, 1955: Agents hold 18 gallons of moonshine that won't liven up any parties that night. Left to right, North Carolina State ABC agents Harold Lilley, Jim Ward, James Ross, and Walter Taylor. They seized this liquor on South Pitt Street in Greenville, North Carolina. *Jim Ward*

These people, their colleagues, and their enemies weren't just playing games. It wasn't just the too-cute "Dukes of Hazzard" eluding the porcine Boss Hogg, or Snuffy Smith blasting away with his muzzle-loader at the revenuers. Ample grim realities—murder victims and poisoned drinkers among them—balance the equation.

Esther Kellner, author of the excellent *Moonshine: Its History and Folklore*, retrieved a cogent passage from Henderson's notebook: "As you sit there, parked along a rutted washcut and faded roadbed, with only the cry of a blue jay or the sound of a cricket around you, you wonder if you are wasting your hours of time on earth . . . Then you remind yourself that this is your world, and you shaped it this way by your own convictions. It is indeed a life that is hard and often lonely as well as dangerous, where glamour has no place."

Although on a basic level, the story of moonshining and rumrunning concerns human characteristics, avarice and ingenuity perhaps foremost, it is also a story of machines: fast cars and speedy boats predominate, linked to the daring and the tactics of the people at the wheel. The nautical "arms race" between the Coast Guard and the rumrunning syndicates—which ended with the latter ordering boatyards to build speedboats equipped with, for example, four 700hp Liberty engines—merits a chapter of its own.

Yet souped-up Fords roaring along Georgia roads, or the speedboat *Mona Lola* ripping across Long Island sound, only fit one niche at one time. They supplied speed and flexibility. Elsewhere, at other times, other attributes in a vehicle were required: size, reliability, or off-road traction became crucial. As a result, trucks, freight trains, sleds, schooners, barges, even toboggans played distinct parts, and played them well.

The players in the drama of illegal liquor offer only a few simple reasons for their actions. A few moonshiners make whiskey because it is cheap and they like to drink. Others have found it to be a lucrative and reliable business, with stable prices and ready markets. In some seasons, moonshine was the only cash crop available. At the end of the nineteenth century, some farmers fired up their stills in order to pay their property taxes. A few of the smalltime, amateur bootleggers and rumrunners were in it for the thrills. Everybody else was in it for the money.

There was plenty to be made, and (especially during Prohibition) it was hard to resist. On the northern border, authorities estimate that as little as 5 percent (and no more than 20 percent) of the illegal shipments were ever stopped. The consensus among rumrunners was that they threw much more liquor overboard than the Coast Guard ever managed to seize, and they landed much more than they ever had to jettison.

The rise and fall of Rum Row became a sort of national soap opera, followed with fascination by newspaper readers around the country, particularly along the coasts. At the end of May and in early June of 1923, for example, the headlines in the Norfolk, Virginia, newspapers were abuzz with reports, speculation, news, and rumor: "Code Messages on Rum Runners Sent As Decoys," one headline said. "*Istar* and Sister Craft Move Up Coast, After Misleading Reports Are Broadcast for Interception By Federal Prohibition Agents; Another Boat On Way to Join Liquor Fleet."

The anonymous reporter dug deep into his journalistic bag of tricks to provide colorful background for his readers: "The story of the first effective raid on the Atlantic coast rum smugglers is but the opening chapter of a history which may be written of the rum trade that has been lifted from the plane of the bootlegger and converted into high finance. It is a history that bids fair to take place alongside those vivid chronicles of the slave trade of the old days, or the ravage of that coterie of romantic scoundrels and privateers headed by Stede Bonnet, Captain Teach and the renowned Captain Kidd."

These articles intensified the curiosity of the citizens ashore. The writer continued: "Since the presence of the rum fleet provided the spiciest topic of conversation of the day, theories innumerable have been advanced by officials, semi-officials and citizens of every degree of prominence." Ensuing articles, often with banner headlines, mentioned mysterious sinkings, mutilated bodies washed up on beaches, and missing fortunes. They provided daily updates on the location and activities of the *Istar*, dubbed the "Flagship of the Rum Runner Fleet."

ATF agents distributed these posters in an effort to mobilize public sentiment against moonshiners, often a losing proposition for the feds. Nevertheless, more stills were discovered and destroyed after being reported by informants were than found by law-enforcement agents poking around in the boondocks. This poster, which shows a good-sized steamer-type still, is from 1954. *Bill Tetterton Collection*

Sources were mysterious, but seemed to provide intriguing information. "Rum Fleet Ready for Fresh Drive Against Patrol; Blockade Runners Are Planning to Land Heavy Cargoes Through Delaware Breakwaters," one headline announced. On February 26, 1925, a spate of articles dealt with the scandal surrounding the seizure of forty cases of liquor from the Navy transport *Beaufort*. The headline trumpeted, "Seizure of Record Liquor Cargo Aboard Transport Results in Naval Inquiry . . . Stir Created in High Washington Circles . . . Mad Scramble to Get Jugs and Bottles Overboard Takes Place on Vessel."

Prohibition made great copy, but historians agree that it was an overwhelming failure. The production and distribution of illegal liquor continued to expand, in spite of the fact that governments and law-enforcement agencies spent more and more resources trying to stem the tide.

Taxes and temperance were the twin incentives in the growth of illicit booze in American history. As far back as the Whiskey Rebellion, some distillers violently objected to federal taxes simply as a matter of principle. Furthermore, in peace and war, excise taxes have repeatedly kept the price of whiskey artificially inflated to such

an extent that even incompetent moonshiners could beat the legal price.

The temperance movement in America has a long and impressive history, a juggernaut building to Prohibition, its finest and most futile hour. Advocates of Prohibition were powerfully convincing, had most politicians buffaloed, and were out of touch with reality. They "looked forward to a world free from alcohol and, by that magic panacea, free also from want and crime and sin, a sort of millennial Kansas afloat on a nirvana of pure water," Andrew Sinclair wrote in *Prohibition: The Era of Excess*.

As should have been expected, this soap-bubble notion quickly burst; from a historical perspective, the temperance movement is a mere footnote, a trifling sidebar to the more elaborate history of drinking and distilling in America. Compared to our forebears, to the people who carved up the wilderness and carried out manifest destiny, modern Americans are downright abstemious.

Two or three centuries ago, Kellner observed, "Rum was everywhere, at weddings,

WANTED

information from **YOU** the taxpayer on the locations of

BOOTLEG STILLS

Moonshine stills in your locality like that pictured above, are robbing you of many thousands of dollars in Federal and State liquor taxes. Help your Government by reporting them, by mail or phone, to

ALCOHOL AND TOBACCO TAX DIVISION, INTERNAL REVENUE SERVICE

All communications held strictly confidential

Form 1793 (8-54)

house-raisings, log-rollings, bed-quiltings, husking-bees; at trading posts, political gatherings, and the founding of churches; in the taverns and on the trails. Rum marched with the armies, fought against the Indians, sustained the explorer, and warmed the traveler; it comforted the lonely and ill and cheered the downhearted." Whiskey, she points out, was used equally by nurses and cooks. "It was administered for numerous ailments, fevers, rheumatism, snakebite, pneumonia, and food poisoning among them . . . Women took it as a 'pick-me-up' when ill, cold, tired, or plain disheartened."

That was all well and good on the frontier, when there wasn't a handy Alcoholic Beverage Control store at a nearby shopping center, but does homemade whiskey retain some magic attraction? Apparently so. At the rotgut end of the scale, where the consumer is less demanding, it is at least cheap. Palatability is another matter. Irvin Shrewsbury Cobb, a Kentucky humorist in the 1930s, gave this definition of "corn licker": "It smells like gangrene starting in a mildewed silo, it tastes like the wrath to come, and when you absorb a deep swig of it you have all the sensations of having swallowed a lighted kerosene lamp. A sudden, violent jolt of it has been known to stop the victim's watch, snap his suspenders and crack his glass eye right across." Yum.

Many discerning drinkers like the taste and the powerful kick that moonshine administers; perhaps store-bought whiskey seems wimpy or adulterated. Some people still believe that whiskey is good for them; as Jess Carr, author of *The Second Oldest Profession: An Informal History of Moonshining in America,* observes, they believe "there is absolutely nothing which the Balm of Gilead will not make sweeter, more pleasant, or more meaningful."

After the repeal of Prohibition, rum-running "sputtered on for a few years more," as one historian put it, then ceased. The rumrunners have long since been replaced (at least in spirit) by drug smugglers. Bootleggers still ply their trade, in a sporadic and reduced fashion. And today's moonshiner faces serious problems: decreasing amounts of truly remote countryside, growing populations, authorities using more sophisticated detection equipment, judges handing out more severe sentences, and a growing public mistrust of impurities and health hazards. But don't be too anxious to write the final chapter of this great American saga.

Attentive reading of the world news yields occasional data that attest to the continuing significance of moonshining. During Operation Desert Storm, for example, an item in the November 22, 1990, issue of *Newsweek* reported, "Because the Saudi Arabians frown on alcohol, soldiers have been given nothing stronger to drink than water or soft drinks. But relatives of GIs tell *News-week* that one of the most requested items from back home is yeast. The U.S. Central Command hasn't had any reports of clandestine desert stills yet, but a spokesperson said, 'If someone's asking for yeast, he's not baking bread.'"

Moonshine even figures into the environmental movement. The June 1991 issue of *National Geographic* had an article about fruit bats. In the southwestern United States, the bats eat the nectar of the agave plant. Their migration routes to Mexico follow a trail of agave species as the plant flowers. "While agaves supply nectar to bats, they also yield spirits like tequila to moonshiners, who are seriously depleting agaves in some locales. This increases pressure on lesser long-nosed bats, which have been classified as endangered in the U.S. since 1988." Thus does humble moonshine figure into the great issues of the day.

In 1869 after the end of the Indian wars, Lt. Col. George A. Custer and the U.S. Seventh Cavalry Regiment were assigned to Elizabethtown, Kentucky. For two years, Custer maintained a hectic schedule of dinner parties and hunting trips, writing his memoirs in his spare time. Some detachments of the cavalry unsuccessfully hunted moonshiners. "While the record of these skirmishes is not clear, the warfare conducted here was even less decisive than that of which Little Big Horn was a part," wrote John C. Chommie in *The Internal Revenue Service.* "Chief Sitting Bull and his Indians were eventually subdued; the moonshiners never have been."

A century later, even the most successful revenue agents were still shaking their heads in frustration at the persistence of moonshiners and the ubiquity of white lightning.

Chapter One

History of Moonshining

This massive operation, seized during the 1920s or 1930s in Georgia, represents a quantum leap forward from the old days of moonshining, when a harried moonshiner could have uprooted and moved his one-man copper still to a safer location when the revenuers threatened. This operation features at least two distilling units (left rear, right center); the massive wooden boxes bespeak permanence. The revenuers have their work cut out for them—the days of the ax were waning, and dynamite was coming into its own as the destructive agent of choice. *Courtesy Georgia Department of Archives and History*

Moonshining in America didn't spring into life as a strange and unusual colonial hobby, invented to while away the idle hours on the frontier. In *Moonshine: A Life in Pursuit of White Liquor,* Alec Wilkinson traced the history of moonshining to Scotch-Irish immigrants in the early 1700s, who were, he wrote, "accomplished and enthusiastic distillers." They made corn into whiskey because distilled spirits were easier to store and transport than grain. They sometimes used liquor as currency.

The intrinsic link between liquor and taxes—the government trying to collect them and the liquor-producers trying to dodge them—wasn't an American development, either, although we may have raised it to new levels. Scotch-Irish settlers "brought with them a pattern of avoidance of an English excise tax imposed on distilled spirits dating from 1643," author John Chommie explained in *The Internal Revenue Service.*

Rum, the contraband of choice for generations of early smugglers, was first produced in West Indies as early as 1650. Al-

Fletcher Slone and Hiram Short fill a bottle with moonshine from a wooden keg. *Photographic Archives, Alice Lloyd College*

A still in operation in Pippa Passes, Kentucky. Photos of operating stills are unusual, for obvious reasons, and this group of nine men seems an extraordinarily large contingent for such a modest-sized operation. The men at right are stirring some mash. *Photographic Archives, Alice Lloyd College*

though the early occurrences of smuggling are murky, rum developed into a major player in world trade during the seventeenth and eighteenth centuries. Shippers sent molasses to New England where it was made into rum; the rum went to Africa, where it was exchanged for slaves; the slaves were then sent to Barbados and traded for more molasses, completing the deplorable cycle. By 1750, Massachusetts alone had sixty-three rum distilleries; more than a thousand ships were engaged in the rum trade out of Boston. Rum remained the most popular form of distilled liquor until the middle of the eighteenth century, when corn whiskey became common.

The popularity of this drink was evidenced on ships of the British Navy. "By 1740 the rum issue, as the daily alternative to beer, was common practice on the West Indies station," A. J. Pack and Kenneth Mason wrote in *Nelson's Blood*. "Seamen drank the raw spirit in drams, one gulp with no heel-taps." The ration was a half-pint per man per day, later ordered to be mixed with a quart of water, so they couldn't gulp it down all at once. Officers didn't permit shore leave because many of the "pressed men" wouldn't come back. "Lack of shore leave brought with it an attendant vice—smuggling," Pack pointed out. "In Jamaica, for example, rum was cheap and plentiful and a little ingenuity ensured its undiscovered arrival aboard." The sailors drilled coconuts, emptied the milk, and refilled them with rum.

Thanks to what seemed to be arbitrary and punitive British tariffs, tax evasion and smuggling along the seacoast was a fact of life before the Revolutionary War. Ships would carry hidden contraband, unlisted on customs declarations; a ship's manifest would be falsified, distorting information about the cargo, the point of origin or the destination; and bribes would be offered to the king's excise officers. Some locales became notorious: in New Jersey, for example, from Barnegat Bay and Cape May to Greenwich, so much contraband sugar, molasses, coffee, tea, and rum came ashore that local folks called it Smugglers' Woods.

These techniques, along with other innovations suggested by local markets and geography, have been "practiced by penny-pinching smuggler-merchants at least as long as there had been customs duties: unload the

Jug Lore Galore

Pottery collector and dealer Phil Wingard of Clover, South Carolina, explained that stoneware jugs for moonshine came in various sizes (ranging from pints to gallons) and shapes, distinctive to various parts of North and South Carolina. Similar types of jugs were used for molasses (these jugs had larger mouths), vinegar, and cider. The hand-thrown jugs had alkaline glazes and ranged in color from light tan to dark brown and olive brown. Some had what Wingard called "tobacco spit" glaze, because the glaze sometimes drooled down the side. They were corked, and were packed in straw for shipment. Similar, factory-made jugs were pressed out of molds by the millions in the Midwest and West. These jugs tended to be light on the bottom and dark on top.

In rare instances, moonshine and pottery were made in the same place (after all, firing a still and firing a kiln are similar operations). Some potters stamped their initials in the jugs, opposite the handle, but stopped during Prohibition to make the moonshine harder to trace.

In any case, Wingard said, "The glass canning jar put a crimp" in the pottery-making business. In his collection, he also has an unusual flat-sided gallon jug (the potter pressed in the sides before firing it), apparently to make the jugs easier to pack.

Potter Billy Henson, who lives between Greenville and Spartanburg, South Carolina, still makes authentic jugs and storage jars "the old way," using a treadle wheel and homemade glaze. Henson's great-grandfather started the family tradition in pottery around 1850, making a variety of whiskey jugs, churns, and storage jars. Henson's grandfather also made pottery, and his father "worked around the shop as a kid but didn't keep it up."

"My grand-daddy quit about nineteen and ten," Henson explained, largely because of two problems: the widespread availability of cheap, glass Mason jars ("That's what really 'bout put them out of business," he said), and the fact that people started getting refrigerators at home.

Pre-1910 jugs have a distinctive green alkaline glaze. After 1910, many potters started using "Albany slip," a brown glaze that was easier to work with and commercially available. It is hard to put a date and location on most of the old jugs. To Henson's knowledge, potters never bothered to sign their pottery or put their initials on it. "It really wasn't necessary," he said. "They didn't care what it looked like, as long as it didn't leak."

Whiskey jugs primarily came in the gallon size and smaller. Very few of the old jugs had writing on them, although some of the jugs for legal distilleries had stenciled names on them. In the South, the old-style handmade jugs had an ovoid shape. They were a solid color, ranging from dark green to chocolate brown. The more modern and more common moonshine jug (a square-sided, shouldered jug called a "jigger mold" jug) was first manufactured in the North in the early to mid-1800s. These jugs were white or two-colored; pottery makers didn't start producing that type of jug in the South until the early 1900s.

high-tariff items surreptitiously, usually onto night-hidden small boats, prior to submitting to inspection at the port-of-entry," Donald Canney wrote in *Rum War: The U.S. Coast Guard and Prohibition.*

The British had their hands full trying to impose and collect taxes before the Revolution; the neophyte American government shared the experience. Apparently, smuggling and patriotism weren't mutually exclusive. The whiskey ration at Valley Forge had been a half-pint per day; soldiers who got it free objected to paying extra as civilians.

An import tax on ale, beer, porter, and wine had been applied in 1789. In 1790, Alexander Hamilton was secretary of the treasury, having been appointed by President George Washington. On behalf of the new nation, he was facing a war debt from the Revolution of $70 million, and the smugglers of West Indian rum weren't help-ing. Part of the solution was to ask the Continental Congress for money to buy ten small ships to suppress the smuggling. On August 4, Congress passed the Revenue Cutter Bill, establishing the Revenue Cutter Service (one source calls it the "Revenue Marine Service"), equipped with ten cutters, brigs, and schooners.

It was a timely maneuver because there were rough waters ahead. The following year, the Act of March 3, 1791 (popularly called the "Whiskey Tax"), levied excise taxes on whiskey (both publicly and privately distilled) and tobacco products; this law took effect on July 1. The tax was fifty-four cents per gallon of still capacity plus seven cents per gallon produced. The tax collectors, a species of detective, were given authority to intrude on private property (which irritated many citizens), and to make matters worse, were paid a percentage of the take. The law also authorized rewards to informers who reported unregistered stills (the use of paid informers halted in 1916).

Whether it was the tax collectors' faults or the principle of the thing, the new law found few supporters. Congressman James Jackson of Georgia called the tax "odious, unequal, unpopular, oppressive." Fittingly, for the subject of this book, the tax was "the first internal revenue statute in the United States," Esther Kellner wrote, and opponents of it (of which there were plenty) "regarded the law as a direct affront to their ideals of justice, a violation of personal and states' rights, and an insult to their integrity." Behind "the high-sounding rallying cries of liberty and freedom lay the memory of the hated excise taxes imposed by the British Parliament," Chommie wrote.

The 1791 excise tax triggered what one historian called "serious opposition" in western North Carolina, and eventually Congress revised the law to exempt small stills. Farther north, the affront rankled to such an extent during the next two years that, by July 1793, a U.S. marshal in Pennsylvania named Lennox was on record as having served forty writs upon still-owners for nonpayment of the tax; as a result, a gang of thirty-six men beat him and burned his home. Two other revenue agents had been tarred and feathered.

Southwest Pennsylvania had developed into a center of distilling in late 1700s. In 1790, of 2,500 known distilleries in the thirteen states, 570 were concentrated in the four counties around Pittsburgh. In that area, visitors reported that there was at least

This detail of the museum-quality copper still shows the "cap" that funnels the distillate to the cooling barrel. The still's owner has twice received permits from ATF in Atlanta to run the still as part of an annual festival of antique crafts (such permits are no longer available). The last time they ran it was 1987. While the mash was working, a couple days before they planned to run the still, several armed, camouflage-clad revenuers (either state or local) showed up, saying that they were going to destroy the still. Several frantic phone calls and display of the permit later, they desisted. As part of the permit process, a federal agent came out, looked at the mash, and announced that they wouldn't get more than 5 gallons out of the run. They had gotten twice that much the time before, and that's how much they got this time. So they hid half of it before he came out to dispose of the moonshine. The agent looked at the jug, nodded his head, and said, "Yep, that's what I figured you'd get." The permit holder asked if he would get in trouble if he had hidden a little bit up in the woods, and the ATF agent rolled his eyes, shook his head, and said, "Don't tell me about that."

Before reaching the late-Prohibition crossroads of successful entrepreneurship and public health hazard, the traditional American moonshiner retained an attractive image. Esther Kellner summed up the glamorous view, describing the mountain moonshiner in Kentucky who had descended from the pioneers: he was a man "of singular character, hardy, strong, and lean, with the wary ears, silent steps, and watchful eyes of the hunter," she wrote in her excellent book, *Moonshine: Its History and Folklore.* "Living in an isolated hollow in the depths of the mountain country, defending himself and his family against the rigors of their lonely life, had endowed him with a proud independence which made him restless, suspicious, ingenious, and unconquerable."

Other descriptions of backwoods moonshiners emphasize this wariness. "The eyes of a mountain moonshiner are always in motion, moving from left to right and back again," Jess Carr wrote, based on his experiences with moonshiners. "Even out of the mountains, this occupation is observ-

This splay-bottomed stick was used to stir up the fermenting mash. It is propped on the still near the opening to the fire box.

able. It is not a shifty-eyed action; it is a sweeping motion of the panorama in view, the constant radar-like searching of the eyes for a movement in the bushes, a sound among the leaves."

This carefulness, while understandable, didn't render the average moonshiner particularly friendly. One researcher found them to be "solemn, businesslike, and frequently downright mean." The physical

In the old days, stills were pure copper, but this recent operation included aluminum, wood, and plastic, illustrating the fact that moonshiners use whatever materials are at hand and whatever seems to work. North Carolina state ABC officer William Boyd is removing the catch basin from this still in Pitt County, North Carolina. *Cliff Hollis,* The Daily Reflector, *Greenville, North Carolina*

tasks involved in setting up and operating a remote still were nothing short of backbreaking, and the constant hazards of hijackers (who would steal the liquor) and persistent revenuers (who would blow up a still and put the operator in jail) hardly combined to make a moonshiner cheerful or relaxed.

Between the nineteenth and twentieth centuries, blemishes began to mar the popular notion of the moonshiner. Some people began to distrust or satirize the character. Although moonshining boomed during Prohibition (it was the main source of illicit liquor by the end of the 1920s, far exceeding the amount smuggled in by land and sea combined), adulterated or toxic moonshine won few friends for the moonshiner. Part of the problem was that during Prohibition, the making of moonshine "was undertaken by an army of amateurs and often resulted in beverages that could harm or kill the consumer," wrote Mark Thornton in "Prohibition's Failure: Lessons for Today." Yet

even these sporadic poisonings didn't put much of a dent in the profits or popularity of moonshine makers.

In modern times, we're left with a trio of contradictory images of the American moonshiner. In their defense, as recently as the 1950s and 1960s, moonshiners in some areas "were looked upon by the local citizens as an asset to the community," according to former ATF agent Charlie Weems, because they were generous contributors to local projects and charities. According to Fred Goswick, who dabbled in moonshine as a young man in Georgia and later built a moonshine museum there, the moonshiners he knew were "just rural people, not gangster types."

The second and opposite facet of the moonshiner, that of outlaw and public nuisance, has always been held by their legal foes, the revenuers. Once a lawman had been beat up, shot at, and frustrated a few times, his view of the moonshiner quickly lost any luster it might have had.

One revenue commissioner's annual report referred to moonshiners as "unlettered men of desperate character . . . sly enough to plead poverty and ignorance of the law." Cartoonists had fun with the moonshiner, but revenuers never found them to be a laughing matter, particularly in modern times when many of them have long criminal records and can't rely on the wrist-slap punishments of former decades. When people asked "Big Six" Henderson why he carried a gun, he said that he wouldn't raid a still operated by his own mother without being armed.

During his career as an ATF agent in Virginia, Bill Tetterton saw both sides of the coin. Recalling his work in the 1960s, he said, "The real old-time moonshiner was a gentleman. If your car broke down somewhere and he saw you, he'd help. His word was his bond. If you captured him and told him to be in court the next day, he'd be there. If you told him to sit still, he'd stay. The younger generation is different. If you have hold of one of them, you better either hold on or handcuff them to a tree."

The third image of moonshiners appears in the mass media, where they tend to appear colorful and harmless. As early as just after Civil War, the southern moonshiner was on his way to becoming a standard, rec-

Tales of the moonshiner as entertainer appear even in the recollections of the lawmen. When they were hauled up before a judge, moonshiners expressed their native cunning with what one historian called "histrionics," "bald lies," and "inane excuses." According to Kellner, "Feigning shame, regret, repentance, and a firm resolve to reform was an old and artful maneuver among moonshiners." Henderson, a very successful revenuer, admitted to Kellner that he found some of the performances very convincing: "Hollywood has missed some wonderful actors out here."

Tetterton laughed when he recalled some of the courtroom scenes he'd witnessed. He has seen violators tell a judge, "Your honor, I'm a sick man, I can't work," while just days earlier Tetterton had watched them carrying 5-gallon jugs of moonshine through the woods, one on each shoulder.

Building Stills, From Tiny to Tremendous

The mechanics and economics of moonshining are quite simple. At the low end of the spectrum was the set-up described in government pamphlets between 1906 and 1915, which described in detail

how to make alcohol from cornmeal mash, apples, oats, bananas, barley, sorghum, sugar beets, watermelon, and potatoes. All you needed was a tea kettle, a quart of corn meal, and a bath towel to capture the vaporized alcohol. During Prohibition, portable 1-gallon stills were readily available in stores for $6 or $7. If you felt entrepreneurial, with a $500 still, you could produce 50–100 gallons per day at a cost of about 50 cents per gallon. You could sell your moonshine for $3 or $4 per gallon. In other words, at full capacity, you'd recoup your investment in four days.

Through the centuries, revenuers have discovered (and destroyed) stills in a spectrum of designs and sizes. The basic design includes a fermenter, where starches in the mash turn into alcohol; the still itself, where the mash is boiled; and a coil where the vaporized alcohol condenses.

The simplest and most common fermenters are made from 50-gallon wood barrels or 55-gallon steel drums; some moonshiners build a 4-foot square oak box. Some amateurs in modern times try to use plywood, but that doesn't work very well because the sides tend to bow out. Modern revenuers refer to the assortment of barrels, drums, or boxes under the generic term "boxes." A "10-box still" would contain ten

Jim Ward's caption for this 1953 photo could almost serve as a moonshiner's shopping list: one 200 gallon copper still, complete; 2 gallons fuel; 500 gallons mash (three 300 gallon boxes); one 100 gallon preheating unit with heater; one 100 gallon slop box; one hoe; one shovel; two lanterns. The still was in the Jones Chapel section near Tranter's Creek in Greenville, North Carolina. The worm has been removed from the cooling barrel (right). *Jim Ward*

ognizable, and rather exaggerated character in the accounts of novelists and journalists who specialized in local-color features, which were increasingly popular. The precise origin of the modern cartoon moonshiner is difficult to pinpoint. In "Li'l Abner," Al Capp depicted them with long beards and bare feet, ignorant and awkward, essentially harmless. The long-running series of "Snuffy Smith" comic strips continued the image.

The original caption for this photo simply says, "Moonshine still, 1922." It is solidly built; a hand-operated water pump is at the right rear, not the ideal method of cooling the distillate. *Sargent Memorial Room, Kirn Library, Norfolk*

separate units, usually multiple fermenters, and one or two boilers. Agents have even found column distilleries that used collapsible Army surplus rubber water tanks as fermenters; they had the twin advantages of being easy to conceal and move around.

Jim Ward's career with the North Carolina State Alcoholic Beverage Control board, from 1937 to 1983, witnessed numerous changes in the size and technology of moonshining. When he began, moonshiners used pine wood for fuel, because it burned hot and didn't smoke as much as other types of wood. Since wood is much too slow and cumbersome for anything but a small, old-fashioned still, moonshin-

ers later started using fuel oil with homemade burners, hanging a can or a wooden keg of fuel in a tree, with a hose or pipe running down to the valve at the burner. They also used coal and coke, and in modern times, bottled gas. To supply water, early moonshiners dug small wells and raised buckets by hand. Later they used hand-operated pumps, and still later, gas-powered pumps.

As boilers, Tetterton has seen lots of steam boilers (both homemade and commercial) made out of fuel-oil tanks, some as large as 550 gallons. Some people preheat the mash with a steam coil, to speed the distillation process. Tetterton has seized stills where the moonshiners were using gravity-fed gasoline (a terrific fire hazard), or pressure-fed gasoline. He has also seen 100-pound industrial propane cylinders on sites.

Some accounts describe 1,000-gallon "groundhog" stills, heated by pressurized gasoline or fuel oil, that could be heard a quarter-mile away. Smaller, gravity-fed gas burners weren't as noisy.

A variant of the standard still design is the "black pot" still, which doesn't have separate fermenters and stills. Mashing is done in the still itself. Some of these stills have capacities of 300–600 gallons, and Tetterton has seen as many as ten on a site.

Small stills are not hard to assemble, with the still cap (a sort of large, inverted metal funnel at the top of the boiler) and the worm (the coiled metal pipe inside the condenser) being the hardest pieces of equipment to make or acquire.

As with Jim Ward's recollections about the stills he seized, the changing eras of moonshining were skillfully captured by Dabney, who discussed ingredients and output with some old practitioners two decades ago. Hubert Howell of Cherokee County, Georgia, made moonshine in the late 1920s and early 1930s, when the age of pure corn whiskey was ending. His recipe called for 500 pounds of sugar and 10 bushels of corn meal, which would yield 50 gallons of whiskey. Howell recalled getting 10 gallons of moonshine per 100-pound sack of sugar, sometimes even 20 gallons. "But using pure corn only, you couldn't get much more'n a gallon of whiskey out of a bushel of meal to save your neck," he told Dabney. Howell made runs to Atlanta to buy 3 or 4 tons of sugar at a time. His moonshine operation, built around three 1,000-gallon fermenters (each holding 20 bushels of mash, 1,000 pounds of sugar, 100 pounds of barley, malt, and yeast) would turn out 400 gallons in an eight-hour day "easy," he recalled. Seven

Although not as effective as a mountain spring, which would provide cool water and the gravity to move it, the shallow well at center worked adequately. This basic still was in Southern Pines, North Carolina. *Wittemann Collection, Library of Congress*

workers were needed: two handled the finished whiskey, two tended the fermenters (mash boxes), and four men kept the fire going and cut wood, which was hauled by mules. "We'd bring it out in sacks—five 1-gallon tin cans to the sack, or 40 pounds," he explained. "We'd take two sacks out at a time and sometimes three sacks—15 gallons [120 pounds]. We were men, then, and we didn't mind totin' it."

Small stills have several advantages: they are cheaper and easier to construct, and they represent a smaller investment if they are destroyed. Revenuers have found some stills that were made to be portable, so the moonshiners could carry them off before a raid. In the mid-1930s, the average capacity of a seized still was 28 gallons per day. By the 1960s, stills had begun to get bigger and more sophisticated; mash seizures, an indicator of still capacity, were up 60 percent.

Small stills are usually one-man or family operations. In rare instances (and more often with large operations, of course), stills are run by migrant specialists who hire on for a few months at a time. Tetterton once caught a frustrated still worker who said he'd been caught at four stills in a row before he had a chance to run off any liquor at all, and he was supposed to be getting paid by the gallon. When Tetterton caught him, the moonshiners were setting up the still, camouflaging it with burlap bags.

Florida revenuer W. George McMullen recalled seeing a tiny still made out of a 5-gallon milk can with a wood cap and a quarter-inch copper pipe as a condenser. At the upper end of the size scale, big-time moonshiners have assembled massive still operations. The last operation set up by Willie Clay Call of Wilkes County, North Carolina, before he retired from moonshin-

The expression on this moonshiner's face indicates that he has seen it all before, but that he isn't too happy about it. Although federal agents were involved in this seizure, on February 13, 1957, this operation is far from the massive, well-organized, syndicate-style operation that was the preferred target. *Charles Abernathy photo file, ATF Reference Library*

ing, included two 550-gallon stills and two 300-gallon condensers, with sixty 180-gallon wood olive barrels for the mash, each holding about 200 pounds of sugar. This rig could turn out 640 gallons of liquor, seven days a week.

Columnist Drew Pearson, writing in the *Washington Post* in mid-January 1956, described his experiences with revenue agents on a well-planned still raid. The agents seized a 600-gallon still that had been installed in a barn that had once been used for packing apples, located in the Blue

Ridge Mountains about 15 miles from Roanoke, Virginia. "I had not realized how much rum-running and moonshining still continues despite the concentrated effort of authorities to stop it," Pearson wrote, echoing the sentiments of observers and citizens for a hundred years. At the site, they found 4,000 pounds of sugar, 100 5-gallon tin cans, dozens of 2-gallon jars. The moonshine cost $1-$2 per gallon to make and was being sold for $12.

Henry Lee, author of *How Dry We Were: Prohibition Revisited*, visited an illegal

This massive, steam-fired still was seized in McDuffie County, Georgia, in the early 1950s. Its size is apparent by the fire hose that was used to pump water from a nearby creek, as well as the pile of sugar sacks, grain sacks, and boxes of jars. A still this size clearly required a truck like the Dodge shown in order to move supplies. Left to right: Boyce Norris, McDuffie County Sheriff Lynn J. Norris, unidentified revenue agent, revenue agent Charlie Tudor, and Robert Phillips. *C. W. Herndon, Courtesy Georgia Department of Archives and History*

distillery in northern New Jersey: the main tank was 75 feet long, 50 feet wide, and 6 feet deep. When he visited, the still was in operation, filled with yeast, water, and cracked corn. A huge mechanical agitator ran on a rail around it to stir the mash. There were eight distilling units located under this swimming-pool-sized tank. This still could turn out 6,000 gallons of alcohol a day, which was dispatched to New York City to make what Lee called "New York Scotch": real scotch, mixed with water and this alcohol, with coloring added. In a bizarre detail, Lee noted that the moonshiners applied an electrical charge to the liquor for twenty-four hours to "take out the bite." The adulterated "scotch" was then put in brown glass bottles, corked, and labeled with the best foreign-looking labels that local counterfeiters could supply.

Legends of huge stills endure in local cultures, circulating like the aroma of mash on a hot summer day. Speaking of the area around St. Croix Falls, Minnesota, former police chief Lloyd Westlund recalled, "The largest still was owned by a Chicago syndicate" that transported the moonshine back to their home turf, about 400 miles away. Equipped with six 50,000-gallon vats and two 500-gallon distillers, it could produce a gallon a minute. The story goes that a trout fisherman stumbled upon it. He told the wrong people about the huge distillery and was promptly shanghaied by the gang, and held as a combination hostage and laborer for a couple of weeks.

Choosing a Site, and Other Stratagems

As we've seen, moonshiners have set up shop up and down the East Coast and throughout the Midwest. Ace prohibition agents Izzy Einstein and Moe Smith destroyed hundreds of stills in New York City during their spectacular careers (see Chapter 8). Huge numbers of stills have been tucked away in remote, rugged, thickly wooded hills and hollows. Small-scale moonshiners have always had to balance ease of access with the need for privacy, and the latter has almost always won hands down.

An 1881 book about moonshiners pointed out that a spring was especially desirable as a source of water, because it stayed cool in the summer. Back then, moonshiners looked for deep hollows, with tree-covered slopes on each side, which, they thought, would absorb the smoke before it reached the summit.

"Wild and woolly country" was what Westlund heard local old-timers describe when they talked about the thirty or so stills that used to dot the nearby countryside.

Although access to a still didn't have to be easy, it had to be tolerable. Moonshiners had to lug in copper apparatus, barrels, tools, shovels, sugar, grain, bottles, and all sorts of ancillary equipment. If they weren't burning firewood from nearby trees, they had to carry in fuel to fire the boiler. And if they were camping on the spot during a run, that meant carrying in food and even more gear. Generally, then, a moonshiner needed at least a rudimentary trail to the still site. And even with a trail, the enormous physical demands are clear. So that you don't imagine a well-positioned still made things easy, listen to Hamper McBee of Tennessee, who recorded some of his memories for author Joseph Dabney: "Ain't no lazy man gonna make no whiskey. Ride the sugar down the mountains and it wet, slippery, and you're falling and a stumbling and getting down there a chopping wood and it wet and trying to get a fire and run that stuff and don't know whether you're agonna run into the revenue or not and then have to pack that stuff back out of the mountains."

Although moonshiners have always been associated with mountains, they are an adaptable breed. In North Carolina in the late 1800s, according to Daniel Whitener in *Prohibition in North Carolina, 1715–1945*, "every indication showed that the practice was widespread. Before 1890, the mountain section of the state, with its numerous valleys and hills, was the main resort of the blockaders. But after that time a larger percentage of them were located along the coast among the bogs, sounds, and inlets that intersected the shore. Like the pirates of old, they suffered little interference on the coast." These moonshiners had discovered

to haul the equipment up. He was caught, incidentally, when revenuers staked out a still run by his father and brother. Johnson had agreed to fire it up for them at about 5:00 A.M., after returning from a race (they fired the still in the pre-dawn darkness in order to hide the smoke). When Johnson talks about his capture, he usually points out, "I never got caught hauling whiskey."

During World War II, Larry Anderson of Norfolk, Virginia, was a boatswain mate on Palmyra Island, a fuel depot about 1,000 miles south of Hawaii. Stiff drinks were hard to come by, he recalled recently as we chatted on his porch. As a result, he and the other sailors made "raisin jack," a fermented alcoholic drink, out of readily available materials. The base commander once found a working batch during an inspection (he smelled it from the exhaust pipe on the roof), but, Anderson recalled, didn't seem very angry. "They knew what we were doing," he said. Another time a seaman blew the roof off a hut in which they were secretly distilling alcohol out of shellac.

Cities and suburbs have hosted their share of booze-makers. On March 2, 1925, for example, Norfolk police found a still at 1348 Chapel Street in an unoccupied apartment on the second floor. In 1971, in Bristol, Virginia, agents seized a 6,300-gallon still and 1,900 gallons on moonshine. This still took up an entire house except for the kitchen. That year in Merry Hill, North Carolina, law-enforcement authorities found an 18,000-gallon still in a mobile home.

Weems once found a still in the attic of a house in south Fulton County, Georgia. "They were usually in basements," he said. "This one was so heavy—all that mash, equipment, hundreds of pounds of sugar— he had to run braces to keep the roof from collapsing. He had run chains from the rafters to the ceiling."

In February 1971, near Dunwoody Country Club (a ritzy suburb on the north side of Atlanta), officers rushed to the scene of a two-story brick house that had exploded and caught fire. They found the remains

that it was easier to build and equip a still carrying the gear on boats rather than carrying it on horseback or muleback or, even worse, their own backs. In Florida in the 1950s, agents found a still that had been built on a platform on an island in a 90-acre swamp; the still was covered with camouflage netting.

Rural moonshiners often used rural dirt roads, and would cut through the bank at a place that sloped down to a source of water. They sometimes used a "still buggy" (a stripped-down vehicle) or a mule-drawn

sledge to carry materials and liquor back and forth up and down the hill.

Junior Johnson, owner of a NASCAR team, and perhaps the most famous former moonshiner, had experience with dirt roads. His illicit career began back when starvation was the alternative. He operated several stills at a time, in an area where revenuers would cruise the roads, looking for tracks and footprints where vehicles had pulled off or stopped to unload equipment or pick up liquor. Johnson and his crews laid planks off the side of a truck onto the top of the bank

The mash in the large square tanks is at work, as evidenced by the thick crust on its surface. Rabun County Sheriff Lamar Queen (in middle) sizes up an indoor still at Timson Creek, a mile outside of Clayton, in Rabun County, Georgia, circa 1950. David Airs and George Carpenter lend a hand. *Courtesy Georgia Department of Archives and History*

mules, guinea hens, crows, and goats. Some moonshiners swear by mules, which will aim their prominent ears at anything unusu-

al in the area and start to bray. Kearins was with an agent once who took off his white hat and laid it down so that it wouldn't attract attention. The problem was that he put it right by the path, and it spooked a mule that the moonshiners were using the carry in equipment. The ensuing commotion allowed some of the violators to escape.

Edward Sloan, Jr., president of the Greenville County Historical Society, recalled, "About 1950 we were working west of Lima Crossroads. Near there I saw a harrow disk hanging in a tree and asked what it was; I was told that it was part of a signaling

system, that a bootlegger's watchman would shoot it with a rifle to signal the approach of the tax collectors."

More sophisticated moonshiners added electronic alarms to their efforts to hide operations or escape arrest: battery-operated buzzers or bells could be triggered by stepping on a board or buried device. A New York garage was once used as a front for an illegal distillery. It had an alarm system triggered when a mechanic laid a wrench across two nail heads on a bench. Another front was a "laundry" that had an entire wall that could swivel outward, and

In this "steamer" type still, raw steam was injected into the mash through the pipe at center. Fermenters are visible at front left. The cooling barrel is barely visible at the back. *Bill Tetterton Collection*

that used laundry-delivery trucks to distribute the product.

Delivery Systems—Low Tech, but Highly Inventive

Once moonshine was successfully distilled and put in a handy container, moonshiners continued the same creative thinking that went into locating and protecting the stills. They also developed some ingenious ways to deliver the product to customers. In remote enough locations, where everyone knew a well-established moonshiner and law enforcement was lax enough, a moonshiner would simply leave a jug and a cup in the brush pile; customers would take or drink their fill, and leave the payment in the cup.

Backwoods moonshiners used "bell trees," sometimes with hollow trunks. A customer would ring the bell and leave his money, and return shortly to collect his cup of white lightning. Other moonshiners would put fresh-cut branches in the road, pointing the direction to a still that was serving up the day's batch.

In *The Black Ships; Rumrunners of Prohibition*, Everett Allen told the story of a man who lived on the edge of town who was obviously selling illegal liquor, but even though the authorities burst in at odd hours they could never catch him with it. He showed Allen how he had rigged a tank of booze in the attic to the kitchen tap, and dispensed it to visitors for the usual fee.

A blind bootlegger in Harlem was once arrested for selling moonshine from a baby carriage that had a wooden box mounted on top with a hinged lid and padlock. In the city, a popular device was called a "carrier's can," a copper container with a pouring spout that fit in a suitcase. The moonshine runner emptied the can into a 5-gallon drum at a speakeasy. At various times and places, folks have sold moonshine out of hot-water bottles hidden in an inner pocket and dispensed through a small rubber hose, and from tire tubes strapped to their bodies.

Although the grand days of moonshining are over, old habits die hard, and new generations find themselves in situations where the urge to drink is strong but the wherewithal is wanting. In Saudi Arabia, for example, where, in spite of a religious-based national prohibition, Los Angeles Times reporter Douglas Jehl pointed out, "Saudi authorities have long turned a blind eye to Western residents' home-based manufacture of beer, wine and distilled liquor for personal consumption."

Diplomats and business people have the time and resources to make safe, palatable homebrew and moonshine, no doubt. Unfortunately, some of the American servicemen who went into Moslem nations during Operation Desert Storm weren't as skillful or as careful—some got caught, and others got sick. An article datelined Riyadh, Saudi Arabia, published in the *Los Angeles Times* on November 10, 1990, said that military authorities had levied "heavy fines" on a dozen American servicemen (including a major and a captain from the Air Force) for violating General Order No. 1, which Jehl called "the stern teetotaling order issued at the outset of the U.S. buildup" in Saudi Arabia.

Revenuer and author George Atkinson, wrote, "The day of the illicit distiller is past." Anti-liquor forces, flush with the success of a moonshine crackdown or simply optimistic, have always made similar pronouncements; the "dry" forces during Prohibition were especially prone to it. Atkinson was writing in 1881. More than a century later, news reports prove him wrong every day.

Chapter 4

The Revenuer

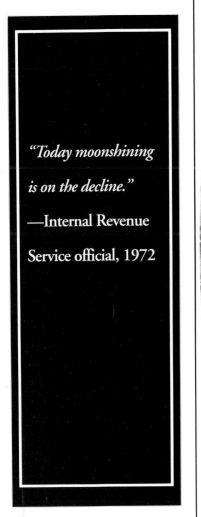

"Today moonshining is on the decline."

—Internal Revenue Service official, 1972

Badges, boots, stogies, and rifles: the tools of the trade during this still seizure, circa 1921 near Edgewood Lake (state unknown). The artillery may be explained by the note scrawled on the back of this photo: "had shootout there." The men were deputies from Jefferson County, including J. W. Howard (second from left) and Bill Burg (fourth from left, with missing arm). If this raid netted 100 barrels of mash, as indicated on the back of this photo, it was a whopper. *Charles Abernathy photo file, ATF Reference Library*

The seemingly endless battle of wits between law-enforcement agents and moonshiners has been described in a variety of ways. In some accounts, it seems to be a sort of game—some days I catch you, some days you get away, and no one gets hurt. It has also been depicted as a sport: old-time revenuers, and modern-day ATF agents, have traditionally been avid hunters and outdoorsmen. In this scenario, the moonshiner appears to be an exceptionally intelligent and unpredictable sort of bear or white-tail deer. In the early days of Prohibition, "there was an element of sport in each battle of wits between agent and bootlegger," Thomas Coffey noted in *The Long Thirst—Prohibition in America, 1920–1933.* Other accounts emphasize the frustration and hazards endured by the moonshine hunters. The section on gunfire in chapter 9 documents the potential for violence.

Bill Tetterton, a recently retired ATF agent from Norfolk, Virginia, said that he rarely had to draw his pistol during two decades of tracking moonshiners. Former ATF agent Charlie Weems recalled that Sheriff Hugh Stinchcomb in Fayette County (there are counties with this name in west central Georgia and Alabama) "seldom carried a pistol." In fact, Weems once saw Stinchcomb stop a fleeing moonshiner by hitting him in the back with a baseball-sized rock. Revenuer W. George McMullen once raided a still in Manatee County, Florida, by sneaking up so quietly that he was able to get right next to one of the moonshiners. He then extended a hand and introduced himself. "The still operator seemed to relax as this was done," McMullen wrote. "I learned over the years that the more casual one is the easier the work." He recalled that he had an "affable working relationship with the violators in the Tampa area."

Revenuers and other law-enforcement agents invariably tried to be professional during their dealings with violators to avoid provoking violence. One extremely successful agent said that if the violator was nice, he was a little nicer; if the violator was mean, he was a little meaner. Whether affable or serious, successful agents had to be able to bluff or brawl at a moment's notice.

"I never had anything personal against anyone I ever arrested," Weems explained. "I was just there to do a job. But the way I feel about it is, I worked on moonshiners too long to have any sympathy for them."

TWO DETECTIVES ALONE IN THE

One of the rewards for this demanding job is emphasized in numerous contemporary accounts: tracking and destroying stills, for some agents, is exciting and challenging—in other words, fun. Weems worked with a civilian pilot who spent hours voluntarily tracking down stills from his aircraft. The pilot's motive? "In a word, it was adventure," Weems wrote in his recent book, *A Breed Apart.* The pilot "loved the excitement of the chase." Balanced against the adrenaline rush of a successful seizure are the long hours of waiting and the boredom of surveillance. During these parts of the job, patience is a necessity.

In the nineteenth and early twentieth centuries, stills were predictably small. Some operators just ran them more often than others. But during Prohibition and certainly in modern times, moonshining stopped being a traditional craft and became a criminal industry. As a result, state and federal law-enforcement agents began to concentrate on large operations. Why spend time

D WOODS.

looking for an old 50- or 100-gallon still when gangs of violators were setting up huge stills that could produce 1,000 gallons per day and run seven days a week?

This chapter explains how the group of local, state, and federal law-enforcement agents, popularly known as "revenuers", carry the battle to the home turf of the people who break the liquor laws and avoid paying taxes. These agents have been freelance or official, civilian and military, amateur and professional; their results have ranged from complete failure to amazing success. At one time, prohibition in North Carolina was a state law that didn't mandate or provide state enforcement. County sheriffs had to do it, but "they had, except in rare cases, neither training, experience, time, nor power to cope effectively with the unorganized liquor traffic violations, to say nothing of the organized rum-runners directed by intelligent men and backed by wealth," Daniel Whitener wrote. At other times and in other places, revenuers fought the moonshiners to a draw, or drove them out of business—at least temporarily.

The battle has been waged by solitary trackers, hiking rugged, bramble-crammed hollows, and in the late 1800s, by raiding parties as large as fifty men mounted and armed with government-supplied Springfield rifles and Colt "round barrel" revolvers. By the 1950s, teams were usually two or four men.

In more modern times, the battle has been waged from the air, with trained spotters in small aircraft scrutinizing woods and fields from 10,000 feet. And it has been waged on the roads and highways, by ATF agents in hot rods they've seized from bootleggers, or in government cars stocked with several sets of local license plates and out-of-state license plates, a case of dynamite, a shotgun, surplus military clothing, binoculars, a shovel and an ax, and what they call "still rations" (pork and beans, canned sausages, crackers, and sodas).

Three Rules for Finding Stills

There is an art to locating stills. Law-enforcement authorities have found and destroyed tens of thousands of them during the past century. Technology has changed, but the basic approach has been constant. You could call it the "3 Ps": look for precedent, pay attention, and prowl around.

As in catching a largemouth bass in a sprawling lake, you tend to fish where you had luck before. "Sometimes we'd just go out and walk an area where we had violators in the past," Tetterton recalled. Since stills require a source of water (to cool the distillate), they usually have to be located near streams. Revenuers have traditionally walked along creeks, looking for mash residue in the water, even tasting the water to check. Horses are said to hate the smell of the mash and readily detect "slops" emptied into a stream.

Top-notch still finders usually like the outdoors and are often hunters. As revenuer Garland Bunting of North Carolina told writer Jane Sanderson, "I just love the woods. I love to get out there when I'm stakin' out a still and smell that wild fern and that swamp." Bunting is an enthusiastic coon hunter, and said that one of the prime hazards to a backwoods still was from hunters, not law-enforcement agents. Chasing his own coon dogs one night, he found five stills.

Agents learn to recognize the particular blend of accessibility and remoteness that are ideal for making moonshine. Legendary Kentucky revenuer "Big Six" Henderson once said, "When you find a path in a place where even a hoot-owl wouldn't go, you can look for a still."

Finding a path, of course, was ideal, and not out of the question. After all, you can't lug in several tons of fuel, metal, tools, grain, and sugar through dense underbrush. If a still is running often enough, the foot traffic will beat down a path (extremely careful moonshiners try to approach their stills from various directions, to avoid this telltale sign).

Another woodland skill that has always been crucial to still hunters is the ability to move quietly through the forest. Excellent peripheral vision is a must, along with a good sense of hearing. Experienced agents learn not to leave footprints when they visit a still.

"One old trick in muddy places is for the officer to walk to the distillery in bare feet as the still hands tread barefoot," ATF agent Jack Kearins wrote in *Yankee Revenooer.* He vividly pictured an agent in this position, standing motionless, and listening: "His pants are rolled to his knees and his feet sloshing in oozing, stinking mud. He is putting one foot carefully before the other in the soggiest places to let watery action efface the pattern of his foot tracks."

As mentioned earlier, moonshiners sometimes strung fine black thread around a still when they left; if the thread was broken when they returned, they assumed that the law had been there. Kearins said he learned to feel threads with his legs (even very fine threads on cold winter days while wearing long johns and heavy pants), back away, and step over them. Sometimes, when he broke them, he retied them, hiding the knot. Once he went into a country store to buy some gloves to wear while changing a flat tire. He heard a moonshiner that he recognized asking for fine black thread, and bragging about what it was for. Kearins called it a "Clark's No. 20 telegraph line" (Clark's is a popular thread brand).

Revenuers, sometimes wearing waders, approach stills by walking upstream or downstream, to avoid snapping twigs. "You only have to crack but one stick," Bunting told Alec Wilkinson. "You make a sound at a liquor still and you let yourself in for a load of buckshot and no flowers on your grave."

Former ATF agent Kenneth Travis described a classic incident of this type that occurred on December 22, 1955. He called it "a sort of disaster in the still raiding business." He was working in Calhoun County (state not known), where, according to a local officer, "it was almost impossible to catch anybody at a distillery." Travis planned to prove him wrong during an upcoming seizure. They found the still in full operation; the still was fired by wood, and they could hear the crackling of the fire before seeing the site. Creeping closer, they saw at least two men at work. Travis led the way down a path.

"We could smell the odor of mash and whiskey and we were excited," he wrote. "I was leading the way and when I got to a point about ten yards from the distillery, I guess I stepped on a stick and broke it or made some noise somehow and one of the violators stopped, looked up at us, turned a flashlight on us and all of a sudden both violators ran off like rabbits . . . We did not know where anything was. Every step was strange and apparently the violators knew where they were and knew just exactly where to run. All of a sudden they were gone and everything was over and it was a disaster. We liked to catch people, but this time we did not."

Successful agents were forced to add electronic skills to their woodland savvy. In the early years, the techniques were predictably crude. George Griffith, a former federal judge and author of *Life and Adventures of Revenooer No. 1*, wrote about tapping a telephone in a Cincinnati apartment. The phone was being used by a criminal syndicate that he called "the Zanaty gang," taking

A Most Exciting Raid

Considerable planning, courage, and endurance were required on the part of revenuers; these traits are illustrated in a successful seizure that former ATF agent Kenneth Travis took part in on April 13, 1957. He called it "the most exciting whiskey still raid of my life." His team of ATF agents had been looking for stills on the Choctawhatchee River, which runs from southern Alabama into the Florida panhandle. It was a tropical area, where the trees were festooned with Spanish moss hanging down on the banks, and alligators patrolled the water. Travis was on the track of a man he called "a very famous bootlegger named Buster Cooey," who operated near the town of Westville. Cooey, who was about seventy years old at the time of Travis' tale, once gave $50,000 to the local school system to keep it afloat during the Depression.

Cooey's modus operandi, like that of another well-known local moonshiner, was to set up three or four stills back in the swamp, fifty to seventy-five yards from the river. He would then post a lookout who would sit on the river bank fishing. Travis and his fellow agents devised a plan to drop down river a couple miles below the suspected area, hike for two hours to reach the river, and walk up to the stills from the opposite direction.

They were dropped off at 9:00 A.M., carrying flashlights and pistols. Hiking through

the swamps, they had to swim three times (holding clothes and guns above their heads). Their efforts paid off: they found a twelve-barrel still right away, and a sixteen-barrel five minutes later. The latter looked ready to run, and had twenty new 5-gallon jugs stashed nearby. They decided to wait until dark to see if the moonshiners came.

The group had neglected to bring along any food, so they split a pack of Lifesavers. At about 9:00 P.M., they heard a motorboat. Men arrived and fired up a kerosene blower under the still. After about thirty minutes, the agents started to creep up on them. The moonshiners, Travis wrote, "saw us coming at the same time. The reaction they gave was something that I will never forget. Each of them put their hands up in the air and sort of shouted like aaah for two for three seconds and then they each turned and ran."

Travis lit out after one of the violators. Reaching a slough, the moonshiner plunged in and slogged through it; Travis elected to run across a fallen tree. "After he got to the other side all soaked and wet, he kept running, but he could not hold out for more than 100 yards or so and he gave out a curse and said the hell with it and stood there and I caught him," Travis concluded. "Once these people are caught, they are not offensive, they are not violent or anything."

orders for moonshine and dispatching the transporters. A sample order in gang code went like this: "Tell Tub to get the lead out and . . . scat me out 100 singles" (this meant 100 1-gallon oblong cans). Griffith listened in on the conversations using a makeshift device that he said, perhaps sarcastically, was built out of a Chevrolet hubcap.

Weems was no more enthusiastic about their radios back in the 1950s,

which he described as "probably the worst of any law-enforcement agency in the country." Once he was on surveillance in Atlanta and couldn't maintain contact with a radio car three blocks away, but he found that he could talk to an ATF vehicle in New Orleans. The ATF had its assigned radio frequency; when violators acquired monitors (which were legal) in order to eavesdrop on the federal agents,

According to the original caption, "Secret Service men" are dismantling this tiny still, which eluded detection for a couple of weeks in the underbrush of the Presidio in San Francisco. Authorities detected it by the column of rising smoke when it was run. Note the condensing barrel in the foreground, feeding into a glass jug. The operators of the still escaped. The men in this photo may have been federal Prohibition agents; if the one at left needed the cane he is holding, he probably wouldn't have been much help pursuing the moonshiners, anyway. *Library of Congress*

the ATF issued scramblers, which made the transmissions sound like Chinese, Weems wrote.

They also experimented with "beepers," small radio transmitters that they planted on suspected vehicles. Weems recalled how they lost the signal from the suspected bootlegger, then unknowingly picked up the signal from a beeper that a man had installed on his wife's car to see if she was cheating on him. Puzzled, they followed the car, and stopped and searched it before figuring out what the problem was. At times, they followed beeper signals from airplanes.

In the 1970s, federal agents started adding high-tech tactics to their arsenal. If they came upon a still that wasn't in operation and couldn't wait for the violators, the agents smeared a fluorescent paste on

shovel handles, fuel line valves, and other parts of the still that the still operators would be likely to touch. "The still operators would touch the marked equipment and rub their hands on their shirts," Tetterton explained. Then, at night, "we'd shine a black light on them and they'd light up bright yellow."

This technique was also tried using a drip-pan (containing a fluorescent liquid) secreted under a suspect's car. It would drip out as the car drove to the still or the moonshine stash, and theoretically the agents could follow the trail with an ultraviolet light. Weems described the device as a small metal box with a tube that hung down. He hooked one of the boxes under a suspected vehicle. It gradually dawned on him how ludicrous the concept was, and after the experiment proved to be a

With their aircraft near El Paso, Texas, are what the original caption called "Uncle Sam's 'Dry-Flyers,'" early airborne Prohibition agents: (left to right) head pilot John Wood, pilots Josef Noyes and L. W. Mendell, and chief mechanic Oscal Wallace. When this photo was published, they had captured fifty stills, a rum boat carrying $30,000, and a number of other aircraft smuggling liquor in from Mexico. The bottom photo shows their aircraft at an El Paso airport. *Library of Congress*

disaster, he sarcastically wrote, "Surely I wouldn't attract attention sitting on the hood of a car moving at five miles per hour, a box in my hands, peering intently at the street." Another problem, he said, was that "motor oil would fluoresce just like the liquid, and most of the time the stuff would all drip out before you even started."

Of much more use, particularly when tracking down large operators, was concentrating on the raw materials required by the moonshiners, especially sugar. Near Peoria, Kentucky, Henderson and other agents once investigated large sales of sugar. At one small grocery store, they learned that 120 100lb sacks of sugar recently had been delivered, and a second load was expected. That night, the agents watched 10,000lb of sugar and 1,500lb of cornmeal unloaded.

Sugar wholesalers came under varying levels of scrutiny, and were required to report large sales. Some comparatively small rural stores sold astonishing amounts of sugar, enough for all the home canning and pie-making for entire counties. A former store owner whose business was located next

to the North Carolina border recalled selling 200 bags of sugar a week—ten tons!

Sometimes surveillance was adequate, gathering evidence against merchants who were breaking the law and trailing vehicles away from them to try to find the stills they were supplying. At other times, federal agents went undercover to buy the raw materials for moonshining, making it clear to the people who sold the materials that the sugar and jars were intended for moonshining.

Weems recalled working with a senior agent named Red Martin, a master of the undercover purchase. Martin was always "casual and unhurried." When preparing to buy a truckload of sugar at a market, Martin first bought Cokes, flashlight batteries, pork and beans, Vienna sausages, and a loaf of bread, the kind of rations that still hands typically bought to take to the sites. Then Martin bought 2,400lb of sugar and forty cases of jars.

Surveillance tested the patience and skill of agents. Finding a still was only the beginning—an "unidentified still seizure," in which no operators are caught, did little to solve the moonshine problem because the

operators almost always set up shop somewhere else. Law-enforcement agents were after the operators themselves, and, if they turned out to be simply hired "still hands," they'd try to get the organizer or owner.

During his colorful career, Bunting staked out stills for as long as two weeks. Some of the nights in the woods were long, dark, and futile, with just the bugs, critters, and the sounds of the forest to break the monotony. At about 2:00 A.M., a truck would rumble up to the still. Someone would inspect the equipment and supplies, to see if cops or poachers had been there. If the still passed inspection, the still workers would start to unload jars. More men would arrive, opening the door to the boiler, lighting off the burner. Serious work would begin—at least until the revenuers burst from the woods to scare the hell out of the moonshiners and grab as many as possible.

Henderson once spent two weeks observing some moonshiners while they built six 800-gallon fermenters for a 1,000-gallon still. Tetterton had similar experiences.

At center is T. B. Turner, a Virginia ABC officer. A. W. Chappell is at left, and state trooper Mike Frank is in uniform at right. Another unidentified seizure; the agents are taking a quick, informal inventory. Agents wear dark work clothes for seizures in the woods; Frank arrived after the original seizure to observe. *Bill Tetterton Collection*

"Some stills you might just walk right in on them operating it," he said. "Another one we watched for almost a year," but were never able to catch the operator. "We kept trying to figure out his schedule or a pattern," Tetterton said, but couldn't do it. When they finally caught him, he told them that he never had a schedule; he just ran the still whenever he got a chance.

Long-time North Carolina ABC agent Jim Ward said that they often staked out stills in Pitt County, North Carolina, but "there were so darn many stills you couldn't watch them all." They picked the ones that seemed most promising. "A lot of times you couldn't get into a piece of woods without someone seeing you," he explained; someone who lived on the road, for example, and who knew the violator and probably would warn him. Ward recalled once watching a 500–600-gallon still for a week without any luck. They finally had to blow it up and move on with other investigations.

Law-enforcement authorities also would stake out storage buildings or transfer points. "The bane of the moonshine runner was to be caught red-handed by revenooers on foot who had been waiting for him at a supply stache [sic] or moonshine terminal," Kearins wrote. "I have heard moonshiners say that it was not fair to catch them on foot when they had gone to all the expense and trouble of buying and maintaining the fastest car they could get."

Aircraft (both fixed-wing and helicopters) proved to be invaluable tools for federal agents. They had been used by the Coast Guard during Prohibition to look for rumrunners (see chapter 6). In the mid-1960s, the Coast Guard (like ATF then, a branch of the Treasury Department) helped its fellow agency look for stills from small aircraft. They always did it in the spring before the leaves came out. In terms of the amount of ground you could cover, riding in an airplane was an order of magnitude better than being on foot.

In Dawson County, the airborne ATF observer in a Coast Guard plane found three stills the first day; two were in operation, and the operators fled as soon as the plane once started to circle above. Weems, who was the first ATF special agent and pilot and who later supervised the Air Operations Section at ATF headquarters in Washington, D.C., became deeply involved in aerial surveillance and searches, at first with a volunteer civilian pilot, and soon with a full-time contract for the services. During the first five months that ATF used a full-time pilot, agents seized seventy-six stills (with a combined capacity of 191,000 gallons) and thirty-eight vehicles.

More than one moonshiner found that airborne revenuers made a major dent in their business. Some days the aircraft would locate five or six stills, as the harassed moonshiners were lucky to get off three or four runs before their stills were seized and destroyed.

Still-hunting from the air was a challenge, Weems explained. One tip-off was finding trails in unusual areas. "You just have to develop an eye for it," he said. He often found stills hidden by camouflaged netting. In time, he developed a special sense when something didn't look quite right. The precise clues were hard to explain; as an analogy, Weems pointed out that "the guys who fly around looking for marijuana say that they can find it by the color."

Informants

Perhaps as important as hardware was the human factor. Tips from informers have always been a valuable part of the agent's arsenal of tricks. Tips come from a variety of sources. In the late 1800s, informers were often motivated by the $5.00 or $10.00 reward, or simply by personal grudges. According to Wilbur Miller, author of *Revenuers & Moonshiners: Enforcing Federal Liquor Law in the Mountain South, 1865–1900,* " many people would walk twenty-five miles to swear out a warrant," but in other cases, next-door neighbors would deny knowledge of stills that were almost within eyesight.

It was once common for marshals (or "fee deputies") to get paid per arrest instead of per conviction, so they would sometimes trump up charges and arrest alleged "moonshiners" just for the fees, or pay professional informers to testify against innocent people.

Anonymous tips often came from women, who were considered by law-enforcement agents to be more reliable than men. According to Bill Tetterton, many informants were interested in "eliminating the competition." Duff Floyd, summing up his thirty-five-year career as an ATF agent in Georgia, said most of the tips they got were from other moonshiners. "A lot of times we had information—we'd get letters or phone

numerous disguises during his career. One of his most successful ploys was to sell fish, traveling a large circuit and attracting lots of attention, singing, dancing, and talking a blue streak. Bunting also swept streets, worked in sawmills and carnivals, and posed as a coon hunter looking for a lost dog. One of his favorite pieces of equipment was an ancient pickup truck that he had seized from a violator. Its fenders, hood, and roof were banged up and rusted. Its paint was splotchy, it had a dog box in the back, a steering wheel from a bus, and creaky doors. Every gauge on the dashboard was broken. It was, in short, a perfect undercover truck. "This damn vehicle probably caught more violators than any other in the state," Bunting told author Alec Wilkinson.

Agents sometimes patrolled by car, cruising moonshine enclaves, looking for anomalies and inexplicable behavior. Much of the job was patience and experience, but luck played a role, too. Tetterton said that in a remote section of Southampton County, Virginia, near Boykins, he and his partner once heard a tractor coming. They quickly backed into a crude road in the woods, and Tetterton immediately saw the smokestack from a nearby still.

While Weems was working for ATF, they often used an old panel truck for surveillance, parking several blocks away and watching suspects through binoculars. At one point his unit also got an "observation vehicle," a large van that looked like a meat truck, outfitted with small windows for shooting photos, a periscope, and an engine that they could start from the back.

Because savvy bootleggers learned to recognize the cars driven by revenuers, law-enforcement personnel had to change cars often to vary the sound of their engines. They also changed license plates.

Agents often had to follow suspects at night, and had noticed that when they were following a vehicle that had its lights off, when the driver hit the brakes, you could see those lights. As a sort of auto-

calls," Jim Ward recalled. "They never told us their names. Sometimes it was other moonshiners, or their enemies."

Of course, turnabout was fair play. Sometimes the moonshiner forces were able to penetrate the law-enforcement agencies, gathering useful information. Or they'd bribe a sympathetic officer, finding out where roadblocks or patrols were planned, for example.

W. George McMullen wrote of an informant who said that he had seen 125 5-gallon jugs in a house. When the police and other liquor agents arrived, the owner of the house let them in, casually announcing, "You may find a little liquor in here." They discovered 112 5-gallon jugs, and methodically broke them all. "It was really a stinking mess by the time we finished," McMullen recalled. Thanks to an informant, he had been part of "the largest seizure of moonshine whiskey I knew of in my twenty-eight years with the U.S. Treasury." In another in-

stance, an informer led McMullen to a whopper still with forty-six 50-gallon fermenters, a 500-gallon vat, and a 300-gallon distilling unit.

Chief Howard Smith of Clayton County, Georgia, once called in Weems when Smith heard that a neighbor, suffering from what can only be described as temporary insanity, had set up a still on the farm in front of Smith's house. Weems, like all agents, found such tips (from either anonymous or paid informants) extremely useful during his career.

Undercover

Just as bootleggers would try to camouflage their loads of illicit liquor, so did revenuers make use of disguises. In the nineteenth century, they often would pose as people trying to buy cattle or fur, or as traveling salesmen. Sometimes they posed as hunters, fishermen, or tourists.

Although Garland Bunting often just blended in with the local farmers, he also used

North Carolina state ABC officer William Boyd tests a batch of mash to gauge how close this still was to "running." The still was seized in Pitt County, North Carolina, in March 1993. *Cliff Hollis,* The Daily Reflector, *Greenville, North Carolina*

motive disguise, some of the government cars were wired so that the driver could turn off the headlights, brake lights, and taillights one at a time, to make it look like a series of different cars. "We learned about that from a violator, who had rigged up his brake lights that way," Weems explained. "Then we improvised from there. It worked. We'd follow for a while, then turn off on a side road, then come back after changing our lights."

The Raid

Arriving at an active but untended still, agents used the condition of the fermenting mash to gauge when to return and seize the moonshiners. Tetterton said most agents simply stick a finger in and taste it, to see how old the mash is and how close it is to being ready to run. If it's sweet and doesn't taste like beer, it isn't ready yet. Weems preferred inserting a finger and letting it dry to see if it felt sticky. If it did, it meant that there was too much sugar in the mash.

Agents also study the condition of the path to the still and the equipment to determine how long it has been there. If the still is fired by wood (a rarity these days) they see how much ash has accumulated. They also see if the surrounding vegetation has been discolored by mash fumes, and how much trash or garbage is laying around (attentive

agents have found receipts for raw materials and supplies).

In the case of smaller stills, the moonshiners visited them periodically until the "run," when the liquor was produced. For extremely large operations, the still hands sometimes lived right there in the woods. In either case, law-enforcement officers wanted to capture criminals, not just find stills. "We were always trying to get the big man, the one putting up the money," Tetterton observed. "We were never trying to just destroy stills—we always wanted to make arrests."

Law-enforcement agents usually prefer a team of three or four people for raiding a tended still—this number enables them to surround it. Once the moonshiners see or hear the law officers, it is every man (or woman) for himself. Sometimes they surrender, sometimes they fight, and many

Looking from the other direction, a ten-gallon wooden barrel (center) serves as the doubler for this still. The metal roofing propped against the still holds in heat and masks the light from the fire at night. The 5-gallon glass demijohns (front right) were one of the favorite containers used in this part of Virginia for bottling moonshine, as were glass home-canning jars (a box of them is visible at far left). *Bill Tetterton Collection*

times they run. "I've been outrun more than once," Tetterton observed.

Jim Ward started out at age thirty-two working with a sixty-seven-year-old former police chief named John Taylor. "He was a good teacher, but he couldn't do much running," Ward said. "I'd run my tongue out." Taylor sometimes fired warning shots to halt fleeing violators; even then, they didn't always stop. Finding the stills didn't seem to be a major problem, particularly when they were so common; it was latching on to the violators. "The biggest trouble we had would be them trying to run off. A few of them would fight you." On rare occasions, revenuers have found moonshiners on site unconscious from drinking too much of their own product.

At a time when revenue agents were paid per arrest, they sometimes arrested people but ignored the still itself, prompting charges that they were simply trying to arrest the moonshiners over and over to collect fees.

In most cases—and always with federal seizures—the stills were destroyed. As early as the mid-1800s, according to Miller, still-raiding parties included specialists called "hatchet men," whose "job it was to smash up a still as quickly as possible, as it was dangerous to stay around a still-house too long." Some stills were seized and carried off to auction, but that was usually impractical or impossible, given the remote locations preferred by moonshiners. In one ATF agent's reminiscences, he recalled a local constable who got $10.00 from the county for every captured still, plus the proceeds from selling whatever tools and equipment he could salvage at the site: axes, hoes, copper pipe, barrels.

McMullen, while working as an agent in Tampa, Florida, recalled that they broke the seized liquor in a specially built trough in the basement of the post office. He said the vapors often got too strong, driving them outdoors for fresh air repeatedly during the job. Ward's biggest seizure was 2,605 gallons. The still had been surreptitiously installed in an empty house; the owner of the property didn't know the still was there, and didn't want the moonshine dumped out on his property. Ward said that they had

A surplus Army field stove forms the base of this still. The moonshiner had inserted a 55-gallon barrel, then put the cap on top. The pipe at left goes to the doubler. Bill Tetterton, an ATF agent then stationed in Emporia, Virginia, was part of the team that seized this still in Greensville County, Virginia, in June 1972. *Bill Tetterton Collection*

Ward said, "they'd bail out and they would be gone."

Weems worked with investigators Jack Berry and Vic Bernhardt, who were both skilled at "intercepting and chasing trippers" who were bringing moonshine into Atlanta. They drove Fords with Cadillac engines "which had been seized while transporting moonshine," Weems wrote. One technique was to park slightly above the level of a highway, and shine a small spotlight on a suspicious vehicle's back seat, looking for large objects covered with a blanket. When they spotted a likely suspect, they'd peel out after him at 60mph, running without lights until they caught up. Then they'd hit the siren and

the lights. Some bootleggers hit the brakes; others hit the gas.

George Griffith also wrote about watching roads. He recalled seeing empty vehicles going one way, and then coming back loaded. Griffith would drop down and follow them without lights. "Some jackrabbited and raced," he wrote. "Some stopped and surrendered." One ATF agent thought that parking by a road and waiting for a transporter was "naive" because they'd be long gone by the time the agent ever got up to speed. He decided that the best way to intercept a bootlegger was to cruise along suspected routes at 60mph and wait for one to pass him.

Once a law-enforcement official spotted a suspicious vehicle and gave chase, the fun began in earnest. Cal Cates, a police officer from Fulton County, Georgia, told author Joseph Dabney, "We could catch up with 'em a lot of times, but then the problem was stopping them." He said they tried to bump them off the road, usually on a curve, making them lose control and wrecking the bootlegger's car. State revenuers welded a steel rail around one car, as a bumper. In one month in 1937, state agents knocked fourteen liquor cars out of commission.

Duff Floyd used heavy iron spikes mounted in a hinged metal base that was about twelve feet long. His approach was to put it at the entrance to a bridge, in order to stop cars that had refused to stop at a roadblock just up the road. Tetterton recalled devices called "wampum belts," which were spiked with hollow steel needles that would continue to release the air from tires. Older bootleggers often refer to the spiked devices

involves gadgets, real or legendary, of the kind shown in television shows such as "The Untouchables."

The cult film *Thunder Road* shows a federal agent's car equipped with a pair of large mechanical hooks, that would latch onto the bumper of a bootlegger's vehicle. Tetterton thinks that bumper grabbers were actually used in the 1920s. Others are skeptical. The film also shows a liquor car equipped with a device that lays down an oil slick (Dabney erroneously calls it "smoke-bomb tanks that would lay down a screen of black smoke"). Smokers were more common in real life. One source says that they burned "oily cloth saturated in moonshine, creosote, hot peppers and crankcase oil." Regardless of the noxious recipe, the devices were effective. Federal agents in Habersham County, Georgia, once plunged into a river during a chase when the bootleggers turned on a smoker near a sharp curve beside a river. The state revenue supervisor in northern Georgia, David Ayers of Cornelia, once chased a smoker for twenty-two miles from Livonia through Royston. He had to roll down the window to try to see, after the windshield wipers got gummed up with the oily smoke. It didn't help much, and the pepper burned and stung his eyes. The bootlegger left him behind, but neglected to turn off the smoker, providing a convenient airborne trail which Ayers followed, eventually getting close enough to shoot out the bootlegger's tires.

Revenuers faced an uphill task even when the transporters didn't have any gadgets. Bill Griffin summed up the consensus of law-enforcement authorities when he observed that the moonshiners simply had better cars. As former ATF agent Joe Carter wrote in his book, *Damn the Allegators,* "I don't recall an agent ever catching a moonshiner car to car, driving man to man." The usual ATF cars during that phase of Griffin's career were six-

as "belts." Tetterton also described "jack rocks," bent and welded steel spikes that you could throw on the road to deflate tires. He heard of strikers using them in the coal fields to disable police vehicles. He also heard that a police department in California is using spiked planks, and recently saw an ad for the device in a law-enforcement magazine.

On rare occasions, agents tried to block cars by pulling one or two vehicles into the road; this technique resulted in some spectacular wrecks (Bill Griffin, an ATF agent stationed at Greeneville, Tennessee, had two brand-new cars wrecked that way). Agents started concentrating on the delivery spots, where they would try to get license numbers, seize the liquor, and pick up the delivery car later if it fled the scene.

The most intriguing aspect of the hardware side of "working transportation"

Virginia ABC officer A.W. Chappell inspects mash barrels that have been wrapped in burlap bags, fencing material, and pine straw, both to hold in heat, speed fermentation of the mash, and provided camouflage. *Bill Tetterton*

A. W. Chappell glances into the woods, perhaps in response to a noise. This still had been partly disassembled (the cap had been removed) when law-enforcement officers arrived. The green container at far left is the fuel supply for the still (the black object in front of the barrel). *Bill Tetterton Collection*

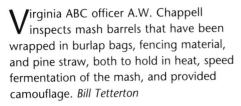

cylinder 1944 and 1948 Fords, augmented by whatever they could seize from the bootleggers. According to federal revenue laws, agents could seize any vehicle used in "the furtherance of" a crime, whether it was used to transport illegal liquor, or even to accept payment for the illegal liquor. In some cases, seized cars were auctioned off. Early NASCAR driver Tim Flock recalled that in Atlanta, seized cars were auctioned on Saturday mornings. Even though the sheriff who seized each car could keep half the money, many of the vehicles were quickly back in the transporting business. "This just run them crazy," Flock said.

In Pitt County, North Carolina, money for auctioned vehicles went to the school fund: "Some of them were good cars, and some were real pieces of junk," Ward said.

Even when the federal agents captured a souped-up car, government funding rarely let them maintain the cars as well as the moonshiners did. Within the ATF hierarchy, the regional special agents got "most of the good cars" that were seized, Weems wrote, so the local agents "were usually left with the rough vehicles" and "clunkers," which were at least good for surveillance.

In spite of disparities in horsepower, federal agents held up their end of the bargain. Tetterton recalled with a grin, "Oh, we used to get out there and run 'em. I've been outrun twice by the same car on the same road. He knew where he was going and I didn't. Plus, I

was driving an old 1962 Ford and I couldn't keep it on the road."

Other things would interfere with agents, too. Tetterton also heard about an agent in Martinsville, Virginia, who was stopped by the local police during a high-speed chase and given a ticket for reckless driving. "Back then the local police were on the side of the violators," he pointed out.

High-speed chases make great movie stunts, but in real life they are extremely hazardous. Six months before Weems joined ATF, two investigators were chasing "Crash" Waller, described as a "known transporter in Haralson County" west of Atlanta. They topped a hill at 95mph and arrived at a T-intersection. Waller, in a "souped-up 1950 Oldsmobile," hit a ditch; his load of moon-

A. W. Chappell at the site of a seizure in Southampton County, Virginia. He may be looking for footprints. The still is the black object at left. The red and green can holds the fuel supply. This still was discovered via an informant. *Bill Tetterton Collection*

shine shifted and crushed him. He was severely injured, and went to prison after he recovered. One of the federal agents was killed, and the other seriously injured.

Yet there were successes, too. In the mid-1950s, working transportation in

Georgia, Weems recalled making forty-four arrests in a three-month period. In 1955, working with Carl Koppe (a former Atlanta police officer and then a Fulton County deputy) and driving a 1946 Ford with a souped-up Olds engine, they averaged capturing two liquor cars a week.

Weems recalled with affection a 1950 Oldsmobile that had a Hydramatic transmission. "If you stayed on the accelerator, it would burn rubber every time it changed gears. I loved it," he wrote. Hazards aside, "Working transportation was always a lot of fun. It gave me the opportunity to experience the thrill of high-speed driving without being arrested."

Although many transporters were wizards on the rural roads of the South in

their home counties, the tables were turned if they ventured north into large cities. "One such guy sent word to me in New York that he would suck my Plymouth up his exhaust pipe," Jack Kearins wrote. "The results were pitiful . . . He was a sitting duck," because Kearins knew all of the shortcuts and one-way streets. He started the chase at 125th Street, crossed Lenox, and caught him at 7th, at which point the revenuer "gave him a light calling card on his rear bumper."

Kearins also recalled chasing a truck that was carrying 1,500 gallons of moonshine. He tried to pull it over, but the truck driver veered into the agent's car, knocking it up on two wheels. "I heard the grinding of

In Sussex County, Virginia, in the early 1970s. Carl Bonds, formerly with the ATF and now a special agent with the Virginia state police, is closest to the camera. Four mash barrels are visible. One moonshiner was captured during this seizure. *Bill Tetterton Collection*

metal and breaking of glass and I felt our car as it started over on its side," he wrote. "I felt the rocking as it settled back on four wheels." The truck plowed through a yard, a cemetery, through some woods, finally stopping when a rear tire went flat. The windows on Kearins' car were jammed shut, but he and another agent jumped out and caught the truck drivers on foot.

Weems also recalled a heart-stopping incident, during which he and another agent had been following a truck at about 50mph, with no lights, and one agent hanging out the window watching the edge of the road. They topped a hill to find that the truck had stopped. Weems had to slam on the brakes and swerve left, almost throwing the agent out the window.

Sweeps and Crackdowns

The routine enforcement of liquor laws, which generally netted equal numbers of stills and violators in familiar places from year to year, was sometimes punctuated by special "sweeps," campaigns, crackdowns, or other unusual enforcement efforts, well-publicized with posters proclaiming such things as, "Remember . . . moonshining is a national disgrace! . . . You can help smash

this million-dollar racket and crime breeder." If moonshiners hadn't been so persistent and mobile, and if laws hadn't been so lenient, and if the demand for bootleg liquor hadn't been so powerful, these special campaigns would have had more than the transitory and sporadic successes that resulted.

In the South in the early 1960s, a number of campaigns were particularly effective, at least on a countywide or statewide basis. Operation Dry Up is usually mentioned as an example. One phase targeted moonshiners in South Carolina in 1963, using air reconnaissance as one tactic. In a second phase, in northern Georgia in October 1965, agents destroyed fifty-six stills the first day, 135 by the end of the third day, and 600 by the end of six weeks, making 165 arrests in the process.

The localized effectiveness of the effort was apparent in 1967, when neighboring

This July 1971 seizure netted a gasoline-fired still. Fermenters are visible at left. The spigot on the still was to empty out the slop after the run. In this area of Virginia, most of the trees are pine, which burns too quickly to make useful fuel for stills. *Bill Tetterton Collection*

Alabama surged back into the national lead for still seizures with 5,864; Operation Dry Up may have worked so well in Georgia that it simply drove the moonshiners across the border.

Authorities worked hard to enlist public support in the campaign; influential newspapers, such as the *Atlanta Journal*, ran a series of articles pointing out that the state and federal governments were losing $70 million in tax revenue every year, because of moonshiners in Georgia. As a result of this phase of Operation Dry Up, still seizures dropped to 1,500 in Georgia by 1967 (the state had averaged between 3,000 and 5,000 earlier in the decade). A third phase of the campaign targeted Alabama in 1968.

Other concentrated efforts have been mounted through the years. In early 1980, for example, ATF conducted what one account called an "aggressive campaign" in Franklin County, Virginia, termed "the unofficial moonshine capital of the United States." Agents arrested more than fifty moonshiners and dynamited ninety-seven stills.

In May 1993, National Public Radio aired a story about a huge still that had been

To one historian, the car seemed "made to order for hauling illicit booze," able to carry 120 gallons (a common load was twenty cases of twelve 1/2-gallon jars), hug the road, and handle easily. Kellner wrote that bootleggers "scoured the country for these cars," paying a premium of as much as $2,000 for them. Dabney quoted an ATF agent from northern Georgia, recalling moonshine transporters in the late 1940s and early 1950s. "Hot rod Fords were *the* thing," he said. "If you didn't have a '40 Ford, you weren't a bona fide violator. You were just some kind of cheap imitation."

"The '40 coupe was the most popular," added Fred Goswick, a former transporter who later operated the Moonshine Museum in Dawsonville, Georgia. "When you saw one, you just naturally thought of moonshine." Early stock-car drivers also grew to appreciate this model Ford, along with the 1939 model. Others cited the 1936 Ford coupe as a favorite vehicle; early stock-car racer Tim Flock once surmised that, in his experience, 1934 and 1935 Fords hauled the most moonshine.

From 1932 through 1948, the Ford V-8 had ruled the roost as the most powerful stock car on the market, superseded only when the big Oldsmobile and Cadillac V-8s

came out in 1949. One source said that the 1949 Oldsmobile 88 took over as the car of choice for some bootleggers. Still others preferred the 1951 Chrysler New Yorker, which had a huge engine but looked more like a family or businessman's car. When Tetterton was working in the western part of Virginia in the 1960s, the most common liquor car was a 1955 or 1956 Ford.

Whatever the make or model, Tetterton observed, one thing was invariably true: "They had more'n we had."

Drivers and cars alike entered local folklore, and reputations grew. "Both the chased and the chaser would often enter into a jargon at some gas station or country store and discuss area moonshine cars as though they were personalities," ATF investigator Jack Kearins wrote in his book *Yankee Revenooer.* "They would talk of the merits and demerits built into those vehicles, and of new trends in racing, and about the legendary figures of the mountain speedways."

Some drivers survived to have comparatively long careers. The cars, however, didn't last nearly as long. Even if they didn't get wrecked or seized, they took a tremendous beating. Dabney interviewed seventy-five-year-old Hubert Howell of Cherokee

County, Georgia, who made moonshine in late 1920s and early 1930s. Howell recalled that in the late 1920s when the liquor market was strong, he would buy a new car every six months. "Tear 'em up," he said. "They wouldn't be worth nothin' when I'd get through with 'um. Driving around on them rough roads, drive just like somethin' after me all the time. Just as hard as I could go. It's a wonder I didn't get killed." Howell preferred Chevrolets, but owned numerous Fords, including a 1927, 1928, and the first 1929 in the county. "I turned it over in Floridey and tore it all to pieces," he recalled.

George Griffith once caught a bootlegger named Tom Baker who, he observed, had "wrecked three new cars since he got out of the pen two or three weeks ago." Recalling his days running liquor in Tennessee during the 1930s and 1940s, one transporter said—which seems certain to be wild exaggeration—that you were lucky if you kept a car a week before it was seized or wrecked.

One transporter wore out a set of tires in less than 200 miles racing back and forth between Dawsonville and Atlanta, and was fired for his trouble. His mechanic from Atlanta recalled that he simply accelerated

North Carolina state ABC officer J. L. Ross and deputy sheriff Marvin Coward were driving this state 1956 Chevy on the night of October 25, 1956, in hot pursuit of a 1956 Buick carrying 60 gallons of moonshine. Roaring down Stantonsburg Road in Pitt County, North Carolina, the bootlegger lost control of his car and caused the wreck that resulted in the damage shown in this photo. Neither Ross nor Coward were hurt. The violator crawled out of his car and took off, limping, and got away. He was later arrested hiding under his bed at home. *Jim Ward*

through corners and curves, never using the brake, and sliding sideways, like a sprint car on a dirt track. Excessive power could backfire, of course. One agent recalled instances in which a combination of spinning wheels and violent maneuvers sheared a rear axle in a transporter's vehicle, stranding the driver.

Dabney quoted a former bootlegger: "I had more nerve than brains. Usta come down out of those mountains in that hopped-up Ford, drove around those curves on narrow roads all the way from up there at Tate . . . I've throwed one of them hopped-up Fords 100 miles an hour around them curves lots of times."

In spite of this horsepower race, ultra-high-speed chases were far from routine, and the colorful Thunder Road era gradually passed into history. More and more law-enforcement officers were equipped with cars that could match the speed of most bootleggers, and improved investigation techniques negated most of the tactics developed by bootleggers. The classic moonshine transporter car, hulled out and with a huge engine, became a rarity. Moonshine had always been trans-

lengths to hide their loads. They quickly discovered that reinforced springs were essential when carrying heavy loads. These extra springs in the rear made a liquor car "stand on its head" when it wasn't "leveled" with a load of moonshine. Griffith wrote of meeting a black rumrunner in Nashville named Son Lockhart; on his car, "the over-load springs made it look like it was tiptoeing." One refinement was to install three extra leaves in the springs on each side in the back, but to have the springs "tempered straight" so they didn't make the car sit up when unloaded. Some mechanics took the springs off a Model T and mounted them to the axles of a 1940 Ford, so it wouldn't sink any more than an inch. Later, they used load

levelers, "clip coils," and air-lift springs. Overinflated tires were a necessity.

With high-riding cars, bootleggers could attach bottles of liquor under the suspension with wires. They could also hide varying quantities in tool boxes, and in spare tires and trunks. Mechanics and sheet-metal experts installed false floors in cars, adding extra-long pedals and shift levers, thereby creating enough space to store 20 gallons of liquor; rumrunners used a similar approach in adding false decks and holds to the boats they used for smuggling. Some bootleggers installed phony gas tanks, tanks within tanks, or false roofs that could conceal 20–25 gallons.

McMullen recalled seizing a car that contained forty to sixty cases, with none in

Packaging jugs of moonshine in paper bags made it easier to transfer or divide up, prevented it from clinking, and kept large amounts of liquid weight from shifting during turns, as it would have in a "tanker" car. *Charles Abernathy photo file, ATF Reference Library*

ported in ways that were more pedestrian and more ingenious.

Bootleggers at all levels developed a variety of ploys that were more effective and more clever than simply mashing the pedal to the metal. Sometimes they were simply brazen. Former transporter Tiny Lund of Taylorsville, North Carolina, recalled one of his first moonshine runs as "quiet" and "sneaky." They drove to a hardware store downtown, unloaded the cases of Mason jars full of moonshine right across the sidewalk, and set them in the store's window. More often, however, disguise and evasion were the key words. Transporters, wrote W. George McMullen, "reached a remarkable degree in the art of camouflaging their loads." McMullen was a customs patrol officer and Alcohol Tax Unit (ATU) agent.

One woman remembered that when she was three or four, she accompanied her mother and her mother's boyfriend on some informal, amateur bootlegging jaunts. The adults would stash the bottles of liquor under the back seat of the car; then she'd go to sleep on the seat. She recalled a police officer shining a flashlight through the window, and her mom politely asking him not to wake her up.

Bootleggers interested in carrying more than a few bottles had to go to greater moonshine runner didn't always end when his car was out of action from fatigue, or crash, or even tumbling end over end on a steep mountainside." Sometimes the chase continued on foot. Fred Goswick never got caught, but said that he "got close to it several times. I could leave a car running right fast."

A North Carolina sheriff recalled a night in 1921 when he had pulled his car across the road, armed with a shotgun and waiting for a moonshine transporter. "The usual method of the trippers, they'd come around a curve and see the road blocked, and they'd jump out and high-tail it and leave the car and the liquor," the sheriff told Dabney. "They figured they could lose every third car and still come out with a profit." In this case, they tried to make a U-turn, the sheriff blasted off their rear tire with the shotgun, and still had to chase them twelve miles.

Goswick was once carrying a load with his cousin, just after the interstate highway near Atlanta was completed. His cousin had gotten off the highway and gone into town, and had parked at the Varsity, a popular drive-in, when the police decided to check him out and inspect the car. Goswick's cousin took off on foot, and the police gave chase. So Fred got in his cousin's car and drove it. They caught his cousin and brought him back, but the evidence had vanished and they couldn't make any charges stick.

A typical multi-stack headline in the May 11, 1924, edition of the Norfolk *Virginian-Pilot* reveals how bootleggers refined their techniques: "City Manager Orders Borland and Ironmonger to 'Go the Limit' in Discovering Real Ownership of Autos Found Full of Liquor; Drivers Abandon Cars; Owners Report 'Thefts'; 'Well Known Bootleggers' and Others Not So Well Known Develop New Methods to Evade Capture; Fictitious Addresses Given." The story dealt with the seizure of a Dodge truck found loaded with 100 gallons of whiskey in a Norfolk warehouse. The article explained, "The latest development in the ramifications of the bootleg industry is the practice of the liquor runner hiring a man to haul liquor in his car, and instructing the man to abandon the car on the approach of the police. The car is confiscated, and shortly afterward the owner files with the police a formal report that his car has been stolen."

Another tactic, used during the early years of Prohibition, was for bootleggers to register their cars with names taken from tombstones, using the address of a vacant lot. These cars, when seized, couldn't be traced.

Without a doubt, liquor runners needed good nerves and good powers of observation. A knowledge of human nature didn't hurt, either. Goswick used to start picking his nose if a police officer seemed to be staring at him for an inordinate amount of time. That proved to be enough to make anybody stop staring.

The Transporter's Technique

In his study of bootlegging during Prohibition in northern New York, Everest found that the largest group of bootleggers were men in their twenties or thirties. They owned their own cars and were self-employed. They sometimes shared information, but ran solo. Another group, he found, "included the eager beavers who could be hired to drive a load across the border," working for organizers in Saratoga, Glens Falls, or New York City. A car might be furnished. They earned a variety of wages: $50.00 per week and expenses, or $10.00 per day, or a flat rate per trip, or even just a case of liquor. Of course, during the Depression, regular jobs paid just $1.50 or $2.00 per day, when jobs were to be found.

A few customs officers left their jobs and became bootleggers. "When they did so they were likely to be extraordinarily tough and skillful, for they knew all the tricks of the trade from the inside," Everest wrote. He mentions a trio of turncoats, including Ralph Hackmeister (he had been known as "the terror of rumrunners" until 1922), who resigned from the service and was arrested for rumrunning the next year; Edward Cronk, who was also later jailed; and Floyd Cool, who was captured in 1931, escaped into Canada, and ended up sentenced to the federal pen in Atlanta.

In the South in the 1940s and 1950s, most bootleggers were young men, some as young as teenagers, others in their twenties. They were rarely self-employed; instead, they worked for other people or groups who financed and organized larger operations. They tended to enjoy mechanics, especially high-performance engines. Kellner, who interviewed several former bootleggers, added two other traits: "they were shutmouthed and wary away from home, and all were devil drivers on the mountain roads."

The mechanics of the operation were reasonably simple. Novice drivers were trained by the organizer or ringleader. They were given detailed instructions, and equipped with special cars, usually a sedan or coupe with seats removed or the trunk expanded or altered. Sometimes workers called "keg-men" had already collected the load of moonshine from the stills and had loaded the car at a secret location before the driver picked up the car. At the other end of the trip, a similar technique was sometimes used. Goswick said that when he was transporting moonshine, he would park the loaded car, get out, and walk down the street. Someone else would take the car, drive off, and unload it, then bring it back.

The existence of "tanker" cars has been a topic of some dispute among writers, revenuers, and bootleggers, especially since the film *Thunder Road* shows this device. Kellner, whose research seems reliable in other areas, writes confidently of cars with a large tank installed in the back seat and trunk, holding as much as 250 gallons of moonshine. The tank had baffles installed so that the liquor wouldn't slosh around.

Charlie Weems remains skeptical. "I've never seen one and never even heard of one. I'm not saying it was never tried, but if you put 200 gallons of moonshine in a tank in the trunk of a car and went around a curve a high speed, the weight would shift and it would be awfully hard to control."

According to former transporter Fred Goswick, "We never used tankers. You needed a separate building to use them. They did exist, but they couldn't carry a large volume. And they took time to unload," an observation verified by other bootleggers, who felt that they ran the greatest risk of getting caught while loading or unloading. The tankers Goswick knew about carried the liquor overhead. Some old Plymouths, for example, had a six- to eight-inch space over the door. Goswick also heard of trucks that had six-inch pipes installed under the rails.

Writer Alex Gabbard, who had made bootlegger gadgets an object of special study for several years, has found just two cases of moonshine tanks in cars—once in a 1957 Ford that had been seized, and in which the gas task had been expanded and converted to hold 35–40 gallons, and once in a 1959 Oldsmobile that had a tank built under the back seat. Gabbard writes about both cases in his book, *Return to Thunder Road*.

A driver had to know his primary route and any alternate routes that were available, down to every bend, ditch,

This 1947 Plymouth is a prime example of a liquor car that has been "hulled out" and packed with moonshine. The sinuous gearshift appears to be custom, but it was standard. The metal cans maximized the amount of liquid cargo. *George Henry photo file, ATF Reference Library*

house, and pothole, as well as every place to hide or turn around. "He drew these on a map and went over them again and again, deciding and memorizing the tactics he would use if an emergency arose at any one of these points," Kellner wrote.

"Familiarity with the routes they were running was a must for both the moonshine runner and the revenooer," Kearins added. Jack Smith, describing the highway from Atlanta to Dawsonville to writer Kim Chapin, said: "You knew where every hill was, where every curve was, and you knew where the dead-end

streets was and where you didn't want to get hemmed up at."

Transporters also learned to recognize the undercover cars driven by local police and federal agents. This precaution worked both ways, but according to Weems, "The violators knew our vehicles even better than we knew theirs."

When these young drivers were caught (as many eventually were) and hauled into court, prosecutors often discovered that the drivers didn't even know the identity of their employer. Sometimes they had earned (or had at least been promised) exorbitant fees, which was still only a fraction of the boss' take after the drivers had assumed all of the risk. Law-enforcement officials wanted the ringleaders.

Invariably, whatever the state or the decade, bootleggers gave similar, simple reasons for their trade; money and prestige were foremost. Some bootleggers developed a curious blend of fame and infamy in their home towns and in the revenuers' reports. Plain old thrill-seeking was a potent factor. Many former bootleggers recall the excite-

ment of the chase more vividly than the money they earned. Few felt any ethical qualms about running liquor—most of them felt Prohibition was unfair, had been foisted on them, and that most of the public didn't support it anyway.

Young men were fearless and felt invincible, but youth also had its drawbacks, which modern revenuer Garland Bunting learned to exploit. "I'd find a young boy who'd just managed to land his first job driving a truck for a still," Bunting told author Alec Wilkinson, "and he'd be so proud, and I'd talk about how many trucks I'd hauled, and how many cops I'd outrun, and when I got through he had to tell me some of his feats— you know how a young man's got to brag—and I'd hear enough and say, 'I believe you're lying. I can *prove* mine, but I believe you're lying,' and many times he wound up taking me to the still."

One of the cast of characters at the famous Roanoke moonshine trail of April 1935 was a thirty-year-old woman named Willy Carter Sharpe, who had been arrested for selling moonshine. According to a magazine account of the trial, she had "a passion for automobiles and developed into a fast and efficient driver. A Virginia businessman at the trial, full of admiration, whispered of her accomplishments: 'I saw her go right through the main street of our town and there was a federal car right after her. They were banging away, trying to shoot down her tires, and she was driving at seventy-five miles an hour. She got away. . .' "

Sharpe worked for former mountain men who had organized convoys of cars on the roads at night. Sharpe testified that she often drove a fast car and acted as pilot. "It was the excitement got me," she said, adding that other drivers, "were mostly kids who liked the excitement." Sharpe said that women, some of them from respectable families, visited her after she had been in jail. "They wanted to go along with me on a run at night. They wanted the kick of it."

Not all bootleggers were daredevils, of course. Many cab drivers found it convenient to dabble in bootlegging. One of them, a New York City cabby named Larry Fay, once took a fare from New York to Montreal in the early days of Prohibition. There, he noted that whiskey was selling for $10.00 a case, so he took a chance and bought two cases. Back in Manhattan, he quickly sold the liquor for $80.00 a case. He headed back to Canada immediately. In just nine months, Fay made enough to buy several more cabs and a few trucks, all making runs between New York and Canadian cities.

It is testimony either to Fay's wiliness and luck, or the laxness of authorities, but he didn't have any trouble with the police until he got arrested in Lawrence by a cop who wasn't sympathetic (others had been). At the station, however, Fay found one who was, and, less cash and whiskey, Fay was soon on his way out of town. In 1922, Fay earned an estimated $500,000 from his taxi and bootlegging operations.

Legend, Myth, or History?

Do the roots of NASCAR and organized car racing reach back to the thunder roads and moonshine trails of the rural South? Was the first engine souped-up to win a bet, a race, or as part of what W. E. Butterworth, in his book *The High Wind: The Story of NASCAR Racing,* called "the unofficial—and perhaps even more thrilling—races between the forces of John Law and John Barleycorn"? Similar questions have proven controversial during the well-documented history of American racing. If you ask enough people, you can find any answer that you like.

In her history of NASCAR, titled *Dirt Tracks to Glory: The Early Days of Stock Car Racing as Told by the Participants,* Sylvia Wilkinson mentions moonshine on the first page, a mere twenty lines into the text: Speaking rhetorically to a car, she asks, "Did your start life loaded with a hundred and eighty gallons of moonshine, rocking like a baby cradle when you sloshed to a stop?" She wrote that "many" of the early race car drivers raced during the day and hauled liquor at night, and were still being caught at it as late as 1971, "although the legend had run its course."

Some historians opt for the quantifier "some" instead of "many." According to Jess Carr, "The occupation of runner or transporter-blockader also helped train *some* of the best race-car drivers in the nation." According to Humpy Wheeler, general manager of Charlotte Motor Speedway, the idea that bootleggers started stock car racing "was partially true."

Jack Smith, interviewed in 1975 in his transmission shop in South Carolina, esti-mated that, of the racers driving in 1946–1948, about 70 percent were involved in hauling moonshine. Smith admitted that he had hauled a little liquor in his time. ("It was fun," was his verdict.)

Other sources are a bit more skeptical. According to Allan Girdler, author of *Stock Car Racers,* the idea that bootleggers (although "they did get real good at driving fast on dirt") were a major force in the birth of car racing has "been overdone ever since Hollywood discovered racing." The "main force behind pre-stock car racing was concentrated on the dusty tracks, the bull rings around which semi-pro drivers raced in stripped and battered Ford V-8 coupes," he wrote. "Some of the drivers in those early days had some practice keeping ahead of those who wanted to catch them," he added in a recent letter. "But the two activities were run under different sets of rules. It didn't take long before the guys who worked hard and thought ahead were faster than those who hauled at night and raced by day." But the legend will remain. "The myth lives because people like it," Girdler wrote, just like the legends about the cowboys and the Old West.

Whether those races stemmed from boredom, bragging, or box-office concerns is another question. According to Wheeler, "informal meetings in cow pastures and clearings" decided who had the fastest car. Without a doubt, the transition from dirt-road liquor transporter to dirt-track race-car driver was an easy and agreeable one. Financial rewards may have been less for the latter, but there was plenty of glory to be had, and it was also legal. Many former transporters agreed that racing cars was easier than hauling moonshine.

There seems to be little question that mechanically, the two pursuits were closely related. Smith recalled, "We had shops for years that never touched nothing except whiskey cars—and race cars." The high-performance techniques applied to liquor cars were also used on race cars, even when those cars were supposed to be "stock." As Girdler observed, up until the early 1950s, a certain amount of cheating seems to have been tolerated on the NASCAR circuit: "The cheating in those days was honest cheating," he wrote. "The cheaters used milled cylinder heads, reground camshafts, or overbored cylinders."

Former bootleggers were well represented on June 18, 1949, at the qualifying trials for the first regular "Strictly Stock" NASCAR race, a 150 miler at Charlotte (there had been an experimental race in February). The fastest competitors included leader Bob Flock (with the quickest lap, just under 68mph) in a 1946 Hudson, with brothers Tim and Fonty close behind. Also qualifying was Curtis Turner, whom author Greg Fielden, in his book *Forty Years of Stock Car Racing: The Beginning 1949–1958,* described as "a womanizing lumberjack," and Hubert Westmoreland, "an eccentric moonshiner."

Glenn Dunnaway of Gastonia, North Carolina, eventually drove Westmoreland's 1947 Ford, moving into first place on lap 151 and winning by three laps. However, NASCAR's technical inspector tore down the winning car, which had caused some officials to remark on its unusual stability through the race's bumpy turns. The verdict? "Altered rear springs." The 1947 Ford was a bootlegger car, and "spreading the springs" was a common ploy. Westmoreland filed a $10,000 suit against NASCAR, without avail.

He stayed active in the early NASCAR races, however. At Grand National Race No. 13, 400 laps at Darlington Raceway in South Carolina on September 4, 1950, winner Johnny Mantz drove a Westmoreland-France 1950 Plymouth. And a month later, at Race No. 19 in Hillsboro, North Carolina, Tim Flock took fourth in a Westmoreland 1950 Plymouth. Curtis Turner won one of his races in a Westmoreland 1949 Olds. Dunnaway, incidentally, was ninth in the 1949 final point standings for the Strictly Stock division.

Yet, as NASCAR grew into the world's most successful racing organization, a certain image-consciousness came into play, and the carefree, anti-authoritarian, and (dare we say it) criminal attitudes of some of the early drivers and mechanics became disreputable skeletons in the closet.

When Sylvia Wilkinson interviewed Bill France, Sr., the czar of NASCAR, she quickly discovered that she wasn't going to find out much from him about bootleggers. The sport's official history, she wrote, deals with the topic "tersely." When she asked if it wasn't true that Red Vogt (the brilliant mechanic who suggested the name of the organization) had been well known for building whiskey cars, France said he wasn't sure, but that it was possible. "Thunder Road, the part that excites the legend-seekers, is a road he never drove down, and one he is tired of hearing about," she concluded.

Here are "snapshots" of some of the folks who did drive that road.

Curtis "Crawfish" Crider

Although not one of the premier names in the early days of racing, in 1962 Crider was twelfth in the Grand National point standings. He racked up three top-five finishes, and was in the top ten eighteen times. Together with his brother, Crider wrote, "we did our share" of hauling moonshine. Once they were taking nine or ten cases of liquor from Greenwood, South Carolina, to Abbeville, then were planning to move on to a race in Aiken, South Carolina. They put the liquor on the front of the truck they were using to pull the race car. Then they piled cases of oil, gas cans, and tires on top of the booze.

They couldn't hook up with their customer in Abbeville, so they left the liquor on the truck. They unhooked the race car and headed to a motel. The police stopped them, suspecting that Crider had stolen the tools and tires on the truck. Crider quickly explained that he was a race-car driver. The officer kept shining his flashlight around the truck, and every time it went toward the liquor (one edge of a case was sticking out), Crider directed it toward some other items, explaining about racing. Police soon sent them on their way.

Crider recalled that he usually drove a 1949 Ford coupe for bootlegging. The busiest times were November to January. In December, they'd load the trunk, break off a cedar branch, and leave it sticking out after tying down the trunk lid with a rope. They hoped that it would look like they were carrying a Christmas tree. Or they would pick up a couple of hitchhiking sailors or aviators, to make it look like they were all soldiers traveling together.

Bob, Fonty, and Tim Flock

Tim Flock—Grand National Champion in 1952 and 1955, and later marketing director at Charlotte Motor Speedway—was one of a quartet of brothers whose names are inextricably entwined with the early annals of racing. They had an uncle named "Peachtree" Williams, described as "one of the biggest bootleggers who ever lived in Georgia." Peachtree brought the brothers (Carl, Bob, Fonty, and finally Tim, the youngest) up to Atlanta to go

to school and haul liquor. Tim recalled that his first job was to ride along to keep the bottles from breaking. They put the jars in a net so they wouldn't move around during the drive; the Flocks earned $40.00 a run, and could make two a day.

With a full load, the liquor car's top speed was 85mph—fast enough to elude the police on straight-aways, but not enough on a hill. If they got caught on a hill, Tim held a gallon of liquor out of the window and let it run out on the pursuer's windshield, which sometimes succeeded in making them slow down or run off the road. The police responded by installing a device that was a cross between what Flock described as a "cowcatcher" and "big old-timey ice tongs," with which they would latch onto a bootlegger's rear bumper. The bootlegger's response was to attach his rear bumper with thin wire, so that it would fall off easily.

Flock also recalled that the police would wait by the side of the road and shoot at their radiators with a shotgun. If successful, the

Tim Flock (second from left), successful both on and off the race track, has never been reluctant to tell humorous stories about his early stint as a bootlegger—a pursuit which he and his brothers learned about in Atlanta from an uncle. His brother Fonty is as left. One of Flock's tales, recounted in the text, documents a bumper-grabbing device similar to one shown in the film Thunder Road. *Halifax Historical Society, Inc.*

bootlegger's car would soon overheat. The transporters responded by installing a steel plate in front of the radiator, or by putting the radiator in the trunk, with air scoops up front. Flock said that it took the authorities several months to figure out that trick.

Bob and Fonty Flock ran whiskey for three or four years. When the racetrack at Lakewood in Atlanta tried to ban drivers who had been arrested (a decision that Flock described as "asking for an empty race track"), the cops once recognized Bob and sent two motorcycles out on the track to catch him. Bob went around a couple times, then jumped the bank, plowed through a fence, and disappeared. He turned himself in a few days later, and was fined $136 ($100 for breaking the no-racing rule, and $36.00 for reckless driving, disorderly conduct, and disturbing the peace).

Incidentally, Fred Goswick said that one of the incidents that prompted the Lakewood rule occurred one night when the announcer said that a driver named Roy Hall "couldn't be with us tonight" because he'd been captured carrying a load of moonshine. "If any of you fans want to go see him, he's in the county jail," the announcer joked. "Everyone cheered and laughed, and the mayor heard about it and got real upset," Goswick explained. The city promptly passed the ordinance.

Because of or in spite of their bootlegging backgrounds, the Flock brothers compiled impressive records in the early days of NASCAR. Fonty won fifteen of the fifty-two NASCAR races in 1948. The 1949 final point standings for the Strictly Stock division showed Bob third and Tim eighth.

Ned Jarrett

Jarrett started his career in Hickory, North Carolina, near Wilkes County, legendary hotbed of moonshining. He once estimated that at least half the drivers that he raced against at local tracks were involved in hauling liquor, and that they seemed to have the best cars. Jarrett was Grand National champion in 1961 and 1965.

Junior Johnson

No history of either racing or moonshining is complete without a mention of Junior Johnson, probably the most successful and well known of the people who lived in both worlds. He has told his family story numerous times: Born in 1931, he survived a hard-scrabble childhood, during which there were times when his family didn't have thirty-five cents for

The fact that the seats hadn't been removed from this early 1950s Ford suggests that it may have been pressed into service on the spur of the moment, or that the driver was an amateur. Metal cans have been long out of use in the bootleg trade, although agents still find old rusty ones in the woods. The containers were originally utility cans, meant for such things as kerosene and fuel oil. *Charles Abernathy photo file, ATF Reference Library*

a COD order of seeds. Making moonshine in the winter kept the family from starving.

His father was sought in connection with a record-breaking seizure of moonshine in Ingle Hollow, Wilkes County, in 1935. Authorities collected 7,100 gallons of liquor (1,113 cases, fifty 5-gallon cans, and three 50-gallon barrels), five stills (with a combined capacity of 2,000 gallons per week), and nearly five tons of sugar. According to one source, the floor of the Johnson home

A young Junior Johnson looks confident, and deservedly so given his prowess as a race driver. He was equally adept as a bootlegger, first transporting moonshine at the tender age of fourteen. Although he was eventually arrested at a family still in 1956 and served ten months in jail, he went on to a glory-filled career without ever being ashamed of his roots. *Halifax Historical Society, Inc.*

collapsed from the weight of the whiskey. Some local news accounts said that the seizure set a record.

Johnson never seems to have done anything halfway, and at one point went into moonshining and transporting in a big way. He had crews working for him, running three or four stills at a time, and hauled moonshine as far as Georgia and Mississippi. He started transporting liquor when he was fourteen, earning a reputation as a fearless driver "If you was ridin' with Junior, you'd have to change britches," Thurmond

Brown told Alex Gabbard. [Curiously, one former transporter said that Junior's brother Fred was an even better all-around moonshine driver.]

Johnson said that if he were being chased, he would sometimes open up a big enough lead, then do a Deluxe Turnaround, flick on his headlights, and calmly drive back toward the pursuing police as if he were just another motorist, uninvolved, heading home from work. Also, to get through roadblocks, he once equipped his car with fake police lights and a siren, which he'd turn on to dupe them into opening the roadblock. Mufflers seemed to be ineffective with the huge engines that powered the bootleg cars. "There wasn't no way you

could make my car sound like an ordinary car," he told writer Bill Libby. Libby wrote, Johnson "sacrificed secrecy for speed, and roared through the nights, waking up sleeping citizens in back country cabins."

Junior has always been careful to point out that he was never caught with a load, and that he lost only one car, when the rear end failed. However, he was arrested in 1956 at a family still and was sentenced to two years in jail (he actually spent ten months and three days at Chillicothe, Ohio)

and was fined $5,000. He couldn't pay the fine, so he signed the "pauper's oath," and served an extra thirty days.

This stint, which Johnson has always discussed openly, proved to be no worse than a minor interruption in his already successful racing career. He was one of the racers to beat in the 1950s and early 1960s, winning the Dixie 500 at Talladega, Alabama, in 1963; the National 500 at Charlotte in 1962 and 1963; and the Southeastern 500 in 1965. He would

eventually win fifty Grand National races, then the third highest total of all time.

Johnson was driving for Chevrolet when Tom Wolfe wrote about him for *Esquire* in 1964, in a well-known article entitled "Junior Johnson Is the Last American Hero. Yes!" He stopped driving in 1966, switched gears, and became what Richard Benyo called "the most famous pit general in stock-car racing." Bobby Allison and Cale Yarborough both drove for his team. He has an official pardon for his bootlegging activities, issued by Ronald Reagan before he left the presidency, displayed with his trophies.

Wendell Scott

Scott was the first black driver on the NASCAR circuit, having been recruited when a race promoter decided that having a black driver would help draw crowds. The promoter went to the Danville police department and asked who had speeding records. They suggested Scott, who had been an active local bootlegger. "Take all the old race drivers; you can't think of one that wasn't a bootlegger," he told writer Sylvia Wilkinson.

Scott recalled having a liquor car that would do 95 in second gear (the top speed of the best of the Danville police department's vehicles), and 118 when he shifted into high. Scott was once caught during a nighttime run, got out on bail, borrowed a friend's station wagon, and finished delivering the whiskey.

For his first race, Scott had to borrow back a liquor car that he had sold when it had become too well known to use in hauling moonshine. He entered his first Grand National race in 1961 when he was forty. He also raced in the Sportsman class. At age forty-nine, Scott entered forty-one races.

The film *Greased Lightning* (made by Warner Brothers in the mid-1970s) was about his life and starred Richard Pryor as Scott; Scott himself did some of the stunts.

Buddy Shuman

Shuman was a top-notch mechanic who allegedly built some liquor cars. He was present at the founding meeting of NASCAR in December 1947. He was later a NASCAR technical inspector. In 1954, Shuman headed up the preparation of Ford's cars for the NASCAR Grand National Series.

Curtis Turner

Of all the larger-than-life characters in a flamboyant cast, Curtis "Pops" Turner took the Oscar. He was born 1924 in the Blue Ridge Mountains in southwestern Virginia; his father was a prominent moonshiner in Floyd County who, Turner once said, bought "whole boxcar loads" of Oldsmo-

biles, converted them to whiskey cars, and ran them in caravans, figuring some would get through. Turner made his first liquor run when he was ten.

He once eluded police on a run by switching on a siren and revolving light. When he finished the run, he counted four bullet holes in his car. "Don't believe any of this stuff about how it was a game and all, and how everybody was real nice to everybody," he told writer Kim Chapin in *Fast as White Lightning: The Story of Stock Car Racing.* "Runnin' was a lot of fun, though. You enjoyed it . . . You get a feelin' after you haul a load of liquor similar to what you do when you win a race."

"Some ol' state trooper ran me thirty-nine times, but he never come close," Turner told Bill Libby, author of *Heroes of Stock Car Racing.* "I used to talk with that ol' trooper between times and he'd say, 'I'm going to catch you with the goods if it's the last thing I do,' but he never did."

During the war, Turner worked at the Little Creek Naval Station in Norfolk, developing a lucrative sideline by stealing sugar (which was extremely scarce in stores) from the base. He'd trade the sugar for moonshine, then sell the liquor to sailors around town. The authorities found out, let him load up with 500lb of sugar, then tried to arrest him on the way out the gate. He crashed through the barricade and took off. Although he lost his pursuers, they notified other authorities along the way. He stopped once to siphon some gas out of a school bus, and eventually made it to Roanoke, where the police were waiting for him. They arrested him, tried him, and he was fined $2,000 and given a two-year suspended jail sentence.

He acquired the nickname "Pops" because he "popped" (banged) other drivers' doors during races. A fellow driver once said that Turner had trouble finding sponsors because they knew that after the race, invariably he would have torn off the running boards and bashed up the fenders.

Turner started late in his racing career and won just seventeen NASCAR races (he won seven of the fifty-two NASCAR races in 1948); however, his reputation and popularity went far beyond these statistics. Turner's successful career as a racer (by his own calculation he won 357 races) was interrupted for four years in 1961. Jimmy Hoffa's Teamsters were trying to organize all professional sports; Turner and Tim Flock joined in the effort, initially enlisting nearly all of the other drivers, who quickly backed down

when threatened with suspension. Turner, who was at the height of his career, refused, and was barred until 1965. Reinstated at age forty-one, he was widely discounted as a contender. But in the 1965 National 400 at Charlotte, acclaimed as one of the best races of all time, he came in third. He then won the 500 miler at the North Carolina Motor Speedway in Rockingham. At age forty-three, Turner was the first driver to break the 180mph barrier at Daytona, winning the pole position in the 1967 500.

Turner later had a spectacular mishap at the Atlanta 500, hit a retaining wall, went what he estimated was about twenty feet in the air, went end over end, then rolled. Describing it later, he said that the distance from where he hit to where he ended up was about as long as a par four in golf.

Turner once drove for Junior Johnson, and was the subject of a biography called *Timber on the Moon.* After retiring from racing, he became an active (although foolhardy) pilot. Race promoter Richard Howard recalled that Turner would put his airplane on automatic pilot, go in the back, and mix a drink. Some people think that's what he was doing when he was killed in a plane crash in October 1970, near Du Bois, Pennsylvania.

Jerome "Red" Vogt

Vogt was involved in the birth of NASCAR in the late 1940s; he was well known as a "tuner" from Atlanta, building racing cars (some for NASCAR founder Bill France) and whiskey cars. He reportedly built moonshiner cars in one section of his garage, and revenuer cars in another area. "Vogt smilingly refuses, even today, to answer the question of whether he did anything different with one set of engines than the other," Curtis Crider wrote in his self-published book, *The Road to Daytona.* According to Allan Girdler, "His garage was where the Atlanta racers started toward the beach [that is, Daytona Beach, Florida] from every year."

Other Vehicles

Mighty machines were by far the most riveting of the bootlegger's vehicles, but they were by no means the only (or even the main) ones. For every jacked-up, supercharged muscle car shown in photos of captured bootleggers, there are also dozens of clunky or oddball vehicles, some drawn by animals, and some that didn't even have wheels. Tabulating the modes of transport he witnessed during his career, Jack Kearins recalled seeing "hearses, tank trucks, wagons, baby carriages, wheelbarrows, [and] push carts."

Deep in the hills in the late 1800s, some moonshiners used mule-drawn sledges to carry their 10-gallon kegs. Bootleggers didn't prefer four legs to four wheels only because autos and trucks weren't available, either. During Prohibition, whiskey was brought up from Mexico on pack animals. At the other end of the country, bootlegging farmers on the Canadian border sometimes used horses in remote areas for smaller amounts of liquor. One former rumrunner recalls a colleague who lost three horses to gunfire from law-enforcement agents. Another bootlegger loaded up a trained horse with as many bottles as it could carry and turned it loose on the Canadian side of the border, letting it find its own way home.

One amateur bootlegger hollowed out two bales of hay, filled them with bottles of whiskey, tied one onto each side of his cow, and walked her back and forth across the border. It was a good gimmick, but he did it so many times that authorities eventually got suspicious and took the cow in for questioning. In the far north during the winter, deep snow made smuggling by car or horse impossible. Rising to the challenge, local bootleggers donned their snowshoes and loaded up toboggans. Farmers also used flat-bottomed produce sleighs to carry loads across snow-covered fields. Police once noticed three men on snowshoes hauling two toboggans over the border. The officers left their car, grabbed their own snowshoes, and chased the bootleggers a mile, eventually making the pinch.

Dabney interviewed seventy-five-year-old Hubert Howell of Cherokee County, Georgia, who told him, "The best liquor car I ever had was a Kaiser-Frazer. You know how big and bundlesome they were. We took the front seat out, and the back seat," so that it could hold twenty-five cases or 150 gallons, "just like a big old hull." Other early automobiles used by bootleggers included Cole-8s, Packards, Lincolns, Franklins, Chryslers, Cadillacs, Buicks, LaSalles, as well as smaller and cheaper Fords and Chevrolets. In the 1920s, one moonshine run could pay for a new Model A.

As long as speed wasn't a primary requirement, all sorts of other motor vehicles proved useful. Fred Goswick, who made more than 1,000 trips in his career as a teenaged bootlegger (he carried his first load when he was sixteen), sometimes used a "sneak car," a beat-up 1936 Ford. He drove a 1938 LaSalle when he hauled his first load to Atlanta. Nothing fancy about it, he said, "just an old car." He hauled his next load in a 1937 Plymouth, a car that became a favorite. "I used that one right smart." He also used 1941 and 1946 Fords, and a 1950 Plymouth. He had a total of five cars, varying them; he ran liquor from when he was sixteen to nineteen years old, ranging from a load a week up to three loads a day. He summed up his approach this way: "I tried to slip it by." For example, sometimes would dress in an Air Force coat and hat, appearing to be a traveler.

Writing in 1969, Kearins said, "The most used form of transportation for moonshine today is the old rundown car." He once caught a transporter while on surveillance on another detail. The agent saw him unload a large, heavy cardboard box from the trunk of a big brown Chrysler, and was curious about the obvious weight of the box, particularly since the outside of the box said "cigarettes." It proved to be non-taxpaid alcohol. The transporter said he'd been delivering alcohol for eight years; the earnings were excellent, and he intended to keep it up until he got caught. He had always kept another job, he explained, and drove "soft and smooth." He said he had been stopped at license check stations several times and had sailed right through.

The undertaker in a small border town discovered that his hearse was "perfectly suited to a sideline in smuggling," Allan Everest wrote—at least until a local officer named John O'Hara "began to wonder about the sudden rise in the death rate." An urban bootlegging gang once organized a long funeral procession, complete with sobbing mourners dressed in black, to bring in several hundred gallons of liquor.

A moonshiner named Cletus told Kellner a yarn about a friend of his, also a moonshiner, who transported jars of moonshine to Cincinnati and Hamilton, Ohio, in a poultry truck. He hid the moonshine among the crates of ducks and chickens. "This went on for some time before an alert investigator observed that the farmer made the trips with unusual frequency, even for a man with an enormous poultry farm," which Cletus' friend didn't own, Kellner wrote. Furthermore, fishily, the crates were always full on the return trip. "It was funny as hell!" Cletus told Kellner. "Them goddamn ducks and chickens rode hundreds of miles!" Small trucks were useful and could

blend in with regular rural traffic. Dabney talked to one tripper who started at age fifteen; his first load was two 60-gallon barrels in the back of a Model A Ford truck. Earning a dollar a gallon, he was soon knocking down $500 a week, a comparative fortune.

A May 5, 1993, story on National Public Radio featured former Virginia ABC special agent Jack Powell, who observed that bootleggers, especially big-time operators, were not so much into racing cars anymore; they often loaded 400 gallons of moonshine in an old camper or a pickup truck and just drove right down the highway, blending in with the regular traffic.

Goswick discovered that you could hide forty cases of moonshine in a truck that appeared to be loaded with two-by-fours, except the ones on the sides were the only ones that were full length—the others were cut off short and nailed together.

Another former transporter started his illicit career by delivering malt. He once burst the tires on a 1965 Chevrolet pickup by putting 3,000 pounds in the back. Many kinds of commercial trucks—usually used for delivering such things as dairy products or sausage—were adapted to liquid payloads. One produce truck had a hidden addition to the back of the cab that could hold several dozen cases, but that was invisible when the truck was full of fruit and vegetables. A grocer once adapted his store's 1947 Chevrolet panel truck by welding a rack along the fenders under the hood, to hold bootleg liquor that was delivered along with the groceries. Another truck-driving bootlegger covered his cargo with manure.

Larger trucks were a necessity once the quantity of illicit liquor got up into the hundreds of gallons. Although the classic moonshine container has always been glass fruit jars in cardboard cases, some transporters found jars "too tedious"; they used 1-gallon "tin cans" for transport, and many preferred 10-, 15-, 20-, and even 50-gallon barrels.

180 of them in a car. Dabney's book pictures a 1929 Cadillac coupe that was seized with a load of 186 gallons, neatly stacked in 1/2-gallon jars, along with a small wooden barrel and two ceramic jugs.

Former North Carolina ABC agent Jim Ward recalled that back in the late 1930s, bootleggers used 5-, 10-, and 20-gallon kegs. The problem with kegs, Ward said, was their weight. Mason jars proved more popular, although some tried using 5-gallon glass demijohns. The problem with demijohns was that "they would break if you just looked at them. And it got real expensive if you broke four or five of them." He also remembered that they once seized three or four loads that were in 5-gallon metal cans, but in hot weather, the liquid and vapor would swell, and the cans would start to leak if they were too full or if the vapor couldn't escape.

Bootleggers used stake-body trucks, covering the cargo with tarps for its trip to the city. Oil trucks (complete with the logo of a national gasoline distributor) and furniture-moving vans were employed. A Coast Guard beach patrol once came upon an eighteen-man bootlegging gang unloading a contact boat, using four teams of horses, several trucks, and three cars. When a Coast Guard officer demanded, rhetorically, what the gang was doing, a bootlegger replied, "Looking for wood."

A headline in the May 30, 1923, edition of the Norfolk *Virginian-Pilot* reveals the truck-sized quantities of liquor involved at the upper echelons of the bootlegging industry: talking about a "Million Dollar Rum Plot," the headline announced, "Eight Hundred Cases of Whisky Found in Plant of Tennessee Corporation, Prior to Discovery of Large Cache in Bronx." The indicted people included a Washington attorney, and the article reported that the liquor (possibly imported from Cuba) seized in the Bronx was valued at $1 million.

Truck drivers developed tactics of their own, since they couldn't rely on pure speed or knowledge of local curves and hills. One common tactic was to stop just over the crest of a hill to see if anyone was following closely without lights. The driver would get out of the truck and pretend to check tires; more than once, law-enforcement personnel who had been chasing the truck (hoping to follow it to the delivery point, thereby capturing additional violators or gathering information about a moonshining syndicate) came flying over the hill with their lights off and slamming on the brakes, thereby tipping off the transporter.

Moonshine packaging showed as much variety as did types of stills and modes of transport. The popular packaging around Atlanta during Prohibition was a rectangular 1-gallon can with a cork top, carried five at time in onion sacks. Goswick often used similar metal cans, carrying 120–200 gallons at a time, except in the summer, when the metal would turn the liquor "kind of blue." Then he switched to Mason jars. In other areas, transporters used 1-gallon glass jugs, Coca-Cola syrup jugs, 5-gallon GI cans, and (in modern times) plastic 1-gallon milk jugs, sometimes packing as many as

Given a large enough vehicle, enterprising moonshiners soon discovered that they could operate their stills on the way to their customers, speeding up the process of delivery while simultaneously saving themselves the worry of whether competitors or revenuers were finding their untended stills back home. During the Civil War, a Confederate Army moonshiner once constructed his still in a wagon bed, using a large cooking tub to hold the mash, and making a worm out of a bugle.

The records of law-enforcement agents reveal seizures of numerous, more modern mobile stills. A 500-gallon still was mounted on a truck bed. Another involved two large vans, one with mash tanks that would hold 2,000 gallons, the other with a 500-gallon still, a boiler, and other equipment. Mobile moonshining units were also discovered in boats, house trailers, and car campers.

Bootleggers were endlessly inventive, and because penalties were often minor or nonexistent (other than losing a load of booze), it didn't hurt to try new and unusual schemes. As early as 1908, moonshiners were shipping their products by mail. On October 5, 1932, the Coast Guard destroyer *Semmes* responded to a disabled Sikorsky seaplane, seventeen miles south of Shinnecock lighthouse. The pilot apparently had been picking up liquor when rough seas had bent the aircraft's struts and damaged a pontoon, preventing it from taking off. The aircraft sank while being towed to shore.

Bigger and Bigger Payloads

As railroads pushed west during the middle and late 1800s, moonshiners gladly used their services, too, labeling jugs of moonshine as "vinegar," for example. Canadian and American authorities were initially preoccupied with smuggling by boat, and it took them some time to begin to appreciate the opportunities offered by railroads. On trains, large and small bootleggers hid liquor in ventilators, light fixtures, under seats or bed springs, behind wall panels, or in trunks with false sides and bottoms. People who filled up their luggage were called "the suitcase brigade."

The railroad freight car was a particularly promising option for large-scale bootleggers because it could carry fifty times as much as an automobile, and the smugglers could conceal their identities behind phony bills of lading. Products such as fish, lumber, hay, and lime were listed on the phony paperwork. Loaded in Quebec and bound for New York or New Jersey, with a thin layer of the phony cargo on top, freight cars could carry 150 barrels of beer. Enclosed cars were sealed for the trip across the border, making detection even less likely.

By installing false ends on a freight car, each three feet deep, smugglers could transport as much as 200 cases of beer. One captured load, ostensibly of hay, actually contained 300 bags of bottled beer, each bag holding twenty-four bottles. In 1931, Montreal authorities discovered a freight car containing eighty drums labeled "white oil"; only twenty drums held oil, and the rest were half full of alcohol, both industrial alcohol and corn liquor. A similar mix was once found among a load of milk cans, which contained 2 quarts of cream on top and 8 gallons of liquor underneath.

Agents once got a tip about a freight car of "pulpwood" consigned to the paper mill at Ticonderoga, New York; agents found 100 cases of liquor on a siding there, hidden under lumber. A customs officer perusing a load marked "apples" had his curiosity aroused because that fruit was out of season at the time. He probed more deeply, and found that the true cargo was ale, not apples.

Reviewing the kinds of vehicles that have been used to transport illegal liquor—animal and mechanical, speedy and sluggish—makes clear the lengths to which bootleggers and moonshiners would go to deliver their tax-free nectar. As we'll see in the next chapter, sea-going transporters were limited to craft that would float, but were no less ingenious.

Chapter 6

Rumrunning: From "Gentleman's Game" to Syndicate Operation

The whole rum running business lent itself to extraordinary feats of seamanship, to intrigue, mystery, and cunning.

—Everett Allen

Four crewmen aboard *Arethusa* display some of the tools of the trade. The man second from left holds a "ham" of liquor bottles, which have been repacked in burlap with padding so that they'd be easier to handle, lighter, and less breakable. The telescope at right had obvious applications in spotting Coast Guard ships, contact boats, and hijackers. Perhaps that's the ship's cook, second from right, holding the small bowl. *Courtesy of the Mariners' Museum, Newport News, Virginia*

The rumrunners who thrived during Prohibition carried all sorts of liquor: brandy, bourbon, blended whiskey, Scotch, and champagne were often on the bill of sale. Plain old rum, however, was what got it all started. In the 1700s, rum was a contraband cargo that was easy to sell and commanded a good price, assuming the ship captain was wily and wary enough to sneak past the tax collectors. Rumrunners of two centuries ago discovered two things: that speedy sailing ships were excellent tools, and that elusiveness was rewarded with increased profits. In the 1920s, rumrunners were reconfirming these two axioms of their illegal trade.

At the outset of Prohibition, before most people realized just how impossible the new law was going to be to enforce, Maj. John Clark Jr., the assistant U.S. attorney in charge of New York smuggling cases, announced, "On the whole, I believe the amount of liquor that will arrive by the water route is not sufficient to cause any real joy to the hearts of the drinking men of the United States."

He was dead wrong. Liquor didn't just "arrive" by the water route, it gushed in by the barrel and by the boatload. In 1922, the Department of Commerce estimated that $20 million worth of liquor was smuggled into the United States that year; in 1923, that estimate rose to $30 million, and $40 million the year after that. In February 1925, the *New York Times* reported, "Since 1919 'Rum Row' is reputed to have delivered 250,000 cases of liquor annually into the country."

Delivering the cargo called for the usual seaman's skills, a dose of courage, and a few extra talents besides. They didn't have to find fish, but they did have to elude the Coast Guard and hijackers. The operators of the huge mother ships had to finance massive cargoes of liquor from Canada, the Caribbean, or Europe, and find customers along Rum Row. The operators of the speedy contact boats that ferried the liquor ashore had to locate the mother ships, haggle over prices, and dodge the law and hijackers both on the way in and while transferring the cargo ashore.

In *The Black Ships: Rumrunners of Prohibition,* Everett Allen described one of the rumrunner captains, whom he remembered seeing around town when he was a youngster: the rumrunner "did possess certain derring-do. The whole rum running business lent itself to extraordinary feats of seaman-

ship, to intrigue, mystery, and cunning." Like his colleagues, this rumrunner was "more silent than talkative, fiercely industrious, exceptionally unafraid." Rumrunners, Allen decided, were "generally unlettered, unassuming, more often than not. They became smugglers not because they were essentially devious or because they possessed any other qualifications for lawbreaking but because they were in the right place at the right time, possessed of the right skills, and they were short of cash."

At least in their memoirs, some of them actually enjoyed it. Before the syndicates moved in and added their usual element of viciousness, rumrunning "was a gentleman's game," recalled Adm. Alfred C. Richmond, who retired as commandant of the Coast Guard. He said that Coast Guard personnel and the rumrunners had an "easygoing relationship," based in part on the fact that "even if the rummies were arrested, there wasn't any great punishment . . . Smuggling liquor wasn't really considered a

Cases of Grand "Old Parr," Grant's Stand Fast, and Sandy Mac Donald Scotch whiskey fill the hold on a captured rumrunner. Some of the cases are stamped "Colombia via Vancouver B.C.," an indication of the paperwork rigmarole attempted by smugglers as they obtained clearances to ship their high-proof cargoes. *Library of Congress*

there were in fact numerous local chapters offshore from the major East Coast cities, from Boston to New Orleans (see chapter 11).

In the boom times of Rum Row, American, British, and other European syndicates bought ships, hired crews, and loaded up with liquor bound for America. Some of the ships carried as much as 25,000 cases. The owners equipped the ships with phony manifests and clearance papers that indicated the ships were "legally" bound for such places as St. Pierre-Miquelon, or Nassau in the Bahamas. Two basic strategies developed: to arrange for sale and transportation of the liquor in advance, then land on the coast and unload. Or, anchor offshore and entertain all customers.

Although Bill McCoy, the ostensible creator of Rum Row, started out as a solo operator, the complex machinery that grew up behind his creation was surprisingly sophisticated. In the summer of 1923, for example, a bootleg ring in Savannah was alleged by that state's assistant attorney general to include a fleet of ships and smaller boats to ferry the liquor ashore, storage caves, a "small army" of laborers, and refrigerated railroad cars for transport.

In researching his book, Allen uncovered the intriguing correspondence of one Thomas Godman, operator of an organization called Schooners Associated Limited of London. Advertising for investors, Godman described his job as "to arrange for a ship to be in certain positions at stated times and then let my customers know where to find her." That ship, of course, was carrying contraband liquor. Godman added that he would know the positions of Coast Guard patrol boats. In a letter from March 1924, aimed at assuring the investors that their liquid investment would be safe, Godman added that the rumrunning crews were carefully warned about the threat of what he called "rum pirates," usually aboard Nova Scotia schooners. His instructions to the

rumrunners were to let no more than two people aboard at a time, and to keep them covered with weapons. Godman said that his company would supply the crews an arsenal that included machine guns and grenades.

In spite of these precautions, the 1924 voyage of the *Tom August*, arranged by Schooners Associated Limited, was a disaster. The plan was to sail from Bremen, Germany, to a point twenty-five miles south of Montauk Point, Long Island, New York, with a cargo of 14,935 cases of whiskey and 1,355 cases of champagne. At $30.00 per case (the price they hoped to get on Rum Row), the cargo's total value was $488,700. The *Tom August* was in fact off Jones Inlet at the western end of Long Island in mid-June.

There the plans started to unravel because, glib promises to the contrary, Godman hadn't arranged the customer end of the operation very effectively. The two supercargoes were arguing with each other and with the captain, and various disreputable middlemen had gotten involved in the scheme. Furthermore, business was decidedly slow. The ship sailed to a point eighteen miles southeast of Block Island, dropping the price to $20.00 per case. Again, business was slow for those rumrunners who lacked connections with bootleggers ashore. Disposing of 16,000 cases required plenty of big customers, and the *Tom August* was dealing with lots of small operators who wanted only ten to fifty cases. By early July, the going price had dropped as low as $15.00.

Hiring new supercargoes only magnified the confusion about how much liquor had been sold. One tally showed 2,200 cases, another said 1,200, another said 1,700. At one point the captain's son went ashore with 210 cases and didn't return. *Tom August* finally sailed to Halifax, Nova Scotia, at the end of August, with about 12,000 of the 16,000 cases sold, and arrived back in England in October. At that point, the captain wrote a blistering diatribe to Schooners Associated, summing up the voyage as "utter confusion" and saying that "the blunders, the mistakes, and the cross-purposes and the double-crossing" had been appalling. Allen quoted the captain as insisting that "the cargo was placed in the hands of some of the biggest crooks in New York."

Rum Row changed and developed during the 1920s, in spite of the Coast Guard's best efforts to scuttle it. One business innovation involved cutting high-quality liquor with water or cheap alcohol, then

criminal act." These attitudes—and the huge amounts of money to be made—gave liquor smugglers both incentive and latitude.

As the business opportunities created by Prohibition became apparent, and once those opportunities were recognized by ship owners who cared only about the letter of the law and not the spirit of the law, a gigantic offshore liquor distribution system arose: Rum Row. Although that new and euphonious noun always appeared in the singular,

These cases and barrels of seized liquor were stored on the deck of a typical trans-Atlantic rumrunner. Liquor was sometimes stored on deck to make it easier to unload, or in preparation for meeting up with the speedy contact boats that ferried it ashore. Most of the liquor that made up a large shipment was of necessity kept below in the hold. This photo is one of a series taken after the capture of a rumrunner by the Coast Guard cutter *Seneca* in 1924.
Library of Congress

rebottling it in counterfeit bottles. This practice, called "cutting," traditionally had been done ashore. But at least one ship on Rum Row, according to historical accounts, was equipped to cut, bottle, and label your liquor on the spot. All you had to do was buy the labels (along with a supply of phony tax stamps, of course) for your customers' favorite brand from your friendly neighborhood counterfeiter and bring them with you to the ship.

Gradually, independent rumrunners were driven out by shore-based syndicates, which were increasingly standardized and well organized. Unlike in the early years, where liquor cargoes were arranged and bro-

kered on short notice and on an ad hoc basis, liquor-smuggling at ports such as Bimini became businesslike and efficient. Skippers checked manifests and supervised loading. A representative from the syndicate doled out the sailing orders, sometimes not until the ship was ready to leave, and then sometimes changed the orders while the rumrunner was en route.

As early as 1923, newspapers were reporting that rumrunners were "nothing more nor less than the privateers of other days, modernized for the sake of expediency." They sailed and steamed in "ships of prey," and there was no honor among thieves. "These are stories of dissensions and disagreements among members of the gang, of distrust, which springs up suddenly and furiously, and of threatened violence," an article declared. The rumrunners were "not derelicts by any means, but members of a powerfully organized combine, with unlimited financial backing and with a definite, well defined program in view." A Norfolk, Virginia, resident who visited the *Istar* said that the people he met "bore evidence of excellent breeding and wealth." The size of the smuggling operations is implied in a local newspaper headline from May 30: "Million Dollar Rum Plot Balked."

Many a well-stocked schooner or ocean-going transport anchored on the various Rum Rows off the Atlantic coast and the Gulf of Mexico. Up north, the St. Lawrence River and the Great Lakes offered hundreds of clandestine points of entry. At these places the riskier, in-shore part of the smuggling operation geared up. The hazards multiplied immediately, including rocks and shoals, several species of law-enforcement authorities both on the water and ashore, and hijackers in the bays and on the beaches. Rumrunners wanted to get their cargoes ashore and on the way to their customers as quickly as possible.

With good shore connections, a load might take just three or four nights to sell out from an offshore mother ship; according to one source, it usually took about three weeks, unlike the *Tom August*'s dismal experience. A spectrum of customers arrived to help lighten their loads. The economics and the mechanics of these transfers varied widely.

Everett Allen interviewed an eighty-two-year-old boatman who had dabbled in rumrunning for several years. He had been a mate on a medium-sized boat, earning $150 a month and an equal bonus. One of his ships had a crew of ten or eleven and could carry 6,000 cases. Sometimes they loaded up in St. Pierre, where gin cost twenty-five cents a quart, champagne one dollar a bottle, and rum fifty cents a gallon. The ship's skipper would get clearance to go to Nassau. Sometimes they would get their

load from a European steamer that would bring 60,000 to 70,000 cases and anchor thirty miles offshore. Their clientele included lobster fishermen, scallopers, and various small-fry customers who wanted only two or three cases. Others arrived in speedboats, buying 600 to 800 cases. Sometimes they would have six or seven boats alongside, up to as many as twenty. Other times, larger

Alastair Moray, supercargo and rumrunner, looking mighty nautical on the deck of the schooner *Cask*. His cruise from Scotland to Rum Row (see sidebar, pp. 106-107) was a catalog of near-calamity, including storms, lost anchors, malfunctioning motors, reluctant and crooked customers, and botched planning.

customers would have the matching half of a torn playing card held by the ship's captain or supercargo.

Manuel "Manny" Zora of Cape Cod was a typical customer of the era; he got into the rumrunning business using his fishing boat. His typical load was 250 cases, which took about thirty minutes to unload from the mother ship. He loaded some below decks, but stacked as many cases as possible above deck, so that he could unload it more easily when he got to the dark beach.

A certain amount of anonymity and trust was usually built into the equation. At the wharf with a typical load, Zora called a phone number in Boston. He didn't know where the phone rang, and never tried to find out. He would talk to someone named, for example, John, and John never acquired a last name. Zora's load would then be reliably picked up and Zora would be paid off. The system worked for months.

If you'll study pictures of rumrunners, you'll notice a surprising assortment of packaging for the liquor. In the early days, smugglers tended to leave the liquor in the original wooden cases; you can see them stacked on the decks of seized rumrunners, especially the mother ships. Smugglers soon discovered that the wooden cases were too fragile and hard to handle; stacking them was time-consuming and sometimes awkward. As a result, rumrunners began repacking the bottles in burlap bags stuffed with straw or cardboard, usually six bottles to the bag. These bags were sometimes referred to as "cases," "hams" (because they resembled the shape of smoked hams), "sacks", or "burlocks." Packaged in this manner, the bottles of liquor could withstand rough treatment. It was, according to one historian, "a very nervous business" and the rumrunners had little time to handle things gently. In the winter, sometimes spray froze on the burlap bags, and if any were lost overboard, the ice-sealed bags would float for hours, sometimes washing ashore to be found by a lucky beachcomber.

Alastair Moray, who chronicled his adventures in *The Diary of a Rum-Runner*, once watched a customer repack the bottles from wooden cases into bags, tying the bags a few yards apart along a long rope, with a "small bladder" on one end. This customer's plan was to shove this contraption overboard if they were chased; the bladder would then float the load and allow them to return and retrieve the liquor.

Sometimes the liquor was shipped in barrels; one seized rumrunner had 3,000 50-gallon barrels of liquor, estimated by authorities as being worth $500,000 (authorities weren't known to be conservative when it came to establishing the value of seized liquor, however).

Lots of rumrunners simply jettisoned their cargoes once the Coast Guard started to chase them, adding to the high-octane flotsam. Syndicates often instructed their contact-boat operators to dump the cargo if chased. Zora did the same thing, as a last resort. "One boat today had to throw overboard 300 cases to escape arrest," Moray noted in his journal. A customer soon arrived at Moray's ship, the *Cask*, with thirteen cases they had found floating.

Of course, liquor that was dumped could sometimes be retrieved. Zora once salvaged a jettisoned cargo of 2,000 cases, grappling for it using Halibut fish hooks. The Coast Guard once inspected a 33-foot former Navy steamer that was posing as a fishing boat but had no fishing equipment. What it did have, however, was six fourteen-foot poles with a combination corkscrew and hook on the ends, obviously designed for retrieving sunken liquor.

A few rumrunners regularly dumped liquor close to shore or in shallow places on purpose, then returned to get it later. Sometimes storms would send loose bottles floating away, or "amphibious hijackers" would raid the dumps. A refinement on this technique was to attach a salt-encased buoy to the load, which was dumped into a marsh or near a shallow beach. The salt would dissolve after several days, releasing the buoy, which popped up to the surface.

Some well-financed rumrunners ditched their ships along with their cargoes before they could be captured and seized. The Coast Guard once found, in a scuttled rumrunner, two six-inch seacocks that had been installed and left open, clearly for just such an eventuality. The sometimes perfunctory destruction of liquor and boats by rumrunners showed the extent of the bankrolls behind the business, and how expendable the loads were.

Most rumrunners made a dash for shore, using as much guile and speed as they could muster. The Coast Guard stationed a cordon of destroyers just outside the three-mile limit, and the rumrunner vanguard would try to dash through. In his book *Smugglers of Spirits: Prohibition and the Coast Guard Patrol*, Harold Waters described the

scene in Florida, saying that the contact boats looked "like so many waterbugs, skittering across the sea, visible only by their bow waves and boiling wakes."

The Booze Ballet

Once the eclectic assortment of liquor containers reached shore, it had to be transferred to cars or, more often, trucks. In New England, the going rate was about $25.00 a night for men to unload the contraband liquor. "Twenty-five dollars was a lot of money to the average guy you found hanging around the poolrooms, barber shops and loafing rooms of Provincetown," Scott Corbett noted.

Smugglers preferred the hours after midnight, when they attracted less attention if they worked quietly. Trucks and men would gather furtively on the beach, with one member of the gang ready to fire a flare if the Coast Guard or police showed up, signaling the incoming contact boat to reverse course and clear out.

One family, as anxious to earn a dollar as any other family during the Depression, lived on a small farm on Buzzard's Bay. An unknown man knocked on their door one night; he said he wanted to use the beach and the road to it two or three nights a week. They gave him permission and never saw him again. But they heard the trucks rolling by in the dark, just as he had said, and their fee would be in their mailbox in an envelope on Saturday mornings, just like clockwork.

Contact-boat operators worked during daytime, if a heavy enough fog shrouded the coastline. One historian described such a fog as "a heavy, blinding pea souper that reduced visibility to less than fifty yards, made to order for contact boats."

Some rumrunners, shunning secrecy, were so brazen as to be foolhardy. The *Hohenlinden*, for example, was a 102 ton, 150-foot trawler of French registry that had been built in Savannah in 1919. It was known to sail up the Narrows in broad daylight, using a variety of names, apparently heading for the Fulton Street Market in lower Manhattan; it would then quickly divert to New Jersey to unload not fresh fish, but cases of booze (it could carry 15,000 cases). Authorities were tipped off by an anonymous phone call, probably from a member of a rival syndicate or someone who had been double-crossed or cheated.

As did their shore-based counterparts —the bootleggers—rumrunners developed an inventory of ploys to foil the authorities. Speed, although certainly useful, was not an infallible weapon. Once fully loaded, most rumrunners were vulnerable because they could no longer outrun the Coast Guard ships. It was far better to evade the Coast Guard entirely, attracting no notice, using no running lights and selecting moonless nights for their clandestine operations, landing on isolated beaches that had good access by road.

Some rumrunners tried to avoid the shoreline entirely, removing the worries of running into reefs, rocks, or Coast Guard sandpounders. Author Peter Mersky recalls his father recounting childhood memories of summers spent in a resort area called Nantasket, south of Boston near Hull. The rumrunners released barrels of whiskey at night to float in with the tide. He watched Coast Guard personnel, carrying rifles, patrolling the beach and seizing the barrels before the rumrunners ashore could get to them.

Other inventive smugglers tried using hollow steel torpedoes that could carry 40 gallons of liquor each. In practice, this ploy was too cumbrous and time-consuming to have potential as anything other than a gimmick. Another bizarre ploy, recalled by a Maine businessman, was "a weekly parachute drop of crates of whiskey into the soft marshes between Capisic Street and Stroudwater." It is hard to believe that it would be worth the trouble, unless the crates were sizable, and even harder to believe that the crates hit the target.

For landing liquor, beach houses with docks were ideal during the months from Labor Day until June, when northern resorts were deserted. Another preferred spot was an isolated beach with good road access. Smugglers were not averse to using commercial docks in small ports, also, as long as no houses were situated nearby. Practiced rumrunners rarely landed at the same place twice in a row, preferring to alternate between four or five places. They usually had a back-up location if problems arose at the initial site. Sometimes they would stash the load and return to collect it later (according to *Portland* magazine editor Colin Sargent, a long-lost cache of bottles was found in a cave in Kennebunk, Maine, twenty years ago).

In the early years of Prohibition, people ashore used flares or bonfires as signals to the contact-boat pilots. Later, colored flashlights and various codes were added. John Durward interviewed a Maine resident who remembered, as a child, seeing rumrunners out in the bay. "The boats would lie out beyond East End Beach in the darkness, waiting for flashlight signals to call them in," he told the writer. "A couple of older boys I knew learned about it and started flashing fake signals to draw the runners in early. Tough characters. I never waited around to see what happened when they came in."

Nautical maneuvers were an obvious technique. Some Coast Guard boats were comparatively easy to elude. A reporter for

Scotch and Water: The Sinking of the *Glen Beulah*

Occasionally, clashes at sea between the Coast Guard and the smugglers were both disastrous and confusing, leaving unanswered the questions of whether a ship had been scuttled, sabotaged, or abandoned. On June 4, 1923, a headline in the Norfolk Virginian-Pilot said, "Mystery Ship Sinks Rum Sloop Off Capes; Skipper Claims Government Tug Ran Craft Down; Coast Guard Brands Assertion as 'Ridiculous'; 1,500 Cases of Liquor Go Down With Boat." A forty-six-ton sloop, the Glen Beulah, had been rammed at 10:00 P.M. the previous Saturday night. Carrying a cargo of at least 1,000 cases of Lewis Hunter whiskey, it had been anchored ten miles south of the Cape Charles lightship, and sank within fifteen minutes. The crew was rescued by a Coast Guard cutter and held for investigation by immigration authorities.

Coast Guard officers claimed the vessel that rammed the Glen Beulah looked like a notorious rumrunning ship called the Istar, but the skipper of the sunken ship claimed that a Coast Guard tug did it. Coast Guard officers theorized that the Istar was pulling alongside to get liquor from the Glen Beulah when the crew heard or saw the Coast Guard approaching, panicked, and rammed the Glen Beulah.

The Glen Beulah's captain, a man named Kelly from Miami, admitted to Prohibition agents that he had been engaged in rumrunning, "but declared that he was bound for St. Pierre, and that he came in close to the coast because of engine trouble," a news article reported. Kelly also said he had forgotten the owner's name. The ship had British registry with "papers obtained in the Bahamas," which had gone down with the ship. Kelly admitted he had been running liquor since Prohibition started, and that he had visited Pamlico Sound. He was "vague" about prices. The federal agents told him it didn't make sense to carry liquor from Nassau to St. Pierre. "Don't you know that you can buy that whiskey in Nassau for twelve or fifteen dollars a case and that it costs less than that in Canada?" they insisted.

More details of the incident appeared in the next day's paper, after Kelly and his crew had spent a day in jail, being held for twenty-four hours as "persons suspected of violating a federal statute . . . Captain Kelly appeared in ill humor," the article said. "In appearance, the grizzled master of the wrecked sloop suggests characters that have been made famous by authors of romantic tales about the sea." One crew member described the mishap: "At 8 o'clock, I was on deck, and the Yamacraw [a Coast Guard cutter] kept circling us, throwing her powerful searchlight upon us." He claimed that it was this ship that rammed the rumrunner.

The Coast Guard version of this incident was that they had been keeping the Glen Beulah under surveillance for several days, although the boat was outside the three-mile limit. "The fact that she should remain so close to the United States, with a cargo which it was quite safe to assume was liquor, led to the belief that she was waiting for an opportunity to land liquor in the United States illegally by means of either transferring it to other craft, by buoying for other craft to pick up, or by running into some convenient harbor," said the commanding officer of the Yamacraw. He said they had observed several suspicious acts, including light signals flashed out to sea, and a tug with no lights approaching it. "Why a vessel bound for St. Pierre, Miquelon, with favorable weather, should continue at anchor with nothing to do but loaf under an awning, was a fact rightfully causing suspicion." He also observed that the boat that rammed the Glen Beulah was "of the small converted yacht type, with a clipper bow, two masts and one smoke-stack."

These seafaring smugglers aboard the *Ouiatchouan* also stored at least some of their cargo on deck. *National Archives*

the New Bedford *Standard-Times* interviewed some former rumrunners in April 1936. One man talked about dodging the big "four-stacker" destroyers; the smaller smuggling boat just went to full-speed, reversed course, and would be a mile away by the time the destroyer got turned around. If the destroyer caught up again, they'd stop and turn off their lights. The destroyer skipper would see the rumrunner too late and futilely go to full-reverse; the destroyer would drift on past as the rumrunner took off in the opposite direction with its lights off.

Another favorite method of evading the destroyers during a high-speed chase, especially if the destroyer had a speed advantage, was to combine a smoke screen with a sudden reversal in direction. The *Black Duck*, although it was equipped with two 300hp engines and could do 30 knots, still used a smoke-screen device and evaded numerous carefully planned Coast Guard ambushes.

Fleeing rumrunners trailed steel cables (several hundred yards long) in their wakes, trying to foul the screws of the pursuing Coast Guard craft. Intimately familiar with their local waters, rumrunning fishermen would lead a pursuing vessel into fishing nets, or throw the nets over behind them, again trying to tangle the screws of the pursuing boat.

Most chases were short and swift; others developed into marathon battles of nerves and tactics. The destroyer *Jouett* once engaged in a twenty-eight-hour chase after a rumrunner named *Yamaska* in February 1931. The rumrunner switched its lights on and off, changed course and speed repeatedly, and tried circling. Twice it deployed a smoke screen, without losing the pursuing Coast Guard vessel. The *Jouett* finally gave up the chase; the captain decided that he had made his point and proven to the rumrunners that they couldn't escape.

December 20—*Moray records that he has $31,760 in the ship's safe.*

December 23—*One of the boats they had sold liquor to the night before sinks. Another boat picks up the four people aboard, then three others from another boat that had broken down. Now overloaded and in treacherous seas, the boat founders, hits a sand bar, and throws ten people overboard. They all drown.*

December 27—*At 7:00 A.M., the Coast Guard cutter* Gresham *circles around the seven rumrunners currently clustered together with* Cask, *then anchors in their midst until the afternoon, halting business temporarily. Meanwhile, Moray's boss and some of the Hamman gang are on their way to shore in a smaller boat that breaks down; ironically, they have to ask the Coast Guard for help, "with the result that they were both taken into New York to explain what they were doing out here," Moray writes. The boss had $46,000 that the authorities were particularly curious about.*

January 7—*"Met the boss, who has had a pretty bad time of it in New York. As far as I can see, nothing but the most artistic lying has got him out of the mess, which appears to be the best way of evading anything in Eastern America."*

January 20—Cask *returns to Bermuda for another round of repairs. The mate's brother comes aboard, saying he has "invested in a schooner in Newfoundland, which is held up by the ice"; he asks to put 200 cases aboard and ride back to America with them. Moray smells a rat. The next day, the chief engineer tells Moray that this guy had asked him, "Will you be on my side if I come off with a boatload of men and rush the ship the next time you are off the coast?" Moray reports this scheme to the boss and Hamman. The mate has also offered to augment the crew with four or five men who just wanted to ride to the U.S. and would work for their passage. A "very pretty scheme," Moray notes sarcastically.*

February 4—*The schooner is back on station, this time twelve miles off the Montauk Light.*

February 22—*"Bos'n down with his kidneys—lumbago he says; 'rumbago,' I think, is nearer the mark." Back in October, Moray noted in an entry that he "broached cargo this morning to the extent of one case of Mr. Dewar. It is quite impossible to expect contentment forward, with all this stuff on board, if the crew are not to have a drink occasionally." The bos'n's definition of "occasionally," unfortunately, is too loose.*

March 3—*What Moray calls a "real sportsman" arrives in an eighteen-foot motorboat with a single-cylinder engine. Moray figures he is crazy to be that far from shore in that kind of weather. The man buys twenty cases, and Moray gives him a $5.00 discount "for coming out this distance by himself."*

April 24—*Hamman's brother tells of unloading 150 cases of liquor at a restaurant near Broadway. The liquor was in a furniture-moving van, which they had usually parked in a garage outside the city until early mornings "when there would be a friendly cop on the beat." But they heard that the feds would be sniffing around the garage, so they drove right in, parked in the busy street, and started handing the cases right across the sidewalk. Pedestrians and diners in the restaurant all lined up to help. The traffic cop on the corner just looked on.*

May 5—*"My birthday, and the thirty-seventh at that. Getting on towards middle age, and, as far as I can see, without much more sense than I had at the age of seven—if I had I wouldn't be here."*

May 17—*Moray visits a nearby steamer, the* Maryville, *that had left home with 95,000 cases at the beginning of December and was nearly sold out. Two weeks earlier, Moray had noted "we have managed to get rid of 8,700 cases, although it is eight months since we started." Perhaps* Maryville's *prices were cheaper.*

June 5—*"Letter from the other side. I can see the shareholders are doing some worrying, and I don't wonder." In mid-June,* Cask *still has 8,700 cases aboard. He still manages to send $39,700 in earnings ashore. In mid-June, a hijacking occurs nearby: a steamer with a drunk crew and 40,000 cases. A gang of forty men attacks and spends seven days clearing it out. As a result, Moray notes, "all the small schooners around here are full up with stolen booze" that they have bought for $7.00 or $8.00 a case.*

July 12—*It is three months since* Cask *left Bermuda the last time, and the schooner still has 6,000 cases to unload.*

July 26—*A speedboat roars past at 5:30 A.M.; a Coast Guard cutter charges out after it, alternately firing and blowing its klaxon. The speedboat driver refuses and heads out to sea. About ninety minutes later, Moray sees the speedboat two miles away, racing back in at about 30 knots; the cutter tries to head it off, firing at the same time. "However, the speedboat knew what it was doing, for after it passed us it kept the* Cask *between it and the Revenue boat, so that we were masking the latter's fire. It did the same until it reached the next boat on the line, and kept these tactics up until it was well away inshore."*

July 30—*With most of the liquor finally sold, Moray balances the ledger and finds that he is only fifty-three cases off. The bos'n probably accounted for most of that disparity, although Moray doesn't say so.*

August 5—*Back in Bermuda, the boss refuses to pay a bonus to the crew; they hire a sea lawyer and sue him, and* Cask *is impounded pending outcome of the trial. Moray testifies and nonchalantly leaves. When* Cask *had sailed the previous September, the organizers had glibly predicted that the voyage would take three or four months, and that they'd make three voyages that year. Instead, the voyage took eleven months. One voyage was enough for Alastair Moray.*

Aircraft were fast and flexible smugglers, but their lack of cargo space, and the fact that seaplanes and flying boats needed calm seas, diminished their appeal and utility. This is an Aermacchi single-engine, dual-seat flying boat, possibly an M.8. It is probably World War I surplus, although that would have been quite rare—the U.S. Navy received just eight of these airplanes after the war. The subject is identified as Captain Ed Music in the photo's original caption. If it is Captain Music, he is standing in an open hatch in the wooden hull of the aircraft, apparently preparing to store a wooden case of liquor. Note the screen installed behind the cockpit, to keep the pilot from leaning back into the propellers. Aermacchi continues as a well-known and thriving aircraft company today. *Courtesy of the Mariners' Museum, Newport News, Virginia*

stateside ports with false colors and registration, changed their appearance every few days with phony masts and stacks, and repainted often. Some even carried phony cargo on deck, with large wooden crates marked as containing vehicles or farm equipment, but that were empty.

One popular rumrunning trick was to load a fast contact boat with empty cases in plain sight of a Coast Guard vessel, luring it into a chase. The Coast Guard would race after the rumrunner, blowing whistles and shooting machine guns and one-pounders until the boat would stop. Then the boarding party would find the empty cases. Meanwhile, back at the mother ship, real contact boats would swarm in and load up. Sometimes, rumrunners would send in several loads at once, with large loads on the faster boats and a small, decoy load on a slower and expendable vessel.

To divert the authorities, rumrunners would call in false alarms to the police stations and Coast Guard stations; the authorities, frustrated and suspicious, nevertheless had to respond to distress calls. Well-heeled smugglers tried to bribe Coast Guard personnel; anecdotes of their alleged success punctuate accounts of the period. One such rumrunner stressed to a potential partner that it was im-

portant to know the positions of Coast Guard boats, and also pay "grafting" to the service personnel; he estimated that their expenses per case (including payoffs and protection) would run about $4.00. With cases of liquor netting $45.00 ashore in the late 1920s, however, that amount of overhead was minor.

Daring rumrunners weren't above sabotage as yet another ploy. Once, twelve converted submarine chasers used by the Coast Guard left Staten Island on a four-day blockade patrol; two of them soon had to return to port, showing evidence of being tampered with. Investigators called it "sabotage made possible through bribery." Another smuggling saboteur sneaked aboard a Coast Guard ship and concealed a fifteen-pound magnet close to the compass, causing a four-mile error in navigation that, it turned out, caused the Coast Guard crew to miss an almost certain seizure. Finally, in what may have been the most audacious ploy, rumrunners stole a Coast Guard boat on December 21, 1925, and used it to land 1,500 cases of liquor on three trips.

In spite of these maneuvers, the Coast Guard routinely managed to stop and inspect suspected rumrunners. On one occasion, a suspicious vessel called the *Elsie B* was ordered to heave to and stand by for

boarding. The skipper vehemently issued the usual denials of criminal behavior, even inviting the Coast Guard personnel to inspect the bilges, which they probably would have done anyway. They discovered, thanks to a long auger with which they bored a hole in the hull, a false bilge, concealing 1,500 cases. Another smuggling vessel, the *Alice*, seized off the Pacific Coast, took a different approach; its owners had twenty two-foot compartments built onto the outside of the hull, near the keel, each holding a case of liquor. A piece of rope was attached to each case, so that they could be retrieved with a long pike.

Although a few big-time rumrunners and syndicate bosses allegedly made fortunes during Prohibition, most of the contact-boat operators and smalltime smugglers probably made a living and financed a few sprees. Zora's career ended when he was forced to scuttle a spiffy new speedboat provided by the syndicate he was working for as a sort of subcontractor. He hadn't been in the racket for the money, anyhow. "From the beginning, the excitement had always been the thing," wrote his biographer, Scott Corbett. "The terrific excitement. What counted was being the Sea Fox and fooling them all. He was poor, yes—but some of the rich ones were sitting in jail!"

Chapter 7

The U.S. Coast Guard Battles Rumrunners

> . . . the kind of
> hound-and-hare
> game they were
> obliged to play
> always gave the
> advantage to the
> smugglers.
> —Everett Allen

Coast Guard Lt. L. W. Perkins of the *Seneca* fires on men in a fleeing motorboat along Rum Row. This is one of a series of photos taken after the seizure of a rumrunner by the Coast Guard cutter *Seneca* in 1924. *Library of Congress*

Before Prohibition, the United States Coast Guard's job was hard enough under the best of circumstances. Rescuing hapless mariners from lethal storms at sea certainly ranks as one of the most severe on-the-job hazards faced by anyone, military or civilian. But the onset of enforced national teetotaling made matters much, much worse. The old but small service was almost completely unequipped for the task dropped into its collective lap.

Several serious problems quickly became apparent. Coast Guard personnel, reflecting American society as a whole, had mixed attitudes toward Prohibition—for every Coast Guard officer or enlisted man who took up the task with an ardent sincerity, many more were lukewarm. In the past, most of the people sought by the Coast Guard wanted and needed help; with Prohibition, the quarry was trying to run away. Bribery cropped up as a persistent problem; as with law-enforcement agents ashore, profligate smugglers sometimes had their way with the comparatively poorly paid personnel who were neutral on the question of Prohibition, or even opposed to it.

Unquestionably, the task ahead was daunting, even to the most diehard, can-do Coast Guard officer. Including the Great Lakes, those immense liquid windows into Canada where distilling and brewing were still very much legal, the American coastline was more than 6,000 miles of beach, bay, cove, and inlet. To patrol these boundaries, in 1920, the Coast Guard fielded just 4,000 people, including those on surf boats, beach patrols, and those stationed inland. As late as the mid-1920s, the Coast Guard had just two revenue cutters stationed at Quebec, with two or three other small craft handling what Everett Allen writing in *The Black Ships: Rumrunners of Prohibition* called "the hopeless task of patrolling the deeply indented coastline of Nova Scotia." Although the Coast Guard mustered its forces along major urban areas, that "hopeless task" in a nutshell, was repeated in many areas of the American coast.

One historian called the early months of Prohibition "deceitfully quiet along America's coasts"; what enforcement there was of the new laws was decidedly haphazard. Toward the end of the first year, the service was becoming better organized. The earliest official Coast Guard reference was in the fiscal 1921 report (issued that June), which mentioned that the Florida coast patrol had been "particularly vigilant" and had made hundreds of trips in support of federal Prohibition authorities. In the next few years, indefatigable Coast Guard pa-

trol ships would make a powerful impression on smugglers, forcing them to develop increasingly sophisticated techniques in their efforts to get illicit liquor to land. The mother ships along Rum Row might operate with impunity, but from there to shore was no Sunday cruise for smugglers.

Between 1920 and 1930, the number of Coast Guard personnel grew 188 percent, manning a greatly improved enforcement fleet (both in terms of numbers of ships and capability). Yet if the Coast Guard put a small crimp in the influx, that was the extent of it. It wasn't a matter of commitment or competence, it was a matter of assets and resources. As Adm. Edwin J. Roland, who retired as Coast Guard commandant, recalled, "If we'd had the equipment to run an effective patrol and stop the flow of liquor, it would have cost ten times as much as it did."

To add insult to injury, the Coast Guard was sometimes criticized for even trying to concentrate on the smugglers. On December 10, 1924, news reports said that the Coast Guard had been disparaged for using its best ships and most of its resources on the rumrunners, and "dodging rescue work," which after all was "the work for which the corps was organized, that of relieving ships in distress at sea." In fact, the Coast Guard had been originally established to keep colonial-era smugglers from avoiding taxes.

Although most of the Coast Guard personnel took their jobs seriously, their ongoing battles with the rumrunners had a lighthearted side, too. Harold Waters, author of *Smugglers of Spirits: Prohibition and the Coast Guard Patrol,* wrote that he and his shipmates came "to regard rum-chasing in the light of sport, as a glorified cops and robbers game." Scottish rumrunner Alastair Moray noted in his journal, "Rowing back we passed close to the cutter, and gave him a cheery wave, to which all on board replied. We are quite good friends with the cutters."

This enforced familiarity sometimes led the Coast Guard and the smugglers to trade good-natured insults. Waters' cutter, the *Tampa,* paid a port call to St. Pierre in the Miquelon Islands, to keep an eye on the rumrunners and gather other information. He wrote that their arrival "was greeted by a raucous, ear-numbing barrage of derisive din. Screaming steam sirens, hooting whistles, clanging bells, noise-making devices giving off sounds suggestive of the Bronx cheer."

Admiral Roland recalled a former skipper of the *Shaw,* Comdr. Gordon Finley, who seemed to particularly enjoy the job of picketing and harassing rumrunners. Finley,

The boarding crew from a Coast Guard surf boat pulls alongside a rumrunner to examine papers and cargo off the coast of New Jersey in 1927. *National Archives*

who was repeatedly frustrated, tricked, and eluded by the smugglers, often ordered his ship alongside and exchanged insults with the rumrunner crews. One day, the rumrunners on a British trawler managed to get Finley's goat. Finley ordered a couple bushels of potatoes brought up to the forecastle, where he and his crew began to pelt the rumrunners. "They really let them have it—about three bushels in all," Roland said. But since vegetables were scarce at sea, the rumrunner skipper didn't retaliate with more insults, threats, or bottles of booze. He thanked Finley, and told him that he'd appreciate some onions, too.

All of this raillery was mere background to the serious job of finding and deterring smugglers. Gradually the Coast Guard learned how the game was going to be played, bounded by the law on one side and the innovations of the rumrunners on the other.

Coast Guard crews soon discerned the locations and operating plans of the Rum Rows that grew at anchor off the coast; they also became adept at spotting likely rumrunners. It was only natural that, especially in the northeast, fishermen would experiment with liquid cargoes (as did cab drivers turned bootleggers ashore). Fishermen were, Waters wrote, "generally up to their necks in the smuggling trade and we kept a close watch on them." With fishermen, the Coast Guard encountered the sort of legal technicality that was to plague many law-enforcement agents during Prohibition. Suppose that the Coast Guard stopped a fishing boat and did an extended search, which was sometimes necessary, depending on how ingeniously the liquor was hidden. If they didn't find anything and the fish spoiled, then the Coast Guard was liable for damages.

Two could play at the technicality game, of course, and the Coast Guard developed its own arsenal of ways to delay and harass contact-boat operators. Unlike the huge mother ships that made the liquor runs from Europe or Canada and anchored off the coast, most contact boats were of U.S. registry, and could be searched and seized. The Coast Guard would stop them (on the outward-bound leg) for safety inspections, which Coast Guard personnel became adept at stretching from what should have been thirty minutes to as much as

The Coast Guard destroyer *Beale (CG-9)* trails a rumrunner in the North Atlantic outside the twelve-mile limit. This destroyer was stationed at New London, Connecticut, part of Division 3 of the Offshore Patrol. *Beale* had triple screws, driven by a steam turbine. *National Archives*

two hours, causing the contact boat to miss its rendezvous.

Another Coast Guard tactic was to interfere with the boats that were bringing provisions to Rum Row; they seized one, charging that it was illegally engaging in foreign trade, but was only licensed for coastal trade; a court upheld this charge.

When smugglers began applying technology to their business, the Coast Guard met them tit for tat. As early as 1919, a Coast Guard cutter was using an improvised radio direction finder to eavesdrop on the smugglers' plans. Direction finders like those used by the Navy were installed two years later; with them, two Coast Guard ships working together could pick up lines of bearing on transmitting rumrunners.

Since U.S. registered vessels were subject to seizure outside territorial waters, the owners of the motley fleet that made up Rum Row registered their vessels in foreign countries. Many popular accounts of Rum Row mention a three-mile limit, which was in effect at the outset of Prohibition. On May 1, 1923, the Norfolk *Virginian-Pilot* ran a pertinent headline: "Court Bars Liquor From U.S. Ports; Vessels Can't Handle It in 3-Mile Limit." The court had ruled that neither American nor foreign ships could bring liquor, even under seal, inside the three-mile limit; the ruling did allow American ships to sell liquor on the high seas.

As a general plan of attack, the Coast Guard stationed a cordon of its boats just inside the three-mile limit, and the rumrunner vanguard would try to dash through. In 1924, some countries agreed that America could extend the three-mile limit to "one hour's steaming," based on the speed of the contact boats. If a boat could make 20mph, it was liable to be seized twenty miles out. This limit, based on typical speeds and distances, is usually referred to as the "twelve-mile limit." The legal maritime agreements were called "conventions," established by the

federal government with the countries that were the principal suppliers of liquor: Great Britain (with which the first such treaty was established on May 22), Norway, Denmark, Germany, Sweden, Italy, Netherlands, Cuba, Spain, France, and Belgium.

The Coast Guard sometimes employed what it called a "test boat," an undercover vessel for making liquor purchases. If successful, the Coast Guard could make a case that involved several apparent infractions of the law: cargo not properly manifested, cargo unloaded without a permit, and cargo unloaded for delivery into the United States. These charges permitted them to seize the boat. One case based on this ploy occurred in October 1924; the Coast Guard seized a large rumrunner twenty miles off the mouth of New York harbor (this location indicates that the "one hour's steaming" law was in effect). They found 43,000 cases out of an original cargo of 100,000, and $26,000 in cash.

The year 1924 marked a major turning point for the Coast Guard. According to one estimate, 160 rumrunners were regularly operating off the American coast, serviced by an inshore fleet of at least several hundred contact boats. Another government

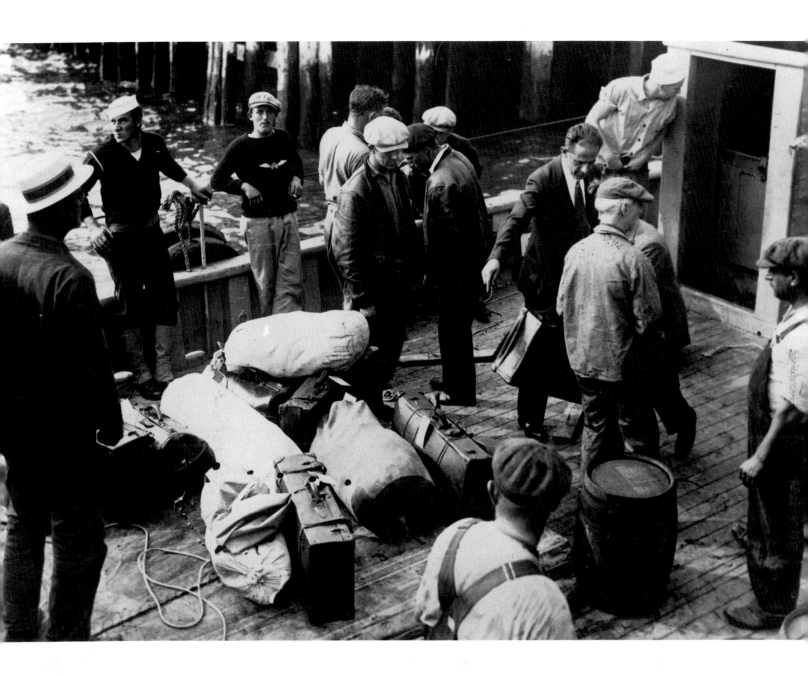

Ten prisoners and $150,000 in liquor were the results of this seizure of the 80-foot British vessel *Nova V* on August 27, 1930. The rumrunners are seen packing their gear for the trip to jail. The vessel was seized off Shinnecock Bay, near Montauk, Long Island. The photo's original caption said it was the "biggest seizure since the raid on New York City's rum-garbage scow *E*," a seizure about which the records are unfortunately obscure. *National Archives*

source announced that twice that number of foreign ships were involved in rumrunning. Government officials estimated that about 100,000 cases per month were being smuggled in from a half-dozen foreign countries. So far the Coast Guard had seized about 150 vessels; service analysts decided that Coast Guard personnel had caught perhaps 5 percent of the smuggled liquor, a total of about 30,000 cases, and had caused another 20,000 cases to be jettisoned.

Dissatisfied with that dismal total, the Coast Guard geared up for a massive upgrade to its fleet. On April 21, it added twenty reconditioned Navy destroyers to its Offshore Patrol Force [see chapter 7], along with 300 other large and small vessels, and 5,000 members. The Act of April 2, 1924 had given the Coast Guard an additional

$12 million in funding; for 1925, its budget for regular activities was $11.7 million, and for anti-smuggling, $8.2 million. In 1926, those figures climbed to $10.9 million and $15.5 million.

Spring 1925 was the opening campaign of a greatly augmented Coast Guard sea patrol, which adopted much more aggressive tactics. A large base was in New London, Connecticut. Other sorties got under way from New York and Boston, with smaller efforts in states such as Maine, where Coast Guard cutters were stationed in Portland, Cape Elizabeth, and Bar Harbor. One historian called it "the Great Offensive," targeting the rumrunning fleets lying north of the Delaware Capes, off

The crew of the rumrunner *Linwood* set it afire to destroy contraband liquor before the Coast Guard could seize it in May 1923. Whiskey fires set off by Coast Guard gunfire were a major hazard to liquor smugglers, who often stored their high-proof cargoes on deck either to make it easier to unload, or because of lack of space below decks. *National Archives*

New York and off Block Island. In mid-May of that year, the government had announced that 385 foreign ships were involved in rumrunning. The drive continued into August, producing what is generally conceded to have been positive, if temporary, results. The drive was said to have dispersed some fifty to seventy rumrunners, most of which returned to Canadian ports.

Newspapers along the Atlantic coast kept curious readers attuned to the movements of the rumrunners and to the Coast Guard's stratagems. On May 5, 1925, a Norfolk newspaper (in a story headlined "Coast Guard Fleet Sails to Begin Offensive; Cutters Will Keep Watch on Every Ship on Rum Row; Fifty Vessels Assigned to Block-ade") reported that twenty-one Coast Guard vessels had steamed out of Staten Island base on Clifton Bay, bound for Rum Row; their goal was to "sweep the liquor armada off the Atlantic seaboard by June 1."

In an oral history, Adm. Alfred C. Richmond, who retired as commandant of the Coast Guard, recalled that "it was almost a 1:1 ratio of rummies to Coast Guard vessels," which made it easier to keep an eye on them. By mid-1925, with the addition of Coast Guard planes, "gradually the schooners were forced out of the business," Richmond said. At that point, syndicates took over, using specially built rumrunning boats, and the same old business continued in a modified form.

According to many sources, the rumrunners were quick to return when the offensive waned. They moved farther and farther offshore, with the Coast Guard using its larger boats to picket them. For this duty, the Coast Guard priority was endurance, not speed, because it was easier to picket the mother ships than chase the contact boats. According to Donald Canney, "the highly visible, dramatic chases close to shore were activities of the second line of defense and of much less overall significance than the dreary, unspectacular picketing going on day and

night over the horizon." The larger Coast Guard vessels would maintain a continuous picket around the mother ships, sometimes a 10 knot circle. The close-to-shore chases were of uncertain benefit, anyway. According to John Durward, one former Coast Guard member who had done duty in the Casco Bay area of Maine stated, "We never caught any. They were like a bunch of spiders in a nest. They all ran away when they saw us coming."

Plenty of chases were recorded, of course, as any reading of contemporary accounts reveals. Scott Corbett recounts a wild story about Coast Guard officers who were surreptitiously paddling around in a dory at night, trying to sneak up on a smuggler, when they came upon their prey, who was also in a dory. The smuggler rowed madly to shore and jumped in the shallow water; the Coast Guard was right on his heels, chasing him down the beach and through the snow for several miles.

The Coast Guard steadily intensified its picketing of the mother ships on Rum Row. Another symptom of its aggressive tactics was the willingness of Coast Guard gunners to open fire with machine guns on diehard operators of contact boats. The Coast Guard also fired "star shells" (white flares) when chasing a contact boat at night, blazing away with tracers and incendiary bullets at the cargoes of whiskey, sometimes setting them afire. Once a contact boat collided with a destroyer and sank within seconds; one of the destroyers had shot away its steering ropes, so the smuggler couldn't control the rudder.

Admiral Roland served his first assignment on the destroyer *Shaw* (Coast Guard-22) in 1929, based in New London. Three or four destroyers patrolled together, one week out, two weeks in, trailing and circling the offshore rumrunners. "We couldn't begin to cover all the activity," he recalled. More positive reports came in from other areas of operations. Three months of anti-smuggling operations in Florida resulted in ninety seizures, and greatly improved prosecutions in federal courts meant that almost all of these smugglers were convicted.

In spite of sporadic or temporary successes, rumrunning continued throughout Prohibition, on a smaller scale, with the Coast Guard trying new tactics in the seemingly endless battle. The new Coast Guard 165-

Coast Guard destroyer *Amhen (CG-8),* one of the famous oil-burning "four-stackers," pickets a rumrunner of the New Jersey coast, outside the twelve-mile limit. "The trailing method proved most effective against smugglers," says the photo's original caption, but the term "effective" was relative; plenty of liquor continued to leak through the blockade throughout Prohibition. *Amhen,* built in 1911, was stationed at Hoboken, New Jersey, the base for Division 2; it was one of the thirty-one Navy destroyers lent to the Coast Guard beginning in 1924. It received its Coast Guard commission on January 22, 1925, and was returned to the Navy on May 18, 1931. *National Archives*

remained a useful option. The Coast Guard gradually got the funding to upgrade their anti-booze armada, enlisting more personnel and building or borrowing better boats. In the mid-1920s, the rumrunners were finding it increasingly difficult to conduct business. Coast Guard crews had become much more adept at picketing and chasing rumrunners, and were able to harass them efficiently. The Coast Guard continued adopting any fast boats they captured, although many of the seized boats were too slow, were

heavily damaged or in ill-repair, or were sold at auction (sometimes to the original owners at dismally low prices). In spite of the fact that, between October 1, 1928, and October 31, 1929, the Coast Guard seized $691,000 worth of boats and launches, fast boats that the Coast Guard could hold onto and convert were rare. Admiral Roland, who joined the Coast Guard at the time, said, "We did operate a number of the captured boats, but we weren't able to fix up enough of them."

Chapter 9

Cast of Characters

A rare photo of skipper Bill McCoy with *Arethusa*'s convincer, which would be used in case of piracy or hijacking, rather than Coast Guard intervention. This photo and the others of McCoy and *Arethusa* in this book are part of a collection of eighty-four photos that were donated by McCoy in October 1937 to the Mariners' Museum in Newport News, Virginia. He was living in Palm Beach, Florida, then. *Courtesy of the Mariners' Museum, Newport News, Virginia*

If we could aim a camera back in time, producing a documentary film of the history of illicit liquor in America, important events, locales, and politics would all play a role. Incidents such as the Whiskey Rebellion, places like the Dark Corner of South Carolina, legal matters such as the Revenue Cutter Bill, all would have to be examined and illustrated. The starring roles in our documentary, however, would be played by a series of heroes and villains, of notorious moonshiners and bootleggers and the steadfast men who tracked them down.

Some of these people attained national notoriety. In the 1870s, for instance, the popular press transformed moonshiner Lewis Redmond into what a contemporary author termed "one of the most distinguished characters, for daring and adventure, of the nineteenth century." The exploits of prohibition agent Izzy Einstein of New York made the front pages of the nation's most prominent newspapers for years. Some moonshine haulers in the 1930s and 1940s, Junior Johnson being the most notable example, went on to fame as race-car drivers. More recently, legendary North Carolina revenuer Garland Bunting was the focus of an excellent book.

The names of other people in the cast of characters are more obscure. Perhaps their fame may have been limited to a particular locale, or they may have been average people caught up in extraordinary events. In the case of lawbreakers, a certain obscurity was not only desirable, but mandatory. Historical accounts often name law-enforcement agents, but assign pseudonyms to the crooks. In his book *Damn the Allegators*, for example, Joe Carter notes that some of the names were "changed to protect the guilty." The better-known violators—such as mid-1950s moonshine haulers Ben Hall and "Legs" Law—appear under their real names. Percy Flowers, named in Carter's book, shows up as "Perry Bloom" in a book by another former ATF agent, Charlie Weems.

Weems changed the name of one particularly disreputable pair of moonshiners in order to protect the rest of the family. "Of

The details have been lost, but Sam Birchfield was prominent enough to merit his own postcard, circa 1910. The exploits of numerous other moonshiners were recorded in news and feature articles, even entire books. *Courtesy of the North Carolina Division of Archives and History*

course everyone in that area knew who it was," Weems said. There were plenty of nephews, uncles, and cousins still around. "I didn't know how they'd take it," he added. When he went to a book signing in that vicinity (at the Fayetteville County Historical Society), a young woman approached the retired ATF agent. "It was the guy's daughter, along with her mother, sister and sister's husband. I thought, 'Uh oh, I'm in for it now,'" Weems recalled, but he needn't have worried. "They were just so taken with the book. They said, 'You made us famous.'"

Through the years, a few of the hares and hounds of the illicit liquor game often developed a grudging sort of respect for each other. Part of the dedication to George Griffith's *Life and Adventures of Revenooer No. 1* is to the "fabled and elusive Homer Payton, the alleged Moonshine King, ruling from his plateau on top of Putman Mountain." At other times, there was no love lost between the opposing sides. "Some of those revenuers were characters, and some of them were just assholes," former moonshine hauler Fred Goswick declared.

In Madison County, Florida, in October 1951, revenuer W. George McMullen found what a news account called "the greatest compliment of his long still-busting career." It was a groundhog still with a brick furnace; etched in the concrete hearthstone of the furnace was the legend, "Mr. Mac. September 28, 1951." The moonshiner who built the still knew that "sooner or later 'Mac' would be around," the article said. Eustace Vanzant was captured at the still site; he "told the agents later that he had been manufacturing the best moonshine in North Florida." McMullen may have appreciated the compliment, but he still had a job to do. "Throwing sentiment to the winds, 'Mac' and agent Frank Watt went ahead and destroyed the copper parts of the still," the article concluded. McMullen called it an "unsolicited honor."

Amos Owens

Few histories of moonshining fail to mention Amos Owens of Rutherford County, North Carolina. He was born in 1822 to a family in which whiskey-making (notably by his grandfather) was traditional. Biographer M. L. White described Owens, as a youth, as having "a rugged, well-knit frame, a constitution like boardinghouse butter, digestion like the bowels of a threshing machine." Owens fought for the South during the Civil War (he enlisted at age thirty-

eight). After the war, he responded to the freeing of the slaves and the post-Civil War liquor tax by joining the Ku Klux Klan and acquiring a 3,000 foot high "mountain stronghold" as a base for moonshining.

In *Mountain Spirits*, Joseph Dabney described him as a "rotund, red-faced. . . hard-drinking, defiant, freedom-loving outdoorsman," who became "one of the most colorful moonshiners to grace a federal court during the post Civil War period." Owens started his fifty-year career as a legal distiller, making a famous mixture of corn liquor, honey, and cherry juice called "cherry bounce," which he sold on Mississippi River paddle steamers. As an illicit distiller, however, he soon ran afoul of the law, becoming a courtroom fixture between the 1870s and 1890, when he was arrested for moonshining and tax evasion numerous times, had nine stills destroyed, and served three terms in the penitentiary.

A judge once told him that he had caused the court a lot of trouble; Owens replied that it was mutual. He remained a colorful and cheerful character to the end. He commissioned his own biography in 1901, a fifty-five-page pamphlet by White, a school teacher from Polkville, North Carolina, who used the pen name "Corn Cracker." Owens posed for a photo, included in the book, wearing a silk hat and standing by a large copper pot still, smoking a corn cob pipe.

Lewis Redmond

Lewis Redmond was another of the well-known moonshiners of the last century. He was active in Whitewater Township, located in northwestern Oconee County, South Carolina, described then as "one of the more isolated regions," with no roads or towns as late as 1880. Redmond, one historian said, was "a sort of Jesse James of the mountains." He built a log cabin, fitted with portholes and stocked with weapons, on a bluff over the Tennessee River, which could only be reached by a pathway along a cliff. During one assault, he escaped up the chimney.

After killing a deputy marshal, Redmond moved to South Carolina with some of his followers. In 1877, a revenue collector captured him at a house, tied up one man, and went for rope; Redmond escaped through the snow. The officers gave chase and ran into an ambush, in which two were wounded. Redmond and nine followers then came after the horse and wagon that the revenuers had captured earlier; they kidnapped the agent's wife and made her cash a

check to pay for the horses. The following year, Redmond and thirty followers stormed a jail in Pickens County and freed a trio of moonshiners. A 100-man posse and a $500 reward couldn't capture him.

In an 1881 book, George Atkinson devoted a chapter to Redmond, describing him as "the best known, and the most dreaded of all the moonshiners in the south. He is today, perhaps regarded as the most notorious character in America." That year, Redmond was finally captured while squirrel hunting in Swain County, North Carolina. Wounded, he was taken to Greenville, South Carolina, where admirers sent food, whiskey, and cigars to his cell. The *New York Times* sent a reporter to interview him. Although he had killed two men, he was tried only for illicit distilling and conspiracy, getting five years in a federal penitentiary in New York. After serving two or three years, and apparently in poor health, he was pardoned. His health must have improved rapidly, however, because in 1890, he was making legal liquor in Walhalla, South Carolina, selling a famous brand under his own name. He lived to be eighty-seven.

Campbell Morgan

Another famous contemporary moonshiner was Campbell Morgan, the son of a Presbyterian clergyman, described as a "wild and reckless" youth who combined exceptional skills as an outdoorsman with an excellent education. During the Civil War, he became a renowned "bushwhacker and guerrilla," author Jess Carr wrote. After the war, his fame took a different turn, as he became "well known throughout the South as the chief of the Tennessee moonshiners." In *The Second Oldest Profession,* Carr commented, "for years he cut a broad and shameful swath in the history of Southern Kentucky and Middle Tennessee," particularly Jackson County. Atkinson called him "Sachem of the Cumberland Mountain Moonshiners."

Morgan was the leading figure in the famous "pitched battle" of August 23–24, 1878, in Overton County, Tennessee. Leading a mob of moonshiners, Morgan surrounded a small band of revenuers led by the equally famous Capt. James M. Davis of Tennessee.

Morgan was eventually arrested and imprisoned by Davis and a large group of revenuers, who attacked and wounded him. Later, he became a deputy U.S. marshal, specializing in moonshiners, and serving under Captain Davis, with whom he became friends. As might be expected, Mor-

Campbell Morgan, "moonshine monarch" of Tennessee in the late 1800s. Initially at odds with revenuer Capt. James M. Davis, the two men were once involved in an epic battle; Morgan later switched sides and joined the revenuers, after which he and Davis became friends. *From* After the Moonshiners *(1881)*

gan was exceptionally successful as a revenuer, once arresting Bill Berong, the head of a clan of moonshiners in Georgia. Berong in turn promised to help them seize other illicit stills in his neighborhood.

The Mysterious "J. R. Turner"

One of the most interesting parts of Weems' colorful memoirs is his account of trying to capture a major violator that he called by the pseudonym J. R. Turner. "Every ATF agent in the Southeast had heard of J. R.," Weems wrote in *A Breed Apart*. He was "the biggest violator in Georgia and one of the largest in the nation."

Turner had been investigated for twenty years by "almost every ATF agent in Georgia," but never caught. Agents would make an occasional still seizure or arrest a still hand, but could never tie him to the operation. They tried using undercover agents, Weems wrote, but Turner "was not going to talk to anyone he didn't know."

Turner was likable, well-dressed, intelligent, and an excellent manager. Turner "had the good will of everyone in the county, contributed to all the social and charity events," Weems said. "He was also paying people off—there's no doubt in my mind about that," he added, mentioning that a couple of state agents seemed likely candidates. "He wasn't above bribing juries, either." Turner had an uncanny ability to detect the presence of the law. Whenever Weems went to stake out a suspected Turner still, "there was never any activity when I was in the area," he wrote.

One operation suspected of being run by Turner was seized eight miles north of Dawsonville, Georgia, in Lumpkin County: eighty-one 220-gallon fermenters, operating full time, which could produce 900–1,000 gallons per day. On another occasion, the Lumpkin County sheriff seized a large still (Weems thought it was one of Turner's) the night after federal agents had located it. Weems figured that Turner decided it would be better to have the sheriff make the seizure with an illegal warrant, go to court, and buy back the still equipment "at about one-fourth the original cost." According to Weems' account, a regional special investigator for the ATF (a veteran agent) was acting as a "mole" for Turner, tipping him off to stills and vehicles that were under surveillance. This agent was later caught in a vehicle with Turner, with a suspiciously large sum of money in the glove compartment. He wasn't prosecuted, however, and they simply transferred him to another region.

Weems worked on the Turner case for three years and never did prosecute. The Turner saga, which Weems promises to continue in his second book, remains a major frustration during a long and successful career. "Of course it would have been much better if we could have caught him and sent him off to prison for forty years, but that's not how it works in real life," Weems said.

Percy Flowers

Joe Carter was one of many federal agents who worked on the case of a moonshiner he described as "the legendary, notorious Percy Flowers" of Johnston County, south of Raleigh, North Carolina. Flowers was the subject of a long investigative article called "King of the Moonshiners," by John Kobler, published in the *Saturday Evening Post* on August 2, 1958. Unhampered by a seventh-grade education, Flowers was already late into a spectacularly successful career as a businessman, farmer, and moonshiner. His annual income was estimated at $1,000,000. He owned a 5,000 acre farm, and was a "philanthropist, pillar of the church and friend of politicians," Kobler wrote.

At that time, the ATF had 400 agents at work south of the Mason-Dixon line. They had destroyed 9,511 stills in the fourteen southern states. North Carolina was the national leader the previous year, yielding up nearly one-fifth of the national total of seized moonshine. And smack in the middle was Percy Flowers, who, Kobler wrote, had been "for years North Carolina's No. 1 bootlegger." Kobler described him as a "stocky, ruddy, balding man of fifty-five, courtly of manner when deferred to, violent when thwarted." Between 1929 and 1958, his name had figured into ten federal and eighteen state indictments for bootlegging and for evading income taxes and liquor taxes. All but one of the indictments ended in an acquittal, a suspended sentence, or a small fine; he was sentenced to three years in jail for assaulting a federal agent in 1936, but even this sentence was later reduced to a year.

He was audited by the IRS in 1951. Flowers had declared a total taxable income of $4,544.44 for the previous seven years. Tax specialists estimated that that represented about one-fortieth of the actual total. He never paid the $285,000 in fines and taxes which federal investigators claimed he owed. His moonshining modus operandi was simple but effective. He avoided bank accounts, instead putting cash in safe-deposit boxes rented in the names of relatives. A witness once testified to seeing, in one safe, a stack of $100 bills "a foot square." All of Flowers' vehicles had fictitious registrations. And, most importantly, he donated heavily to charities, community projects, and local political campaigns.

In 1955, a member of Flowers' organization named Signal Wall shot a suspected informer (in fact, Wall's own brother). Wall was arrested and got twelve years at hard labor; he soon escaped from a road gang, however, and was at large for six months before he was eventually captured at a cottage behind Flowers' farm. Flowers, however, avoided any direct involvement.

That year, the ATF assigned "two of its crack agents," Leonard Mika and Roy Longnecker, to concentrate on Flowers. During that time, Flowers had the audacity to complain to them that they were ignoring some moonshiners in neighboring Wake County, who were undercutting his prices.

During the course of their extensive investigation, agents seized five stills on Flowers property, destroying about 6,000 gallons of liquor in the process. One still gave up 1,800 gallons of whiskey and 47,740 gallons of mash. In July 1957, on a Flowers tenant farm, Kobler wrote, "the agents brought off the biggest single seizure anywhere since Prohibition": 3,019 gallons. At one point, Flowers offered Longnecker a job at twice his government salary.

At the end of the campaign, the federal agents handed in a 216-page report on the activities of Flowers and sixteen of his hired hands and associates. His alleged offenses, if he were found guilty, would put him in jail for nine years and call for fines of $30,000. In February 1958, the federal agents produced sixty-eight exhibits and thirty witnesses during the court case. Result: a mistrial, although Flowers was slapped with an eighteen-month sentence for contempt of court. At a grand jury hearing five months later, Flowers' four lawyers got him out of every charge except contempt. Of the codefendants, one had died, five were discharged, and seven got suspended sentences. Three others were not present.

Eleven indictments in Johnston County Superior Court remained. He entered no plea to eight of them, "theoretically exposing himself to a lifetime in prison," Kobler noted, but the judge blithely fined him $150 and gave him eighteen months, later reduced to a year. During sentencing, the judge said, "While we're dealing with a man who hasn't had half the respect for the law a good citizen is supposed to have, he has a lot of good qualities, too."

When it was time to take this exemplary citizen to the penitentiary in Atlanta, the officers must have felt that the clock had been rolled back a century to the time of Lewis Redmond. According to Kobler, they "took unusual precautions to keep the date of departure and the route secret, lest his cohorts attempt a rescue."

Alvin B. Sawyer

On February 25, 1990, the Norfolk *Virginian-Pilot* ran an article entitled "Still at it? Legendary moonshiner gives law the slip," datelined Elizabeth City. The article said that Alvin B. Sawyer, another well-remembered name in the history of moonshining, was "on the lam" after eluding police who had arrested him for having a still in his backyard, barely a year after he'd gotten out of prison for moonshining. "You could smell the mash from the road," a local police corporal told a reporter. Local officers had been investigating Sawyer's most recent moonshine foray for five weeks. The article called the seventy-two-year-old Sawyer a "northeastern North Carolina legend."

Sawyer had started crying when he was caught. The officers knew him from previous arrests, and they let him go in the trailer to "collect himself." He escaped out the back door. He had been making whiskey for fifty-five years, and had escaped on numerous occasions. (He once ran out of a shower and through the woods naked to escape officers.) The article pointed out that his newest still was in a "makeshift shed" next to his trailer, and that he appeared to be making 45 gallons a week, selling it for about $20.00 a gallon.

"Despite the escape, the atmosphere around the Sawyer yard Saturday morning was almost jovial," the article said. Police were sure they'd catch him again. "Alvin genuine[ly] loves to make whiskey," said veteran lawman Bennie V. Halstead after Sawyer was convicted in 1987 for making and selling bootleg whiskey. Halstead, now retired himself, "nearly made a career out of chasing Sawyer," the article continued. "He'd make it if he had to make it in a little old still in his front yard," Halstead said after the 1987 conviction. Sawyer had been making and marketing small "ministills" as a novelty item, selling for $175, along with a card that said "Greetings from the moonshine king of eastern North Carolina."

Although the rogue's gallery of moonshiners is mainly male, a few representatives of the opposite sex have cracked the gender barrier through the years. At the end of the nineteenth century, Lucy McClure was

sought for eight years "as one of the most persistent and daring of West Virginia's moonshiners," Wilbur Miller wrote in *Revenuers & Moonshiners*. McClure was twenty-four years old, athletic, a good shot, and a skillful horse rider. During Prohibition, Jennie Justo earned a reputation as "queen of the bootleggers" in Madison, Wisconsin, selling homemade wine at a speakeasy that catered to college students.

Drivers

Moonshine haulers also attained transitory local prominence. Conrad LaBelle was described as a "notorious Canadian smuggler," reputed to have had a fleet of twenty cars and drivers. In upper New York state, Allan Everest wrote in *Rum Across the Border*, "the 'king' of bootleggers won the title by unusually daring and successful exploits." Dick Warner of Saratoga was the first, but was arrested in March 1920 for bootlegging, charged with six counts, and got two years in the federal pen. He was caught again immediately after getting out of prison. He escaped from the detention room of the customs house in Rouses Point, New York, was captured again in Canada, and jailed in Plattsburgh, New York, where he almost escaped again by sawing through the bars. He served eleven months and, just over a year later, was caught acting as a pilot car for two other bootleggers who ditched their loads and escaped. Warner pleaded guilty, was fined $14,000, and got three more years in jail.

According to Esther Kellner, Jaybird Philpot of Manchester, Kentucky, "handled his tanker-car like a jet-propelled demon." One night he came upon a roadblock the police had set up for him, two cars across a narrow road with the rear ends in the ditches and the front ends hardly more than a yard apart. He jammed his foot down on the accelerator, crashed into both cars, slicing off the hoods, spun one of them out of his way, and escaped.

On another occasion, the sheriff got a tip about the route Philpot would take that night, and when he would make his run. The sheriff and his deputies built a heavy rail barricade across a bridge, hid in some bushes, and waited. Soon after dark, Philpot came roaring over the hill; he saw the roadblock but didn't even hesitate, crashing through it at full speed.

One night his luck ran out. He raced around a curve to find three police cars pulled across the narrow road. He threw his car into the Big Turnaround and sped back in the opposite direction. However, two other police cars emerged from hiding places along the roadside and drove straight at him. He kept right on coming, and they crashed. There were no serious injuries, but, Kellner wrote, "the Pride of Manchester had made his last moonshine run."

An early race-car driver named Lloyd Seay earned a tragic sort of prominence in the pantheon of moonshine transporters. Driving a two-door 1938 Ford (what Dabney described as "an Atlanta-based trip car with its manifolds drilled") on Armistice Day 1939, Seay won the first car race held at Atlanta's Lakewood Speedway. He also won the National Stock Car Championship on that same dirt track on September 1, 1941. The next day, a cousin killed him near Dawsonville, Georgia, after a dispute over a load of sugar. In his book, Dabney shows Seay's tombstone, which depicts a 1939 Ford coupe; Seay was twenty-one when he died.

Revenuers

On the right side of the law were the enforcement agents, who wrote their names in the history books through persistence, dedication, and courage.

Because revenuers had much longer careers than moonshine drivers, they were able to put together some eye-popping career totals. An early southern revenuer of note was Jacob Wagner who, in 1875, fielded a twelve-man civilian posse, armed with rifles, and equipped with tents and camp gear. They seized an average of twenty-five stills per month.

Capt. James M. Davis

In George Atkinson's 1881 book, *After the Moonshiners: By One of the Raiders,* chapters twelve and thirteen are about Capt. James M. Davis of Tennessee, "the noted Raider and Scout" (Atkinson himself was no slouch, destroying more than 200 stills in his career). He described Davis as "the beau ideal raider": shrewd, active, daring, strong, and an excellent tracker. Davis had first worked in Tennessee tracking escaped convicts and arresting horse thieves, "two classes of malefactors whom the most of criminal officers desire especially to avoid. He was intimate with nearly all the bypaths and deep recesses of the Cumberland Mountains . . . When entering on a man's trail, he acquaints himself with all that man's habits and movements, and all this time never allows his intentions to be discovered." He could also travel for four days without food or sleep, Atkinson wrote, and was an outstanding marksman. As a result, "The individuals against whom he has operated for violations of the law, quake at the bare mention of his name."

Capt. James M. Davis, one of the earliest revenuers whose deeds were chronicled in print. Davis implacably pursued Campbell Morgan, perhaps the most infamous moonshiner of the time. *From* After the Moonshiners *(1881)*

Davis captured more than 3,000 moonshiners and destroyed 618 stills during his career. He killed three men during that time, one of them in Tennessee where Davis was arrested and charged (unsuccessfully) with murder. During the famous, oft-recounted "pitched battle" between federal agents and moonshiners in Overton County, Tennessee, on August 23–24, 1878, Davis led the revenuers. He was ambushed and murdered in 1882 while taking a moonshiner to court.

Isadore "Izzy" Einstein

When it came to the energy and brilliance with which a person attacked a job, Isadore "Izzy" Einstein had one of the twentieth century's most appropriate names. He was a genius at coaxing bartenders into selling him illegal drinks.

An enforcement agent for the Federal Prohibition Bureau in New York, Einstein was also an actor. He was called "the man of 1,000 disguises," "the mastermind of the federal rum ferrets," and "the Lon Chaney" of the bootlegger busters. The prohibition bureau was widely criticized as being at best inefficient and at worst incompetent, but Einstein was astonishingly successful—both at nabbing crooks and headlines.

Born in Poland in 1880, he had come to America when he was fifteen. He got married, fathered four sons, and went to work as a postal clerk on Manhattan's Lower East Side. When the Volstead Act took effect and the federal prohibition-enforcement mechanism geared up, Einstein decided that he wanted to be an enforcement agent. When he strolled in to apply for the job, he must have been the least prepossessing applicant of the year: he was just five feet tall and weighed 225 pounds. Later, after Einstein became famous, Herbert Asbury described him like this: "When he walked, his noble paunch, gently wobbling, moved majestically ahead like the breast of an overfed pouter pigeon."

The recruiter didn't see the nobility or the majesty, however. He sized up Einstein as a slob and turned him down because he "didn't look like a detective." Einstein convinced them that was an advantage, got the job, and proceeded to prove his point several thousand times during the next few years.

For his first arrest, he put on his dirtiest and most worn clothes, went in a blue-collar saloon in Brooklyn where several other agents had failed to buy drinks, and got one. This modest ruse set the tone for his meteoric career. "Izzy liked disguises," Thomas Coffey wrote in *The Long Thirst—Prohibition in America, 1920–1933.* Einstein believed that the primary skill of a dry agent was to be able to look and act as if he weren't one. Einstein "was an adaptable man and a skillful actor. He could be a fast-talking salesman, a happy jokester, or a timid farmer bewildered by the city." He spoke three languages and could pass for several varieties of immigrant, Polish and German among them. Searching out speakeasies and buying glassfuls of evidence, Einstein posed as an iceman, laborer, fisherman, farmer, and Italian fruit vendor. He wore a tuxedo to mix with the uptown folks, or overalls to blend in with workers.

He acquired a partner, Moe Smith, a perfect bookend at 5 feet 6 inches, 250 pounds. The good publicity was fine, but their rapid rise to fame was also a curse and a challenge. The bootleggers were soon on the lookout for them. Conspicuously corpulent, Izzy and Moe had to devise what Coffey called "an ever-changing variety of ruses to outwit their intended victims." They put on athletic gear and smeared themselves with dirt to pose as football players (linemen, presumably). They pretended to be selling coal, fruit, and vegetables, to be truck drivers, longshoremen, college students, streetcar conductors, even musicians. Late in his career, in what may have been a crowning achievement, Einstein became a member of a private club for actors on Forty-eighth Street, using the name Ethelbert Santerre; then he promptly raided the place.

Einstein once grabbed a shovel, masqueraded as a gravedigger, and hung around Woodlawn Cemetery to keep an eye on a nearby house that had aroused suspicion. When agents made the resulting bust, they found two 110-gallon stills, several barrels of whiskey, and 200 gallons of alcohol.

He and Smith once darkened their skins and spoke "negro dialects" to infiltrate a Harlem delicatessen. The store had developed passwords for illegal sales of liquor—"tomatoes" meant gin, "small can" meant pint, "beans" meant whiskey. The agents posed as customers for several days; eventually, a helpful and trusting employee spilled the beans.

At other times, Einstein donned disguises as an automobile cleaner, a milk-truck driver, fisherman, horse dealer, a churchgoer in a Palm Sunday parade on Fifth Avenue, a grocery wholesaler, and, according to Charles Merz, a "thirsty motorman . . . a patron of a suspicious pawnshop, an iceman catering to saloons in Brooklyn," and a trombone player.

The Manhattan office of the Federal Prohibition Bureau was responsible for the southern part of the state, and soon Izzy and Moe took their act on the road, eventually ranging into neighboring states. In Detroit, posing as dock workers, they made fifty arrests. Einstein arrested eighty-five people in Mobile, Alabama, and seized $100,000 worth of booze. The pair, along with twenty-four other agents, went to Providence, Rhode Island, in September, 1922. That state was one of only two states to refuse to ratify the Eighteenth Amendment, and had overtly ignored the law for several years. In other words, it was a perfect stage for Einstein. Coffey relates a typical exploit: "At one saloon, Moe Smith told the bartender he'd give him a useful tip in exchange for a drink. 'Tell me the tip,' the bartender said, 'and we'll see if it's worth a drink.' 'The tip,' Moe said, 'is that there are federal agents on the job in this neighborhood.' Moe soon had a glass in front of him, after which the grateful bartender learned that the tip was embarrassingly accurate."

Izzy and Moe visited one bar that had been hard to infiltrate. Noticing the street was torn up in front, they returned to Providence to procure work clothes and shovels. They worked for a few minutes, then strolled in and ordered a drink, successfully, adding another arrest to the forty-six the two agents tallied during their three days in Rhode Island.

Einstein carried a stopwatch and calculated how long it took to get a drink in the various cities he visited during his official perambulations: Chicago, twenty-one minutes; Baltimore, fifteen minutes; Pittsburgh, eleven minutes. The record was in New Orleans, where he once got a drink from a cab driver in thirty-five seconds.

Einstein's success was not unalloyed, however. He became a sort of King Lear with a badge; the seeds of his downfall were sown. By 1925, the pair had so dramatically outshone their colleagues that it was humiliating (they had investigated or taken part in 20 percent of the arrests in the New York district since the beginning). Their enthusiasm and triumphs highlighted the lackluster performance of their superiors and their peers. According to some accounts, the higher-ups were jealous of their publicity. The cat-and-mouse game of the early days of Prohibition had become much more serious. Influential customers got tired of being inconvenienced by raids that closed down their favorite speakeasies. The crime syndicates got organized and gathered political influence. Untold numbers of revenue agents took bribes and grew to depend on the income; when the guys paying the bribes were arrested by an honest agent, they didn't like it. On numerous counts, Izzy and Moe were pests. They were more than unpopular; they had bona fide enemies on both sides of the law.

Push came to shove in November 1925, when 180 agents in Einstein's division were asked to "resign" as a "formality" pending reassignment and changes in official titles. Izzy and Moe had raided 3,000 speakeasies, routinely busting fifteen or twenty places a week (they'd once made seventeen raids in one night). They had arrested 4,900 people, and confiscated 5 million bottles of bootleg liquor, conservatively valued by one historian at $15 million. Nevertheless, during the 1925 reorganization, thirty-five agents were not reinstated—Izzy and Moe were among them.

Historians agree that Smith was fired; one reference adds that Einstein stayed on for a "few more years" involved in other investigations. In defense of the persistence and ingenuity of the liquor smugglers and merchants, Coffey observed that in spite of Izzy and Moe's "tireless efforts, New York had infinitely more bootleggers and speakeasies now than when they had begun." At any rate, both men ended up as successful life-insurance agents in the late 1920s—less exciting, no doubt, but at least they didn't have to wear disguises.

Einstein got at least one more dose of publicity: he wrote his autobiography, *Prohibition Agent No. 1,* published on October 26, 1932, by Frederick A. Stokes. By his own demand, Moe Smith wasn't mentioned or even pictured. Izzy Einstein died in February 1938.

W. George McMullen

McMullen, mentioned throughout this book, started his career in 1931, spending a decade as a customs officer in Florida, South Carolina, New Jersey, Louisiana, Mississippi, and Alabama, during which time he was involved in the seizures of 145 stills and fifty-three cars. He then spent five years in Tampa with the ATU, adding to his tally another 129 stills, sixty-eight cars, a tractor-trailer, five horses, and a bicycle. A final dozen years in Tallahassee brought another 260 stills and 157 automobiles into his clutches.

William Bernard "Big Six" Henderson, perhaps Kentucky's best-known revenuer, holds an item from the bottle collection he worked on after turning in his badge. Moonshiners claimed that he could smell a still ten miles away, but Henderson modestly estimated that two miles was closer to the truth. He raided more than 5,000 stills and sent more than 5,600 moonshiners to prison. He credited part of his success to some advice given him by the federal agent in charge of the Louisville office when Henderson first went to work as a revenuer; the senior agent said that although some of the moonshiners they would try to catch couldn't read or write, Henderson should "give them credit for having at least 10 percent more brains" than he had. *Charles Fentress, Jr., the* Courier-Journal, *Louisville, Kentucky*

William Bernard "Big Six" Henderson

The name and reputation of William Bernard "Big Six" Henderson looms large in the annals of enforcement. He was born in Hardin County, Kentucky, and grew up in Jasper, Indiana, but would become leg-endary for his work around Louisville and in the hills of Rockcastle County. He started out as a lawyer, but when he got an obvious-ly guilty client set free during his first case, he quit. "I decided if I had to make a living that way I might as well be a holdup man and at least be honest about it," he told journalist Jules Loh.

He joined ATU as an investigator in 1941, and began working in the Coe Ridge area in March 1942, making more than 200 raids into the area. According to Kellner, he "knew woodlands, wildlife and weather like Daniel Boone," and was "as silent and alert as any pioneer hunter. Many a time he walked right up to a moonshiner without breaking a twig or stirring a leaf." He was as-signed to the notorious Golden Pond area in April 1942 as part of a serious crackdown.

Henderson was a big man, 6 feet 4 inches, and his reputation grew to match. At times he would chase violators as far as two miles. Violators claimed that he could smell a still ten miles away ("Actually about two miles if the wind is right," he told Loh). He was said to be a crack shot, able to shoot a pistol out of a man's hand at a hundred yards; he acknowledged that did happen once, but he had been aiming at the man's belt buckle.

Up to 1960, he sometimes made eight raids a week; he once arrested twenty-seven violators in one day, and arrested one viola-tor thirteen times. By his own count, he raided more than 5,000 stills and sent more than 5,600 moonshiners to prison. In a ca-reer spanning twenty-eight years (after serv-ing with ATF, he worked for the Justice De-partment's Marshal Service from 1970 to 1975), that equates to roughly a still every other day. Loh wrote, "Big Six Henderson busted up more stills in his time than anybody in history. If that is not so, at least it is the legend. When moonshiners talk about Big Six Henderson, the line between truth and legend blurs."

The moonshiners that he tracked down respected him and feared him. Some named their children after him. One moonshiner painted the name "Big Six" on his mash barrel; Henderson caught him talking to it one day. Henderson also earned a reputation for fair play. "I never regarded them as doing something evil, just illegal," he told Loh. He retired in 1968.

Henderson's closest friend was a fellow agent named Everett Liley. Henderson once described Liley as "an investigator who should have been in a book." Liley had an "Indian skill at tracking and following a trail. He could track like a Comanche and was so stealthy and quiet of foot he could have slipped up on a jackrabbit."

Garland Bunting

A revenuer who did get in a book is Garland Bunting of Halifax County, North Carolina. "In the minds of many people he is the most successful revenue agent in the history of a state that has always been enormously productive of moonshine," wrote Alec Wilkinson, author of *Moonshine: A Life in Pursuit of White Liquor*, which brings Bunting to life far more effectively than can be accomplished here.

Bunting started his colorful career as a county police officer in North Carolina. He served in the military police during his time in the service, then embarked on what would prove to be three decades of what he called "undercover all over this state."

He is an exuberant, jowly man, with a protruding belly, and deep creases and smile lines in his face. He is nothing if not creative and ebullient, and possesses the classic gift of gab. "Rural people are just plain leery of strangers," he once told writer Jane Sanderson. "If they see somebody just hangin' around who ain't got something interestin' to talk about, they wonder, 'Who is he?'"

Whether he was posing as a fish seller or a coon hunter, he was invariably successful. In Gaston County in 1954, for example, he and another agent hauled 177 moonshining cases into court and got 176 convictions (one man died before he could go to trial). His success in undercover work is all the more remarkable because he is arguably famous: he was once written up in *People* magazine, for example, and appeared as the sports announcer in the film *Bull Durham*.

Bunting was "a good undercover man," said Jim Ward, a former North Carolina ABC agent who worked with Bunting several times. Ward smiled and shook his head when asked to describe Bunting: he was "just a plain old guy, but he carried on more crap than you'd think thought possible." At times, Bunting's antics made him appear, perhaps misleadingly, to be "a real clown." But he was "a good buyer [of moonshine]—he could buy from anybody," Ward said. "He'd get him an old pickup truck and a load of fish on the back" and go to work.

A classic Bunting anecdote is one that he told Wilkinson, introducing it by saying, "Throughout life it looks like things have just worked out for me." He offered as an illustration a yarn about an incident in Martin County, North Carolina, in 1962. An ATF official told him that a local moonshiner named Hugh Pitts had just gotten a new 1963 Ford that he was using for transporting moonshine. Bunting vowed that if that information was true, Pitts wouldn't get away with it for long.

On his way home from the ATF office, Bunting decided to stop at the bootlegger's house to check his license plate number. When he was almost there, he met Pitts coming the other way. Pitts gunned the car, and Bunting turned around in pursuit. They careened around several curves, and Pitts finally went off on a dirt road, lost control, shot up a bank, and landed in a field, where he abandoned the car and lit out on foot, carrying several gallons of whiskey. Bunting caught him before he could reach some nearby woods. Bunting then called the ATF office and reported that he had kept his vow.

He is unexpectedly modest when it comes to describing his career: "You might say my job is a regular old raw life, nothin' all that interestin', but catchin' a moonshiner takes bein' sort of shrewd, bein' persistent and bein' dedicated," he told one journalist. Dedicated, indeed; at last report, Bunting, now in his mid-sixties, hadn't yet retired.

Duff Floyd

Another prolific modern-day revenuer was Duff Floyd who, according to Dabney, "for thirty-five years was one of the most productive 'still busters' in north Georgia, a tall, rangy outdoorsman who during his career literally worked around the clock in an evangelistic commitment to slowing down the flow of moonshine whiskey."

Floyd started his long career on February 1, 1929. During some years, he and his colleagues seized three dozen stills a month, averaging more than one a day. He had ample opportunities, since his longest tour of duty was in Jasper, Georgia, where his territory included two of Georgia's most notorious moonshining counties, Gilmer and Dawson. His longtime nemesis, John Henry Hardin, was known as the "king of the moonshiners" in Cherokee County in the 1930s and early 1940s. Hardin ran a pair of steamer distilleries, making 300–400 gallons a day.

In 1936, Floyd crashed into a stump while driving, broke his neck, and spent six weeks on the horizontal. He also suffered a severe cut on his head in the crash of a private plane, which cost him an eye. Nevertheless, he became adept at flying aerial patrols to hunt for stills. In radio contact with agents on the ground, he could direct them to a still in fifteen or twenty minutes. It got to the point where the moonshiners would start running if they just heard an airplane.

Most localities, sooner or later, produced revenuers of note. Former moonshiner Willie Clay Call mentioned a law-enforcement officer named Bill Queen of Greensboro, North Carolina, that he "dreaded awful bad." Call also remembered Jim Malt of China Grove, who drove a 1959 Pontiac with two bumpers on it, which he used to try to knock moonshine haulers off the road. The powerful Pontiac had been seized from a transporter. Malt was dreaded by the moonshiners in his county. He had the reputation of being able to spot a whiskey car "twenty miles away." One former transporter said that when he got a call from someone in Malt's county who wanted to buy some moonshine, he made the customer meet him at the county line. He didn't want to go into Malt's territory.

Rumrunners

Rumrunners of note were a mixed lot. Some garnered headlines, and a few developed a localized fame. Retired Coast Guard Admiral Edwin Roland recalled that most of the rumrunners he dealt with were Canadian (since that country's distilleries thrived during Prohibition).

Like Garland Bunting, at least one rumrunner had a book written about his career: Manny Zora, a Portuguese fisherman from Provincetown, the subject of Scott Corbett's *The Sea Fox*. The book's title was taken from the nickname given to Zora by the Coast Guard crews who tried to track him down (Zora meant "fox" in Portuguese, and he was also an extraordinarily shrewd smuggler). Zora

Bootlegging Fueled Capone's Rise

If Prohibition didn't plant the seed of organized crime in America, it certainly provided a tremendous fertilizer. Organized gangs had existed in the big cities for a century, and criminal syndicates were already deeply involved in gambling, loan-sharking, brothels, and extortion when the Volstead Act took effect. Crooked politicians and bribed police were already widespread in the early part of the century, particularly in Chicago. "Chicago is unique," said University of Chicago professor Charles Merriam in 1917. "It is the only completely corrupt city in America." If possible, Prohibition made this worse, and making, smuggling, hijacking, bootlegging, and selling beer and whiskey kept scores of gangs busy. These activities also led newspaper headlines to refer to gangsters as "beer barons" and "booze kings."

It was against this backdrop that a gangster named Johnny Torrio and one of his protégés, Umberto (Albert John) Capone, would soon soar into prominence. Making and smuggling beer and whiskey rapidly became a major part of the criminal's portfolio. Most of the bars and roadhouses in and around Chicago stayed open after Prohibition, their operators on the lookout for sources of liquor. Bootlegging was a natural for most gang leaders. Some had laid in supplies of whiskey before the Volstead Act took effect, while others made arrangements with moonshiners and smugglers.

An early criminal combine, the six Genna brothers, operated on Chicago's South Side in Little Italy. They obtained a government license for handling industrial alcohol, which they redistilled and flavored into a barely palatable (but highly popular) liquor. They also set up hundreds of tenement dwellers as moonshiners. "Alky cooking became the cottage industry of Little Italy," John Kobler wrote in Capone. At one point, the Gennas were netting $150,000 per week, a substantial part of which went into payoffs to the police. Bribery on this scale helped create the situation described by Charles C. Fitzmorris, Chicago's chief of police during the early years of Prohibition, when he admitted, "Sixty percent of my police are in the bootleg business." Several years later, Johnny Torrio would try to bribe Chicago's chief of police by offering him $100,000 per month, but was turned down.

Capone's inauguration into the festivities began in 1920 when Torrio promised him half of the profits from the gang's burgeoning business. Whiskey smuggling was a major part of that business. A lesser known, aspect involved breweries. Brewers wishing to stay open had few options. They could either make near-beer, go out of business, or stay in business by affiliating with gangsters, who would buy protection, pay off cops, and fight hijackers. Torrio was one of four partners in a chain of nine breweries (including the Sieben Brewery on the North Side, one of the city's largest). He also arranged a series of agreements among rival gangs for the production and delivery of beer and liquor to bars and brothels. In 1922, Torrio and his partners grossed an estimated $12 million from these arrangements.

The truce was broken when Spike O'Donnell, leader of a rival South Side gang, returned from prison and added another chapter to what Chicago's mayor, William Dever, had referred to as a "guerrilla war between hijackers, rum runners and illicit beer peddlers." O'Donnell ignored the loose syndicate that Torrio had arranged. He began hijacking beer trucks and forcing bar owners into buying illegal beer from him. He thereby triggered what came to be known as the "beer war" of 1925, during which at least five of his beer-truck drivers were ambushed and killed by Torrio allies. According to Kobler, "In several of the beer war massacres Al Capone was placed at the scene by eyewitnesses, none of whom, however, would so testify under oath." The beer war was simply another outbreak of the bloodshed that became the hallmark of that era.

Business boomed for Capone. Beginning in 1926, Kobler wrote, he began "expanding his bootleg operations on a national scale," developing " a network of interstate alliances" reaching to Detroit, St. Louis, and Philadelphia. He was getting large, regular shipments of smuggled liquor and selling it throughout the Midwest. Occasionally gang members got greedy and paid a predictable price. One gangster who worked for Capone, Frank Yale, was supervising ship landings on Long Island and the ensuing truck shipments to Chicago. In the spring of 1927, many of the trucks were being hijacked before they got out of New York. Capone suspected Yale of double-crossing him. On July 1, 1927, Yale was killed by a barrage of fire from revolvers, shotguns, and the first tommy gun used to kill a New York gangster.

Early the following year, a rival gang run by Bugs Moran began preying on Capone's operations, hijacking truckloads of liquor coming from Detroit, an entire cargo of whiskey from a Canadian ship, and bombing six saloons that were buying beer from Capone. Capone's revenge went down in the annals of brutality as the St. Valentine's Day massacre. It was set up, appropriately enough, by the promise of a truckload of hijacked liquor. Moran was not among the seven victims.

Although, in 1928, liquor produced most of Capone's profits, Capone kept his other criminal activities active, as well. At one time he and Torrio owned nearly two dozen brothels. And with the approaching demise of Prohibition, Capone became more heavily engaged in racketeering. Bribing politicians and police, of course, remained mandatory. In 1928, Frank Loesch, head of the Chicago Crime Commission, said, "Al Capone ran the city. His hand reached into every department of the city and county government . . ."

That year, when the Prohibition Unit became part of the Department of Justice, twenty-six-year-old Eliot Ness was appointed to run a special unit targeting Capone in Chicago, a city that then had 20,000 places to get a drink. Ness' accomplishments, Kobler says, were "later melodramatized" to a great degree, thanks in part to Ness' own strong sense of publicity. The "Untouchables" did harass Capone and cause him some financial loss, but they did not destroy him, and they came nowhere near drying up the city.

didn't start rumrunning until two years after Prohibition started, and continued to do some fishing for several reasons: he enjoyed it, he needed a cover for his income, and he always wanted the Coast Guard to suspect that he might just be going fishing.

At least one woman gained distinction as "queen of the rummies." She went by the moniker "Havana Kitty," owned fifteen boats, and was once arrested on the beach at Coconut Grove, Florida, supervising the unloading of a smuggling boat called *Kid Boots*.

In 1986, the newspaper in St. Pierre-Miquelon ran a long article on the death of eighty-three-year-old Henri "Le Bootlegger" Moraze, who had been born in 1903. Before he was eighteen, he was making liquor runs to the West Indies; one shipping point was Demerara in British Guyana, a twenty-five-day trip, where he bought 7,000 gallons of liquor for twenty-five cents a gallon. He would then smuggle the liquor onto the American and Canadian coasts, finding customers in Newfoundland, the Maritimes, and Quebec.

Moraze spent twelve years as a rum-runner and made "millions of dollars," the article said. He met both Al Capone and Bill McCoy, "the man who discovered by chance that St. Pierre—that small part of France—could be a great sheltering port and distribution centre for liquor shipments heading to the U.S., Canada and New-foundland," wrote John Calver.

In 1939, he was forbidden to enter either America or Canada, and could only leave the island on direct flights to France. Yet his nefarious past didn't keep Moraze from becoming a prominent citizen. He became a storekeeper and shipping agent, and was elected to the regional council in 1946, later serving as vice president. He also directed the French Administrative Fleet for a decade.

Numerous gangsters became famous during Prohibition, including William "Big Bill" Dwyer, a New York "sportsman" and part-time legitimate businessman. He went to prison for violating the Volstead Act, charged with what one newspaper called "directing a vast rumrunning syndicate"

with two dozen vessels, speedboats, and an airplane. His rumrunning operations were once estimated at bringing in a gross income of $20 million a year.

Another New York mobster, Charles R. "Vannie" Higgins, earned as much as $4 million directing rumrunning activities. He owned the *Cigarette,* described as "the fastest of the rumrunners in the New York area." Higgins called himself a "lobster fisherman," but the newspapers referred to him as "the prominent Brooklyn wet goods importer."

Bill McCoy

Bill McCoy's father was in the Union Navy during the Civil War, and had served

D eck loaded to the gunwales with cases and hams of liquor, *Arethusa* steams in the open sea at the beginning of one of it famous voyages. *Courtesy of the Mariners' Museum, Newport News, Virginia*

138

Moonshiners, rumrunners, and bootleggers—along with their opponents on the other side of the law—have been regularly glorified in books, articles, and films. The characters tending the stills appear as harmless, drunken yokels, or as savvy backwoodsmen. Rumrunners are charming buccaneers; bootleggers are peerless behind the wheel. Most of the revenuers are tenacious and clever; or, in the case of "Snuffy Smith" cartoons, a few are blundering flatlanders. Most members of the Coast Guard are dedicated and fearless. Prohibition agents are untouchable. These caricatures and prototypes swirl around in a nip-and-tuck, cat-and-mouse contest that (at least in the media) seems more sporting than serious.

In actuality, the game has rarely been a game at all; it has always been fraught with peril and tinged with disaster. Not all the crimes were victimless, and not all of the shots were fired in the air as harmless warnings. Honor among thieves was the exception rather than the rule. Bribery, corruption, a hamstrung legal system, lethal gunfire, car wrecks, murder, piracy, amateur and professional hijacking—these were just a few of the things that drained the glamour away, leaving a hard, nasty business behind.

Perhaps the tone for the Volstead era was set at 1:00 A.M. on January 17, 1920. A scant hour after the midnight deadline that ushered in Prohibition, six men wearing masks drove a truck into a freight yard on the south side of Chicago. Working with efficiency and purpose, they tied up a watchman and the yard master. They locked six other workers in a shed. Then they stole $100,000 worth of whiskey from two train cars. "Obviously some of Chicago's hoodlums viewed the onset of prohibition as a business opportunity," Thomas Coffey wrote. And good-old, brazen theft, which had been around for centuries before and would be around forever after, was part of the strategy.

It was, without question, a business opportunity: for people making booze (in crude stills or high-tech Canadian distil-

This small arsenal of rifles, pistols, and ammunition is arrayed in the cabin of a rumrunner seized by the Coast Guard cutter *Seneca* in 1924. There's a bottle of champagne in the drawer, along with boxes of Peters .30-.30-caliber smokeless and .45-caliber automatic ammo. *Library of Congress*

leries); for people hauling booze (in an A-to-Z cavalcade of anything that would roll on wheels or that would float on water); for people selling booze (by the shot, pint, quart, gallon, or barrel).

High Seas Hijacking

Liquor-law infractions weren't the only kinds of crimes that skyrocketed in frequency during Prohibition. Some crooks opted to bypass the "making" part and most of the "carrying" part; they jumped into the process late in the game, hijacking shipments afloat and ashore. Rumrunners had to keep an eye peeled and an ear out for the Coast Guard—the other eye and ear were devoted to pirates. Take the case of the *Yankton*, a luxurious 214-feet British-built vessel once known as the "Queen of Rum Row." It had served as a gunboat in the Spanish-American War and had sailed around the world with the Great White Fleet in 1908; despite these grand precedents, by 1923, authorities knew that it was engaged in running liquor between Nassau and the U.S. On one trip, the boat anchored east of Ambrose Channel Lightship. A group of customers arrived, bearing forged credentials that appeared to be from the bootlegging syndicate that had contracted for most of the *Yankton*'s cargo. The so-called customers had a phony cable ordering the ship to move up the coast to a position off Montauk Point, where it was met with phony contact boats, which lightened the *Yankton*'s load by 2,000 cases and even gave the skipper a phony receipt. The boat returned to Rum Row, where a different gang of hijackers (more violent and less clever) looted it of its remaining cargo. Running out of food and fuel, the crew began chopping up furniture, teak decks, and rosewood paneling, and limped into New York, where the captain turned it over to authorities, along with papers that proved valuable to Coast Guard intelligence. Shortly thereafter, the ship ran aground during a blizzard and was lost.

The saga of Rum Row is rife with similar tales of treachery. The *Mulhouse*, a rumrunner of French origin, had 35,000 cases in its holds when it was boarded off Ambrose Light by a con artist who fobbed himself off as a representative of the owners. Talking smoothly and convincingly, he reported that the Coast Guard blockade had become too strict, and that the newest instructions for the skipper were to head down the coast to a spot twenty miles east of Atlantic City. There, hijackers in contact boats stole the *Mulhouse*'s entire cargo in two days.

In Norfolk, the *Ledger-Dispatch* reported on June 4, 1923, about the mysterious case of the sloop *Glen Beulah*, which was rammed and sunk after 1,800 cases of illegal liquor apparently had been taken. The Coast Guard cutter *Yamacraw* had constantly circled the sloop, shining a spotlight on it at night. George Kelley, captain of the sloop, claimed it was a Coast Guard tug that rammed him. The cutter's skipper, however, said that he saw a ship fleeing the scene, and that it looked like a well-known local rum-running vessel, the *Istar*. Kelley claimed that he was on his way from Nassau, Bermuda, to St. Pierre, New Brunswick, and that his engine had broken down; officials said that the sloop, which drew just ten feet, was waiting to slip in to shore to unload the liquor. Kelley's credibility was extremely low,

however; for example, he said he had forgotten the name of the owner of the sunken sloop.

The newspaper offered three theories: first, the cargo was hijacked, then the ship was sunk to hide it; second, the cargo was delivered, but then the ship was sunk to avoid payment; third, the ship was sunk by rival rumrunners because it didn't belong to the syndicate that controlled that section of the coast.

Sometimes the hijackers used surprise and brute force; at other times, guile and subterfuge proved effective. The *Hankenson*, a 1,000-ton Canadian banker, was once boarded off Boston Light by three hijackers wearing uniforms of the U.S. Customs Service. The gang (which, according to some accounts, numbered as many as thirty peo-

ple) promptly shot the skipper and another sailor, and stole the cargo and the ship's safe (which contained $25,000 from earlier sales). One version of the *Hankenson* episode says that the gang spent three days clearing it out, and even had the gall to sell cut-rate liquor to customers during the hijacking.

Starting in April 1921, Norfolk readers were engrossed in the sensational trial of four men charged in the murder of a Japanese crew member, Hadie Sesaki, during a hijacking on the *Kaisho Maru* at Lambert's Point. The four men had been arrested in January; the murder had taken place on Christmas, 1920. A sample headline gives the flavor of the media coverage: "Letter from Woman to Graham Bombshell Hurled at Defense in Japanese Murder Trial." Ernest

Graham, one of the defendants, had denied knowing anything about the murder, but had left a letter in a toolbox in his car that showed him to be lying. Graham's three cronies—named Jones (a former Norfolk police officer, who did the shooting), Ennis, and Seymour—were members of what the newspaper referred to as "the notorious Colonial taxi-cab stand." The Japanese ship had had 300 cases of liquor aboard; the Norfolk men had arranged to buy forty-five cases for $3,000.

At one point Ennis denied knowing the meaning of the term "knocking off" and said they never used it. The prosecutor asked, "Don't you know that 'knocking off' ships has been a favorite pastime around this port for months?" Gradually, the defendants admitted to what the newspaper termed "pi-

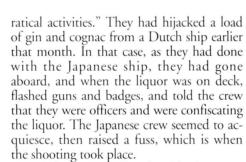

Tourists fool around on the battered remains of *Annie L. Spindler*. The craft was built in 1910 in Lunenburg, Nova Scotia, and was owned by Henry Amiro of Yarmouth. On December 1922, near Cape Cod, it foundered with a cargo of liquor, which was promptly plundered by the local populace. *Courtesy of the Mariners' Museum, Newport News, Virginia*

ratical activities." They had hijacked a load of gin and cognac from a Dutch ship earlier that month. In that case, as they had done with the Japanese ship, they had gone aboard, and when the liquor was on deck, flashed guns and badges, and told the crew that they were officers and were confiscating the liquor. The Japanese crew seemed to acquiesce, then raised a fuss, which is when the shooting took place.

"This system [of hijacking] has been employed on board foreign steamers by organized gangs of bootleggers in the Norfolk harbor on numerous occasions," the newspaper account said. "At one time during the late summer this traffic reached such proportions that it threatened to drive away commerce from this port."

The crew of a Coast Guard patrol boat once found the Canadian two-masted schooner *Levin* twenty miles east of Montauk Point Light, heading to shore. They carefully tracked it until the ship was definitely inside the twelve-mile limit, then fired the usual warning shots to make its skipper heave to. However, the ship kept coolly sailing straight in toward shore. Upping the

ante, the skipper of the Coast Guard cutter fired a couple of blanks from a one-pound gun across the schooner's bow, again to no avail. Pulling closer alongside, the Coast Guard crew swept their searchlights over the schooner; eerily, they found the ship's wheel lashed down and no living person in sight. The Coast Guard skipper swore an oath. "We've been trailing a ghost ship," he reportedly exclaimed. Going aboard to investigate, the Coast Guard found the usual signs of a violent hijacking: bullet holes in the masts, a safe that had been blasted open, and evidence of a wide-ranging struggle that demolished the ship's cabins, scattering furniture and papers everywhere.

On May 30, 1923, the Norfolk *Virginian-Pilot* ran a story entitled "Money Missing From Body," datelined New York a day earlier. It said, "Investigation into the mysterious sinking of the rum lugger *John Dwight* off Vineyard Haven, Mass., with a loss of nine lives early in April, has revealed that James A. Craven of Lyndhurst, N.J., one of the victims, had $100,000 in his possession when the ship sank, Federal authorities said tonight. The money was missing when Craven's mutilated body washed up on the beach." The ship's cargo had been Canadian ale; the boat was "reported to have capsized due to her heavy cargo." Although all hands were initially thought to be lost at sea, the captain was later reported to have been seen in Havana, Cuba. "Authorities expressed the belief that liquor pirates, knowing that Craven was carrying the large sum of money, attacked the vessel after she left Newport, killed several members of the crew and scuttled the ship," the article said. An added paragraph, entitled "Mystery Explained," pointed out that the Coast Guard crew at Cuttyhunk had seen a vessel flying distress signals on April 6 just as a heavy fog lifted, but it sank before Coast Guard could arrive. They found eight bodies "floating amid barrels of bottled ale."

Seagoing hijackers were known to come upon a rumrunner that was having engine or steering trouble and offer them a friendly tow. Then they would pull alongside the disabled vessel, swarm aboard with guns blazing, and loot the boat. Sometimes they would kill the crew and sink the boat, too. Hijackers played dozens of roles. They posed as fellow rumrunners in distress or in need of directions. As evidenced in the previous stories, they often pretended to be customers. Sometimes they even wore Coast Guard uniforms, using boats that looked like picket boats or cutters.

This isn't to say that the crews aboard the rumrunning mother ships were simply sitting ducks. "Rummy crews often fought back, and occasionally in these wild melees it was the pirates who were wiped out," Harold Waters wrote in *Smugglers of Spirits*. "Captured hijackers were shown no mercy by their captors. They were trussed up like chickens and unceremoniously 'dropped over the wall.'"

In the early days of Prohibition, seagoing hijackers were particularly active at the Rum Row off the coast of New York. They usually selected ships that were alone at sea as their victims, ideally ships with crews that were both drunk and unarmed. The rumrunners responded by allowing just one or two customers aboard at a time, and by upping the number and caliber of the weapons they had aboard. As big bootlegging syndicates and ruthless professional criminals gradually took control of Rum Row, their retribution for hijacking was increasingly merciless, so the problem diminished.

The safest approach was to convert the brown bottles to greenbacks as quickly as possible. Once a contact boat had brought the illicit cargo ashore, the problem was by no means solved. Assuming a Coast Guard cutter didn't nab the contact boat inbound, and assuming that a Coast Guard shore patrol didn't discover the unloading operation, the truckloads of liquor were hardly home free. With an armed guard riding shotgun, the heavily laden trucks would rumble up the lonely beach roads toward the highway. If the cargo had landed in Cape Cod, for example, it had, in author Scott Corbett's words, "its own special problems ahead of it. Between them and Boston lay infinitely various possibilities of double cross, trickery, and ambush."

Just as moonshine transporters and bootleggers developed ingenious ploys to deceive the authorities, so did hijackers to entrap their prey. One trick was to deliver an anonymous, bogus warning to a contact-boat operator known to have some booze aboard ("The cops are after you, better unload your liquor in a hurry"), then shadow him to see where he had it stashed. "What they hoped was that the rumrunner would dump his load someplace in shallow water to get it off his boat, someplace where they could then fish it out for themselves," Corbett wrote. Angling for burlap bags of liquor was a popular pastime during Prohibition in the shallow waters off American coasts.

Some enterprising hijackers wore caps that looked like those worn by customs officers; they stopped bootleggers at night, occasionally going so far as to fire warning shots in the air. With luck, the bootleggers wouldn't pause to argue; they would simply abandon their cars and head for the woods. A pair of high-class New England hijackers drove a Cadillac touring car from which they had removed the back seat; they specialized in surprising groups of men who were unloading contact boats on the beach. If the smugglers fled, the hijackers filled up the back of the Cadillac and took off.

Although ruthless professional hijackers were the major worry, amateur hijackers could also do some damage. At least the victims ashore didn't have to worry about becoming shark bait. Describing the inhabitants of Provincetown (on the tip of Cape Cod, Massachusetts) during the Prohibition era, Corbett points out there was no reason to expect them to be more or less moral than anyone else. Yet, he wrote, "Jungle law prevailed. It was the only kind of law that affected most persons' attitudes toward liquor. . . The possession of liquor was illegal to begin with, so how could it be wrong to swipe something that its owner had no business possessing in the first place?"

And swipe they did, the "they" being just about anyone who found out where someone else had cached some booze. As Manny Zora discovered early during his career as a rumrunner, "a man with liquor stashed ashore could never have an easy moment." He recalled a local character called "Papa" Perera, who dealt lavishly in bootleg liquor, but never kept it in his house. Rather, he always went outside and buried it somewhere among the yards and pastures on his farm. Perera's only problem was that he didn't have a very good memory, and would sometimes forget where he had cached a particular kind of liquor. Long after Prohibition was over, he was still rubbing his head and bemoaning his losses. Sometimes he would hit a bottle when planting a garden or field.

Three rumrunners went aground during a violent northeaster in December 1922, near Cape Cod. The Coast Guard rescued and captured the crews of two vessels. A large crowd, braving the wind and rain, gathered on the beach to watch one of the vessels, the *Annie L. Spindler*, break up in the surf (this incident is described more fully later in this chapter). They weren't merely curious or sympathetic; they were hoping to share in the informal salvage of the boat's bootleg cargo.

The saga of rumrunning is replete with similar instances. Often, as Coast Guard cutters bore down on a contact boat, the smugglers were forced to dump large loads of liquor in accessible spots, hoping to return and retrieve it later (assuming they managed to elude the authorities). The top speed of the pursuing Coast Guard vessel wasn't their only concern, however. If word reached the local citizens, it spread like smoke on a windy day.

Once, Manny Zora had to explain the fate of just such a load to a representative of the syndicate that owned the mother ship. "You see those little boats out there, too, look like ducks on the water, they so thick?" Zora asked the gangster as they peered out into the harbor. "Well, that's just about everything under sixteen feet that floats on these shores . . . out there is everything from old ladies in canoes to little kids in skiffs, all trying to hook a case or two for themself."

According to Corbett, "As usual with any piece of news involving booze, the word had traveled like wildfire; and everybody who could handle an oar or a paddle and could find something which could be bailed fast enough to keep afloat was out at the fabulous fishing hole dropping a line and trying to hook into burlap."

One time off Orient Point (a summer resort in Long Island), seaside tourists and beachcombers witnessed scores of people, many fully dressed, wading and diving in the water. Other people were out in skiffs, probing the bottom with oyster tongs; on the beach, men, women, and children carried sacks of salvaged liquor on their backs, up and over the sand dunes. The intoxicating treasure-trove was from the *Artemis*, which had jettisoned its load close to shore during a hot pursuit.

Land Hijacking

If liquor wasn't safe on the bottom of a bay, it obviously wasn't safe on dry land. Recounting an incident from Manny Zora's career, Corbett tells about the time that Zora paid an acquaintance five dollars per case to store 200 cases of liquor in his barn for a few days. The liquor belonged to a syndicate for which Zora ran a contact boat. Local freelance hijackers found out about the cache; fifty of them showed up one night, broke into the barn, and simply stole all of the booze. Zora shrugged his shoulders, briefly regretted the syndicate's bad luck, then grabbed a couple for himself. When he got back fifteen minutes later, only six cases remained on the dusty barn floor. "Manny contemplated the brilliant accomplishment with a sort of perverse pride," Corbett wrote. "He would put Provincetowners up against anybody. For men who made a mere avocation out of hijacking, they were great performers."

It wasn't that the salt air made people extraordinarily rapacious. Small-scale and large-scale hijacking was the order of the day throughout America. In 1924, on the so-called "Rum Trail" in northern New York state, three Prohibition agents captured a bootlegging caravan of four cars. Next, they saw a Cadillac approaching; the driver tried to turn around, but the agents stopped the car with a bullet in the gas tank. Finally, the agents halted and seized a truck that was also carrying liquor. Unfortunately, the agents didn't have time to congratulate themselves on their good fortune. An unruly crowd had gathered, and people started to snatch bottles from the seized cars. As the agents struggled to restore order and maintain control over their contraband, things went from bad to worse: a member of the crowd, clearly not content with a few measly bottles, jumped in the truck and roared off.

On April 1, 1924, a train hit what appeared to be a furniture van near the village of Eighty-Four, eight miles east of Washington, D.C. For some reason, bystanders and spectators suspected that the truck belonged to bootleggers. Their suspicions were confirmed when they bored a hole into the false bottom of the truck and found fifty 5-gallon containers of whiskey. "Soon large quantities of the contraband were siphoned into every kind of vessel," the *New York Times* reported the next day.

As rumors of rich strikes circulated during the gold rushes to the Black Hills, California, and Alaska, so did stories (on a smaller and more local level) circulate during Prohibition—except they concerned fifths, not nuggets. Bootleg liquor wasn't quite as valuable as gold or silver, of course, but it was readily negotiable, easy to barter or sell, and all in all a great thing to stumble on for free. As a result, "Rumor placed liquor caches everywhere, not only in the woods but far out among the dunes and even in the ponds," Scott Corbett wrote. "Before Prohibition the only visitor to the woods, the dunes, and the haunts of coot and tern had been the solitary bird watcher, the gentle nature lover, the artist, the photographer. Now these once lonely retreats began to crawl with human beings of all ages and both sexes, nosing around stealthily on a hundred-proof Easter egg hunt."

These "Easter egg hunts" were just one of the myriad hazards of the liquor trade (whether you were a bootlegger trying to sell it or an officer trying to confiscate it). Lucky locals finding a few bottles represented the amateur end of the hijacking spectrum, which spelled instant bankruptcy or death for victims of the more organized efforts. Other problems faced by enforcement agents included uncooperative citizens and courts, nonsensical laws, minuscule budgets, and ridiculously small numbers of personnel.

The case of the rumrunner *Annie L. Spindler* illustrates two of these problems. *Annie* was a rumrunner of British registry that ran aground in a winter storm in the early years of Prohibition, carrying a huge load of illegal liquor. "The news went through town like wildfire, and something like the race into Oklahoma took place as everything on wheels began rolling in the direction of Race Point," Corbett wrote. The captain of the rumrunner marched into the local Coast Guard headquarters and demanded protection for his cargo. He was, of course, equipped with papers showing that he was outward bound from a port where liquor was legal (Nova Scotia or Nassau, for example), and that he wasn't heading toward an American destination. "Although unencumbered by any naive illusion as to the nature of the affair, the station captain was forced to do his duty toward a foreign vessel in distress"—in other words, the Coast Guard had to duly protect the cargo of booze from the freelance hijackers who were gathering like vultures on the beach. Coast Guard personnel stored the booze in a warehouse and later had to transfer it to another British ship with phony papers.

Ham-Strung and Snake-Bit

Some of the obstacles faced by law-enforcement agents dated back decades before Volstead became a household word in the 1920s. In the insular centers of moonshining throughout the South, the aggressive lack of cooperation with the authorities mirrored what would take on national proportions during Prohibition. As early as 1888, in small towns in Murray County, Georgia, the folks who made and transported moonshine (called "blockaders" back then) had formed a secret organization called the "Distillers' Union." The booze-makers in Gilmer banded together in the Working Men's Friend and Protective Organization; in Pickens, they joined the Honest Man's Friend and Protector. Members of these secretive societies swore to provide alibis for each other, to find other members innocent when serving on juries, and to make informers move away or kill them.

No enforcement agency had enough people during the years when the Eighteenth Amendment was in force. There were dramatic shortfalls in numbers of personnel in the Coast Guard, the Customs Service, the Internal Revenue Service, and every other law enforcement agency. In 1927, Seymour Lowman, head of national Prohibition enforcement, said that "enforcement in New York alone would need 30,000 agents instead of the existing 300," as well as twenty new federal courts. Needless to say, neither more agents nor new courts were forthcoming in the waning years of enforced temperance.

Although the laws about liquor seemed clear-cut and all-encompassing, law-enforcement authorities often had their hands tied by the same sort of legal technicalities that allowed American citizens to own and operate rumrunning ships flying a foreign flag a mere three miles off the East Coast, selling liquor with impunity. Outside the three-mile (or, later, the twelve-mile) limit, the general interpretation of the law was that the Coast Guard could only seize ships or boats of American registry, and only then if they found liquor or other contraband on them. First, of course, when approaching a possible smuggler, they had to make sure it was a rumrunner, something that wasn't necessarily easy. Once a rumrunner was identified and arrested, they had to make the charges stick. The Coast Guard did experiment in court with various interpretations of "conspiracy to commit" and a few technicalities of their own, with limited success.

Ashore, local police chiefs had no authority to board vessels, even when the boats were tied up at a pier: they had to summon the Coast Guard, a time-consuming process that usually allowed the smugglers to unload and vanish.

Although Coast Guard crews were well armed, they were also issued ample supplies of blanks, which they often fired as their opening gambit in trying to make a contact boat heave to. Sometimes, thanks to savvy navigating by the contact-boat skipper, they had to use blanks in order to avoid hitting innocent vessels. In January 1930, as the Coast Guard chased a speedboat, the crew found that they could only fire blanks because the contact boat ran behind a pair of handy shields: first, a tug that was towing a barge, and next, the Cuttyhunk Lighthouse.

In Pippa Passes, Kentucky, a group of moonshiners display their tools of the trade: Clalse Short, Randolph (R. B.) Reynolds, Curt Short, Has Short, Fletcher Slone, and Hiram Short. The original caption said, in part, "They look plum proud of themselves." *Photographic Archives, Alice Lloyd College*

Often, the hazards faced by the authorities weren't a factor of technology, technique, or technicality; they were more personal. Former ATF agent Bill Tetterton of Norfolk, Virginia, always enjoyed tracking down stills and moonshiners in the woods during his extensive career in Virginia. He was never afraid of the humans; what preyed on his mind during his early years was

snakes. "I used to be terrified of them," he recalled. "I'd spend more time watching my feet than looking where I was going." At night, watching a still site in the woods, "It was incredible the amount of sounds you'd hear," he said. If he heard a large insect rustling through the leaves, for example, he couldn't help but suspect it was a serpent. Tetterton's fears weren't groundless, either—

in a single day, revenuer "Big Six" Henderson and four other agents killed fifty-two copperheads and four rattlesnakes while searching for stills in Kentucky.

Revenue agents all say that they enjoyed the job of tracking down stills, although it was difficult and at least slightly dangerous. They were tough outdoorsmen, and savored the challenge of matching wits with wily violators. Nevertheless, there were many aspects of the job that were far from glamorous or exciting. Describing Henderson chopping up a still, Esther Kellner wrote that it "was filthy work, and by the time it was done Henderson's raiding clothes were covered with dirt, ashes, mud, spray from the mash, and soot from the cooker . . . During one raid he was photographed in this grimy and disheveled getup standing next to the moonshiner" who was neatly dressed. The news editor who received the photo thought that Henderson was the one who had been arrested.

In the late nineteenth century in the South, military units sometimes took part in moonshine raids over large areas, sometimes covering several hundred miles during extended sweeps. Their accounts detail traveling on horseback at night in cold and rainy weather, riding through dense underbrush over steep, rugged trails. Such duty hardly qualified as adventure.

Gunplay

Discomfort wasn't the only hazard; although most moonshiners put their hands in the air and surrendered peacefully once they were caught in action, some fought back with fists and guns. While doing research in state archives about prohibition during the late nineteenth century, in North Carolina Wilbur Miller found that "most of the correspondence of several southern federal district attorneys was concerned with the difficulties in collecting the whiskey tax and dealing with violent resistance." In 1877, in the course of seizing 596 illicit stills in North Carolina and arresting 1,174 people, twelve officers were killed or wounded.

The 1878 annual report from the Internal Revenue Service said, "So formidable has been resistance to the enforcement of laws that [in various districts of Virginia, North and South Carolina, Tennessee, West Virginia, Arkansas, and Kentucky] I have found it necessary to supply the collectors with breech-loading carbines . . . the officers of the United States have often been treated very much as though they were emissaries

from some foreign country quartered upon the people for the collection of tribute."

Writing in *Revenuers & Moonshiners*, Miller described the situation as "perpetual guerrilla warfare" in some regions between revenuers and moonshiners. On behalf of the gun-toting, itchy-trigger-fingered moonshiners, an anonymous mountain man is on record as threatening, "Come out and tell me who ye be, fer if ye be one of them damned revenuers, I'll mince yer shivering slats with the contents of my barker."

Several full-scale, long-term shoot-outs appear in the documented history of illicit liquor, in such books as George Atkinson's *After the Moonshiners: By One of the Raiders,* published in 1881. In the late 1800s, revenue agents in a southern state once ran into some moonshiners who had an old Civil War cannon loaded with metal and nails, but they fired too high.

From July 1876 through July 1905, fifty-four "revenue raiders" were killed, thirty-five in the six years from 1876 to 1882. In the early 1900s, another historian wrote, "shoot-outs between moonshiners and investigators reached such violent proportions that the words 'raid' and 'killing' became synonymous." The statistics of fatalities and seizures, however, show that this statement is exaggerated.

The use of handguns—at least as props, but often as weapons—skyrocketed during Prohibition. Bootleggers packed guns to defend themselves against hijackers and occasionally to trade shots with law-enforcement agents. Police were already armed, and thieves had to ante up with weapons of their own if they wanted to bluff or scare bootleggers into surrendering their contraband cargoes. Some accounts of the period make it sound like the shoot-'em-up television version of the old Wild West.

According to the New Bedford police chief, during the years before Prohibition, his department issued about 100 permits for handguns annually. However, between December 1920 and January 1921, he received 1,800 applications. Clearly, an arms race of major proportion was under way.

Bernard Weisburger quoted a Presbyterian minister who said that the Volstead Act should be enforced "if every street in America has to run with blood." Few criminals or cops took liquor-law enforcement quite that seriously. Shooting at night, from the deck of a speedboat bouncing through the waves, or from the window of a car careening down a crude highway, wasn't exactly a marksman's dream. Nevertheless, people on both sides of the law (and in the middle,

if that is the location of innocent bystanders) were killed by gunfire.

Describing the action along the boundary with Canada in *Rum Across the Border,* Allan Everest wrote, "The wilder and more desperate of the smugglers did not hesitate to shoot to maim or kill their pursuers, and shooting frays became commonplace along the border."

Other accounts depict a much less bloodthirsty scene. Describing the action around Provincetown, one former rumrunner pointed out that, since the smugglers and the Coast Guard personnel were all natives—sometimes even related—casualties were held to a minimum. "They don't believe in killing each other over any such foolishness as the Eighteenth Amendment," he said.

Jumping ahead several decades, this attitude persisted in other parts of the country. Speaking of the local moonshiners, a local sheriff told Kellner, "These fellers are my neighbors, and some are my kin. Sure, I hunt down the stills, but I shoot over the shiners' heads and give 'em plenty of time to get away. I ain't aiming to hit none of 'em or take 'em to the jail-house, either. As long as they live decent, they don't bother me none. Anyway, some couldn't keep cornbread on the table without making moon." Tim Flock recalled, "I never did know of any killins . . . The sheriffs was proud of us, really."

During his long career as an ABC agent in North Carolina, Jim Ward never fired his weapon at anyone. He was shot at a few times, he said, "but I think they were trying to scare us off." Once a spent bullet bounced off his leather jacket because he was too far away from the gunman. Sometimes, he explained, gunshots were signals, not offensive fire; "they knew the law was in the woods," he said, and were spreading the word.

Although hardly commonplace, shootings were recorded at sea, too. In many accounts, gunfire is listed as a serious occupational hazard for Coast Guard personnel, along with the usual storms, shipwrecks, and collisions. In April 1925, a chief boatswain's mate, who was at the wheel of a Coast Guard patrol vessel near Race Rock Lighthouse in Long Island Sound, was killed by machine-gun fire from a contact boat that escaped. Two Coast Guard men (one source said that one man was a "secret service agent") were killed while trying to seize a motorboat in August 1927. They had boarded it to find 160 cases of liquor, and were shot while trying to subdue the crew of the contact boat. The captain of the speed-boat, a rumrunner from Lee County named Alderman, who had shot the Coast Guard men, was overpowered, arrested, tried, and finally hung in a hangar at Fort Lauderdale's Coast Guard Base Ten in August 1929.

The Coast Guard was well armed, of course, as were the rumrunners, as evidenced by an article published at the end of May 1923, in a Norfolk newspaper: "Guns on Board Rum Ships May Affect Status; International Complications in Liquor Traffic Loom As Rifle, Mounted on *Istar*'s Aft Deck, Is Sighted from [the Coast Guard vessel] *Mascoutin*." The gun was either a six-pounder or a three-inch rifle; seagoing yachts were permitted to carry smaller guns, mounted forward, for purposes of saluting, but the rumrunners' ordnance was clearly not meant to render honors.

The hazardous fire wasn't always hostile, in the heat of hectic pursuits on pitch-black nights. "More than once we came very close to firing into one of our own ships," Harold Waters recalled. Most contact-boat skippers preferred trying to outrun the usually underpowered Coast Guard boats, or jettison the cargo before heaving to. Moonshiners in the South were generally peaceable, as well. Although one historian describes gunfights and casualties as "common" as liquor-law enforcement increased, most moonshiners preferred to use their wits to avoid arrest.

Many people who lived through Prohibition remember witnessing high-speed automobiles chases, or at least heard tales about them. But being a spectator was more than simply exciting—it was downright dangerous. "Being a passer-by was a particularly hazardous condition in those days of deplorable marksmanship when the Prohibition men so often aimed at tires and hit people," Henry Lee wrote in *How Dry We Were*.

Another rare but costly mistake involved cases of mistaken identity, as amateur or poorly trained law-enforcement agents failed to make sure of their targets, or began firing out of fear or frustration. A well-known case occurred in May 1928, at Niagara Falls, New York. The secretary of a local Elks Lodge refused to stop for two out-of-uniform Coast Guard personnel. They opened fire and hit him in the head, inflicting serious wounds. He later said that he had mistaken them for "highwaymen." He died four months later. No liquor was found in his car. Military personnel and police alike were vilified in the press when they killed bona fide bootleggers; the outcry

A Coast Guard picket boat pursues and fires on a rumrunner in the North Atlantic, March 1927. *National Archives*

when an innocent citizen was killed must have been shrill, indeed.

The actual body count during Prohibition is hard to gauge, depending as it does on the sympathies of the historian or reporter. According to one source, whose sympathies are clear from the phrase "trigger-happy Prohibition agents and associated enforcers," between 2,000 and 3,000 officials, suspects, and bystanders were killed "during raids or wild auto chases."

One historical account pointed out, "in some mountain counties of Kentucky or

Tennessee, four or five moonshine-related homicides per month were reported during the Prohibition years." Another estimate appeared in a pamphlet distributed by the Association Against the Prohibition Amendment, which claimed that enforcers of the prohibition law had killed more than 1,000 people in ten years. According to one historian's assessment of the official records, however, a combined total of 286 federal officers and private citizens were killed, at roughly a 1:3 ratio. This total is close to that of another writer, who cited Justice Department totals at the end of the Prohibition era, reporting that ninety-two federal agents and 178 civilians had been killed. The same source stated that $129 million had been spent trying to enforce the unpopular law, and that

more than 500,000 people had been tried in court for offenses.

The end of Prohibition didn't mean the end of gun battles, unfortunately. Between the time that the Eighteenth Amendment was repealed, and 1948, twenty-six agents of the Bureau of Alcohol, Tobacco & Firearms were killed in the line of duty. According to another source, between 1934 and 1966, thirteen agents were shot to death. Another 506 were injured in car accidents ("some deliberately," the source said). ATF had added some new and dangerous responsibilities by then, of course, so moonshiners weren't to blame for all of the mayhem.

A particularly memorable account of death in the line of duty appeared in the Norfolk *Virginian-Pilot* on March 10, 1938.

The story involved a Norfolk police officer named John F. Estes, a federal Alcohol Tax Unit agent named J. W. Jackson, and a pair of bootleggers, including a trigger-happy, six-foot, five-inch man named Bernard Royals. The article said it was "perhaps the most lurid tale in the annals of the Alcohol Tax Unit here, the story of a running gun battle, fought by Officer John F. Estes with the killers of Jackson, in which Officer Estes, driving at full speed in pursuit of the killers' car, emptied his own revolver at the fleeing machine and then continued the fight with a revolver he took from the holster of his dead companion." He was "miraculously untouched by the buckshot charges which tore away the right half of the windshield" of his car. Estes, the article continued, was

"known as one of the most fearless drivers and efficient officers cooperating with the Tax Unit, has figured in many thrilling pursuits and captures."

The bloody affair unfolded when Estes and Jackson received information from a "stool pigeon," whom they met in a nearby city and who rode down to North Carolina with the two officers. Estes said he knew both of the bootleggers, and recognized them as they watched them load up the liquor from a quarter mile away. Driving a 1937 Ford V-8 coupe, the two agents trailed the moonshine transporters (who were in a 1931 Buick sedan) from North Carolina, intending to let them cross the Virginia line. The bootleggers stopped short. As Jackson opened his door to get out, he was immediately hit by five pistol shots. Estes pulled Jackson's body back in and took off in pursuit of the fleeing vehicle, steering with his right hand and shooting out of the window with his left. When he had emptied his revolver, he reached over and took Jackson's, shooting that one too. After Jackson was shot, Estes said, "I had to go after them. I shot at them all the way from North Carolina into Virginia," firing a .44 caliber pistol.

As Estes told reporters, "I emptied my gun, and the bullets tore out most of their back window. Once their car started to zigzag and I thought, 'I've got 'em,' but they straightened out and went on . . . I fired three shots from his [Jackson's] gun. I knew there were three more in it. I saved these. I was hoping to get alongside the whisky car and finish the case with the bullets."

Shotgun blasts from the fleeing car riddled Jackson's dead body during the chase, which lasted for seven or eight miles, and finally punctured Estes' radiator, forcing him to stop. "Not only was the windshield riddled on Jackson's side, but there were bullet or slug marks inside the car, inches from where Estes' head was at the time of the shooting," the article continued. Agents later found 100 gallons of moonshine in the abandoned "rum car." After Estes' car was knocked out, the killers went home. Estes knew where they lived. "The other officers took my gun before we went over there, because I was going to kill one of them," he recalled. Royals and his partner were arrested, tried, and convicted. Royals "broke down and cried when he met his mother" in court, the article pointed out. Both of them got life terms in prison. Estes says, remarkably, that one of the two men is still alive, is out of jail, and is living in Portsmouth, Virginia.

Estes, who was ninety-four years old when I interviewed him in 1994, served with the Norfolk police department from 1926 to 1960, first as a motorcycle cop ("They used to call me Tom Mix—I'd jump from my motorcycle onto a car's running board," he said), later as a patrol officer and sergeant. The fatal chase occurred when he was detailed with the federal officers for two years. "I drove the road car, the one that chased speeders," he recalled about one of his police duties. "I wrecked two or three of them—run them in the ditch." Recalling the Jackson killing, Estes said, "That was the worst one," although, in the course of his long career, he said "I've been shot at and everything else."

The gunfire wasn't always one way. "I shot a man down at a still. I told him to put his hands up, and he reached back for a flashlight. I thought it was a gun and shot him in the chest." The bullet didn't kill him. "I caught the same guy a year later. He threw his hands right up. He said, 'I'm not going to give you a reason to shoot me again.'"

The headlines in Estes' scrapbook depict a colorful and controversial career: "Driver Is Pinned in Wreck of Auto By Jug of Liquor"; "Millan and Estes Are Injured In 5-Car Liquor Chase Smash" (John Millan was the head of the Norfolk branch of the federal Alcohol Tax Unit); "Furious Chase Through City"; and "Estes Rides Again." Numerous editorials praised Estes' bravery and dedication, but implored the police department to put a leash on him, alleging that his exploits (such as that described in an article entitled "80-Mile-an-Hour Chase With Blazing Gun Through City Streets") amounted to reckless endangerment of innocent bystanders. "Whiskey Agents Face Charges; Accused of Reckless Driving," said another headline.

Most of these newspaper clippings appear in Estes' own scrapbooks, carefully compiled and well worn with decades of thumbing. Some of the clippings appear in the material donated to ATF archives by Millan. Millan's career was twice touched by shooting deaths. While stationed in Fairfax, Virginia, he shot and killed a moonshiner in Loudoun County near Stirling, Virginia, in July 1935. An article in the *Washington Herald* on August 1 reported, "The score between raiders and Loudoun County moonshiners stood even today following a raid yesterday afternoon on a still in a wild and desolate section of the county." A Loudoun County grand jury "refused to indict" Mil-

lan in the case, ruling that it was self-defense. His testimony explained the events that led up to the shooting.

Using information about a still (which, ironically, would turn out to be a small, 5-gallon device), Millan and a fellow agent followed a path toward the suspected site, coming across a car that had its upholstery removed, cracked corn and rye spilled on the floor, and no license plates. They followed the path toward a stream called Broad Run; fifteen yards from the still, one man (later identified as twenty-three-year-old Delmas Duncan) looked up, turned, and started to run. He leaped into the creek, with Millan five or six steps behind. "When he was about half way up this bank his foot slipped and he threw out his left hand to catch himself and as he was getting to his feet again he half turned around with his right side towards me," Millan wrote in his statement. "He was still partly off balance and as he pointed his arm towards me I could see that he had a gun in his hand. I jumped sideways towards a tree that leaned over the creek and as I jumped I heard the gun snap but it did not go off."

Duncan turned and started to run again. Millan pulled his pistol and cocked it, ordering the fleeing moonshiner to stop. Duncan turned his gun toward the agent again, and Millan fired. Duncan yelled, stood up, and dived into some brush, which turned out to be the bank of another creek. Millan went back to get his partner; they returned to find Duncan face down in a small creek.

Accounts of flying bullets, are invariably balanced by credible testimonials that depict an opposite view. "I made hundreds of arrests, but I never had to shoot anybody," Weems said. "Oh, I might have to tackle them and struggle with them a little, maybe. But most of the violators knew they'd get in a lot more trouble if they shot at you or hurt you. Of course there were a few that were just plain mean."

Sometimes the hazards faced by revenuers were less direct than a bullet, but potentially just as fatal. One undercover agent, trying to buy $400 worth of moonshine, was robbed southwest of Chattanooga, tied up, and left in the boondocks. "Liquor law violators were not all innocent, good-natured victims of poverty, trying to feed their children," Weems wrote. An ATF area supervisor named Doug Denney was killed when he crashed headlong into a car that had been racing in the opposite direction. The fatal accident occurred in Dawson

County, Georgia, which, as Weems observed in his book, *A Breed Apart,* was "noted for its liquor car drivers and strangely they were looked upon as local heroes." The wreck occurred on Highway 53, two miles east of Dawsonville, a stretch of road with lots of curves and small hills, and more than two miles of "no passing" zones. Denney's car was hit head-on by a Chevrolet going 75mph. The driver of the Chevy was seriously injured and later died; his passenger was also killed. This driver had, starting at age seventeen, compiled a ludicrously bad driving record: he'd been involved in a slew of accidents, had earned four speeding tickets, had had his license suspended twice, had been arrested for drunk driving and driving without a license—hardly the credentials of a hero.

In the 1950s and 1960s, gunfire was rare during still seizures. ATF agent Bill Tetterton said he hardly ever had to draw his weapon during his thirty-year career. He recalled that once someone fired into the trees over his head from a house. He also had a moonshiner come at him with an ax on the path to a still in Southampton County, Virginia, near the North Carolina border. The moonshiner was drunk; Tetterton drew his pistol, which calmed the moonshiner down considerably. Physical confrontations were more common. "Once in a while you'd have to fight one, wrestle with him," Tetterton said.

For the record, between 1954 and 1964, twelve ATF agents were killed. Two agents, Joe Cooper and Ralph Holt, were killed in Alabama in 1964 by a liquor shothouse operator. "Almost every agent who worked in the Southeast was injured, either by direct confrontation with liquor law violators or in their pursuit," Weems wrote.

Going to Court

Let's assume that the guns weren't drawn, that the moonshiners or bootleggers didn't escape by sprinting through the trees, and that they ended up safely behind bars to await justice. Having successfully navigated all of the preceding hazards, the authorities still had to make the charges stick. That wasn't as easy as it might sound. Before and during Prohibition, most courts were notoriously lenient with liquor-law offenders, if not downright hostile to law-enforcement agents. Local judges and juries tended to be much more sympathetic to local offenders than out-of-town revenuers or prohibition agents, who were sometimes accused of being corrupt or getting carried away.

Revenuers in the Old South seem to have had the hardest time of it. In several states in the late 1870s, prosecuting attorneys sometimes arrested revenuers for trespassing (as the revenuers prowled around private property sniffing for the telltale scent of mash), for carrying concealed weapons, even for murder (if a typically wild shot managed to find a mark). Between 1876 and 1879, 165 revenuers were prosecuted in various state courts for these offenses. Georgia tallied the highest number, forty-eight cases. And even if the revenuers weren't found guilty, the trials destroyed morale and incentive.

This reverse-justice phenomenon cropped up during Prohibition as well. For example, a trooper named Samuel Dickson was charged with first-degree murder in Plattsburgh, New York, for killing an alleged bootlegger, Otto "Big Swede" Eske. The case was remanded to federal court, where the charges were dropped.

Trials for moonshiners in the South, on the other hand, tended to be a slap on the wrist. Writing about trials in Georgia in 1891, Wilbur Miller found that moonshiners sometimes got a minimum penalty of a month in Atlanta's Fulton County jail. They might have been fined $100, but they could get out of paying it by swearing a "pauper's oath." (During Prohibition, captured bootleggers could sign "the poor man's oath" as an alternative to fines, serving a sentence of thirty days in jail instead.) Moonshiners could also reduce the length of their sentences for good behavior. The Fulton County jailer, Miller wrote, "seems to have been generous in his definition of good conduct. He recommended William Bowen of Rabun County for the reduction, adding to the printed phrase that he had 'uniformly conducted himself with propriety except that he once tried to escape.'" Perhaps multiple escape attempts were required to exasperate the jail wardens.

Thirty-day sentences were hardly severe, but some lenient jailers made them even less rigorous. At the Hall County jail in Gainesville, in northern Georgia, a judge

Mug shot of a killer: six-foot, five-inch Bernard "Big Boy" Royals, twenty years old, described in local newspaper accounts as a "giant Norfolk County youth." *John Millan photo file, ATF Reference Library*

discovered that prisoners were routinely turned loose to lounge around town, drinking at local saloons or visiting their homes. Bill McCoy, the "founder" of Rum Row, ran into a similarly comfy deal during his prison term in 1923, but it backfired. When the Coast Guard turned its attention from the rumrunners in the north Atlantic and deployed units to Florida, they encountered what service historians reported as corrupt officials and bribed district attorneys. As a result, seemingly clear-cut cases of Volstead infractions were repeatedly thrown out of court, and the rumrunners were back in business in a matter of days.

In the early years of Prohibition, even when the Coast Guard seized a contact boat and was upheld in court, a legal loophole allowed the boat's owners to simply buy the boat back at auction for a very low price

and, like the Florida smugglers already mentioned, be right back in business. The steamer *Underwriter* was seized four times in one year, three times by the same Coast Guard vessel, but each time it was auctioned off and quickly went back to running liquor.

In a July entry in his journal, rumrunner Alastair Moray noted that the penalty for "whisky running" was confiscation of the boat and cargo, and a $100 fine. "The boat is generally put up for auction the next day, and the owner generally gets it back for a song, as no one bids against him," Moray wrote.

Powerful syndicates and corruption were other hindrances. "Even when a rumrunner was foolish enough to be overtaken with liquor still on board, the courts were incredibly lax about handing out punishment," Scott Corbett wrote. An engineer on a rumrunner told the story of a smuggler who was caught, was out of jail at 11:00 A.M. the next day on a year's probation, was caught *again* the next night, and was promptly let out again (with—you guessed it—another year's probation).

Like southern revenuers, Coast Guard personnel received volleys of public criticism

R-DISP[...]

22 PAGES

[...]N—JUNE 4, 1923

um Pirates Sink Ship
After Seizing Cargo

Captain and Crew of Lost Rum Runner

COAST GU[...]
FLEET SAI[...]
TO BEGI[...]
OFFENSIVE

Will Keep Watch
Every Ship On
Rum Row

[...]els Will Be
The Blockade

[...]5—(A. P.)—Twen-
[...] the United States
[...] out of Clifton
[...]ase, this morn-
[...]ow to open an
[...]eek sweep
[...] Atlantic

[...]cut-
[...]Red-
[...]ere

RAM SLOOP
AFTER 1800
CASES ARE
TAKEN OFF,
IS BELIEF

Federal Agents Work On
Theory That Sinking Was
Conspiracy

Rescued Captain And The
Crew Questioned By Agents

More Coast Guard Cutters
Sent To Search For Ship
In Collision

M FLEET READY
OR FRESH DRIVE
AGAINST PATROL

[...] Runners Are Plan-
[...]o Land Heavy Car-
[...]Through Delaware
[...]waters, According to
[...] Reports

[...]Y SURROUNDS
[...]OCATION OF ISTAR

[...] of Outlaw Fleet,
[...]ed and Scarred by
[...] Usage and With
[...]s Depleted of Fuel,
[...]ears From Coast

of rum-running British sloop Glen Beulah [...]
[...]riday night and his crew of eight being [...]
[...]federal building for questioning by Prohibition [...]
[...]m prohibition charge against them as their [...]
[...]e limit when sunk [...]
[...]n on the left wearing a white jersey.

Photo by Ledger Dispatch Staff Photographer

Alleged Slayers of Federal Agent

IS ACCUSED
OF RUNNING
LIQUOR
BLOCKADE

Engineer Of S[...]

TWO[...]
DE[...]

[...]pers
[...]office
[...]

The OOD, his temper at the boiling point, contradicted Waters and insisted on touring the ship to show that Waters was exaggerating. They started at the forward living quarters, located directly under the wardroom. The officer was shocked, but Waters merely shrugged: full-scale parties were under way in all three crowded compartments, tables littered with bottles of Scotch, bourbon, rye, rum, cognac, brandy, and champagne. Lacking ice to properly chill this latter delicacy, the Coast Guard crew had tied lines around the bottles and lowered them over the side into the harbor slush:

The intoxicated crew members, brimming with good cheer, invited the officer and chief to join the fun. This scene, Waters wrote, "was only the beginning of the most unforgettable night in my entire Coast Guard career." Crew members from scores of Coast Guard ships had joined in the well-lubricated fiasco, and soon, Waters estimated, at least 1,200 men were involved. By midnight the situation was plainly out of control. The snowy pier was like a carnival, as drunken men carrying hams of booze stumbled and guffawed along the piers. Snowball fights and bonfires broke out. The chain of men who were supposed to be unloading the rumrunner had dissolved, and nearly all of the liquor was going straight to the Coast Guard fleet. Patients from a nearby Coast Guard hospital came out to join the revel, adding crutches to one large bonfire.

Waters' officer ordered him to collect all of the drunks from the Tucker. It was not possible—they had vanished, passed out, or disguised themselves in the snow. At about 3:00 A.M., order was finally restored. Officers who had been at home or on liberty had been recalled and had set up watch on the gangways of the Coast Guard ships. Drunken crew members were frisked; if they were carrying any booze, they were charged with "Smuggling intoxicating liquor aboard a vessel of the Coast Guard"; they lost three months'

pay and were reduced to the next lower rating. Waters estimated that 150 men were caught.

For months after the affair, bottles of booze turned up in obscure nooks and crannies aboard Tucker, in lockers, storerooms, and tanks. Drunken crew members, seeking to protect their embarrassment of riches, had hidden their loot and couldn't remember where after they sobered up. "It was like finding treasure trove," Waters concluded.

Is Waters' account accurate? Good stories have a way of becoming better, with retelling, and sea stories are no exception. Newspapers in New London did carry stories on a "Sunday afternoon in early January of 1930" about the event. On January 3, 1930, the Washington Herald reported on the Coast Guard inquiry to the affair, which produced court-martial proceedings against six men for having participated in "a drunken orgy on confiscated liquor." The article also pointed out that New London had been "peculiarly flooded" with the predominant type of liquor that had been aboard Flor del Mar, Golden Wedding rye whiskey, ever since the vessel was seized.

Acrimonious debate about the affair reached the halls of Congress, as Prohibitionists lambasted the Coast Guard for a criminal lack of supervision. A defender of the accused men, Rep. Carroll L. Beedy of Maine, replied that "these men, gobs, as we call them, ordinary seamen, yet red-blooded American boys, stood in the water for hours on that cold December night unloading this liquor. In the explosions which had occurred on board the ship, some of the boxes had been broken open and some of the gobs, to relieve themselves from the cold and suffering, opened the bottle and drank something out of it." An observer at this point noted, "The speaker here was interrupted by a gale of laughter, which swept the floor and galleries."

got a year out of it. And a finer feller than Lonny never wore hair.'" Sometimes, informers had to weigh short-term gains against long-term losses.

Other Hazards

Smuggling liquor was far from an innocuous pastime, although popular accounts persisted in making it sound like a mere lark, a spot of adventure. Things could get serious in a heartbeat. Five contact boats were lost in storms at a single location over the course of two years. A tug being used as a "puller" got overloaded, listed badly, and capsized off the Atlantic Highlands in New Jersey. A few foolhardy rumrunners dabbled in gunrunning into Cuba for revolutionary foes of the dictator; the Coast Guard found them dead in their craft, with their hands tied behind their backs, their throats cut, and their boat adrift.

For the operators of mother ships, mutinies were an unusual but still very real hazard. The British ship Tyneside, which had started its rumrunning cruise with 75,000 cases of Scotch, found business to be slow, and began running out of provisions. Once the crew had to start subsisting on "salt horse" (beef and pork stored in casks of brine), and "dog biscuits" (ship's biscuits), morale went south in a hurry. With only about half of the cargo sold, the crew mutinied, forcing the frantic skipper to ask Coast Guard for help. Because the Tyneside was not of American registry, however, the Coast Guard could intervene only in the event of a riot.

The skipper of a three-masted Icelandic schooner had an even more unusual tale of woe to tell the Coast Guard. He asked permission to come aboard a Coast Guard vessel, where he told the sad tale of how he and his crew had invested their life savings in 15,000 cases of Scotch. They were fishermen, not financiers, but had successfully sold the liquor on Rum Row for $400 a case, an astonishingly high price if their account was true—alas, their customer paid in crisp, convincing confederate money.

By the middle 1920s on Rum Row, the twin plagues of pirates and payoffs got worse and worse. Bill McCoy, who had a year's worth of smooth sailing thanks to disorganized law enforcement and a lack of competition, noted that pirates had started to become an increasing hazard even before his retirement from rumrunning. He added machine guns, repeating rifles, sawed-off shotguns, and Colt .45 pistols to his equipment list for his later voyages.

Once ashore, a rumrunner's problems weren't over. Other bizarre hazards arose, in addition to hijackers. In one case, rumrunners stored so much liquor in a beach-front cottage that the floor broke, sending 1,100 cases crashing, tinkling, and leaking into the dusty cellar.

For bootleggers making the 350-mile trip from Canada to New York City, high-speed encounters with customs agents and sheriffs were only an occasional threat. Monotony was the more common problem; more than one bootlegger, having navigated the patrol cars and customs stations, fell asleep and wrecked his car.

A grim undercurrent always eddied through the world of illicit liquor. Sometimes the excitement turned to fear. Sometimes the games of cat-and-mouse or hare-and-hound, played out in a gentlemanly fashion by careful cops and persistent booze smugglers, turned serious, and there would be one less mouse or hare in the ranks of the smugglers. Kellner told an apt tale: "In 1965, in the small Indiana town where I live, a man told me that he had been offered $500 per run to transport moonshine from eastern Kentucky to Cincinnati," she wrote. He had to furnish his own gun, which was no problem, and the travel didn't bother him. But he wondered, 'Why had the previous transporter quit such an easy and lucrative job?' 'Oh, he didn't quit,' was the answer. 'He was found in the Ohio River, floating on his face.'" Kellner's informant opted for a more mundane career.

The passage of years has a way of editing memory, dispensing with the negative aspects, leaving a version of action and event that is more entertaining, more fun. But many rumrunners and bootleggers recall the hazards clearly and without much relish. A former rumrunner named Gaston Monette told author Allen Everest that the dangers he experienced were "so close they are still almost scratching my back."

Chapter 11

Moonshiners in the Media

Moonshiners were a predictable, peripheral, and amusing addition to the "Andy Griffith Show." In this publicity photo from an episode called "The Haunted House," moonshiner "Big Jack" Anderson (Nestor Paiva, at right) and regular cast member Otis Campbell (Hal Smith) find that Sheriff Andy has turned the tables on them. "Big Jack" had hidden his still in the cellar of the haunted house; Andy has just scared them by making an ax appear to float in the air. Shortly after, he carried the ax down to the cellar, telling Deputy Barney, "We've got a still to chop up." Otis is holding a corked bottle of the moonshiner's product. *The Andy Griffith Show Rerun Watchers Club Collection*

For a variety of reasons, much of the mythology of American moonshining has found an enduring focus in the film *Thunder Road*. It has a great title and a theme song that proved to be a minor hit when it was released in a later, gutsier version, yet the films almost bizarre production qualities make it an unlikely choice to have become one of Robert Mitchum's more memorable films.

It was Mitchum's sixty-first film, released in 1958, and coproduced by Mitchum's film production company, DRM (for "Dorothy and Robert Mitchum") and United Artists. Mitchum had an unusually deep involvement in the film, having written the story on which it was based (the screenplay was by James Atlee Phillips and Walter Wise), and cowritten the song with Don Raye. He discussed the project in a short magazine article published in November 1957, revealing that he considered naming the film *The Whippoorwill*, which is the nickname of the film's hero (another alternative title was *Jack O'Diamonds*). His sixteen-year-old son Jim played his younger brother, Robin.

Although Mitchum seems ideal as the film's hero, Lucas Doolin, the film was originally intended for Elvis Presley. Elvis, however, was getting $150,000 per picture by that stage in his career, and the budget for *Thunder Road* was only about $300,000. Furthermore, according to Jerry Roberts, author of *Robert Mitchum, a Bio-Bibliography*, Elvis' advisers felt he should continue to exploit his success in musicals. The film's final cost was between $350,000 and $750,000. To some extent, playing the antihero character of *The Whippoorwill* seems appropriate to Mitch-um's colorful personal history: hopping freight trains, serving three terms in jail (the first for vagrancy when he was a teenager, the last on drug charges that were later rescinded after his sixty-day sentence), and doing a short stint as an itinerant boxer. As an actor, he once recalled, his first break was "working for Hopalong Cassidy, falling off horses." The year before *Thunder Road* he had made *Fire Down Below*, in which he played a smalltime smuggler in the West Indies. *Thunder Road* was "made before Mitchum was perceived as a respected iconoclast rather than a Peck's bad boy who got his name in the newspapers too many times," Ray Starman noted. Mitchum claimed to have some personal understanding of southern moonshiners, although the details of this information are blurry. "I had a smattering of knowledge

John Schneider as "Bo" in the television series, "The Dukes of Hazzard," which ran for more than six years. Schneider is perched on their car, the "General Lee," a central figure in the series. The popular television show was developed from a less well-received film called *Moonrunners*.

about that part of Uncle Sam's domain; I was raised there," Mitchum wrote in a short article. He said that Phillips, the screen writer, "spent five weeks at the Library of Congress in Washington, just studying folk music," he added. "Research takes time, but we wanted it right. Now it's right and tight."

The film has a peculiar authenticity, something that may have helped make it a drive-in theater classic, but that left most critics unimpressed. Critic Richard Thompson wrote that the film was "designed for ozoners and grind houses" and that "by any accepted critical standard the film is garbage." In *Robert Mitchum on the Screen*, Alvin H. Marill was kinder, calling the film "memorably off-beat"; although it originally received "scant—even scornful—notice," he wrote that it was "huge-

ly successful among what *Variety* lovingly terms 'the yahoo trade.'"

Thompson accurately describes the film's look as "a cheap Hollywood imitation of newsreel style"; details such as the voice-over that introduces the film, pointing out that "millions of gallons" of moonshine poured out of the Southeast in one year and that the federal Alcohol and Tobacco Tax Unit seized more than 10,000 stills and 3,000 vehicles every year, add to this effect. The film was directed by Arthur Ripley, an "enigmatic and eccentric" figure, according to Starman, and "a shadowy cult figure in the world of American crime and gothic films of the forties."

Thunder Road is rich in moonshiner terminology. Consider this dialogue on the police radio in a federal agent's car, after a typically unsuccessful chase after Doolin:

"What license number?"

"Never mind that, I'll bring you his back plate, it's hanging on our car now."

"The Kingpin again?"

"That's right, the real stampeder."

The agent, played by Gene Barry, had just latched onto Doolin's rear bumper with a grabbing device. The bootlegger, driving a

'50 Ford two-door coupe, responded by pulling what he later called a "drop lever," which released the bumper and allowed him to speed away. This exchange leads to a later piece of dialogue between Doolin and the federal agent, who said, "I've got a bumper that belongs to you."

"Well why don't you give it back?" Doolin responded. "That's just like stealing, ain't it?"

Other moonshiner lingo, like that found in the glossary at the end of this book, includes a comment from a mechanic in a garage who buys moonshine from Doolin. He shook some in a jar and announced that it had "pretty good bead." He paid $1,400 for 250 gallons. Luke called his car a "blockader"; everyone called engines "mills." And the federal agent, trying to threaten Doolin with how close he was to getting arrested, told him, "You're standing pretty close to the horse's head right now."

Numerous scenes are also quite genuine. Early in the film, Poppa Doolin has fired up the family still. He is shown putting the cap on it and setting a big rock on top, then sealing it with some paste that he scoops out of a bucket. Later scenes, during the revenuer's crackdown, illustrate chopping up stills and blowing up several others. At one point, Doolin repainted his car gray and put a Tennessee license plate on it. The scene of dancing to guitar music on the porch at Ledbetter's Store is particularly evocative of the times.

Several other bootleg gadgets, like the releasable bumper, are depicted in the film, as well. At one point, Doolin pulls a lever that lays down an oil slick on the road behind his car. The car driven by the pursuing gangsters flips over, catches fire, and slams down a steep hill and over a waterfall. Later in the film, Doolin pulls his loaded car into a garage that has a trick, corrugated wall that moves up and down. Doolin is driving a tanker car, a device that generated a good deal of controversy in real life. The car is also equipped with a drain on the bottom of the trunk, and also a high-volume "dump" with which Doolin could allegedly drain 250 gallons of moonshine in two minutes. Gimmicks like these prompted Mitchum to explain his sources: "We've used the Treasury Department's Alcohol and Tobacco Tax Division files; we have case histories that'd curl Yul Brynner's hair."

"The rum runners and moonshiners by the tens of thousands saw that picture, over and over again," wrote George Griffith in *Life and Adventures of Revenooer No. 1*. "I've heard that they cheered Mitchum endlessly, and some who saw it, expended tidy sums equipping their cars with bumper shedders. To the extent of my knowledge, no other revenooers ever used any kinds of bumper hooks. The police in some cities did." In several published interviews, however, early stock-car racer Tim Flock spoke colorfully and convincingly of a "cowcatcher" device that revenuers used successfully (until Flock and his cronies

started attaching their back bumpers with coat-hanger wire).

Griffith was less enchanted with the film than these audiences. He said that he had been visited by the screen writer, who, instead of paying attention to accurate accounts of actual cases, instead "lifted from my reports 'our' successful tricks and attributed them to the brilliant criminals."

Aside from questions of accuracy and art, the film did accomplish one thing about which there is little dispute. It was promised in the ads for the film, which blared, "Mitchum roars down the hottest highway on earth." Today, the film is "considered the grand-daddy of road movies," according to author Jerry Roberts. The nighttime chases are heavy on the screeching wheels; one of Doolin's rivals admits, begrudgingly, "You can always tell it's him when you hear those pipes of his come grumbling down the road." Cogan, the criminal villain who is trying to take over moonshine distribution in the Rillow Valley, has an office at The Speed Shop in Asheville.

Stunt driver Carey Loftin performed the scene where Luke crashes a 1957 Ford Fairlane hardtop through two cars that are blocking the road. During this scene, although the car's hood was wired down, it buckled so badly that Loftin couldn't see a marker that had been set up as a guide in the middle of the highway. He followed markers along the side of road, which had been installed as an alternate plan. According to an article by Clarey Barbiaux in the

A "Dukes of Hazzard" lunch box—just the thing for the aspiring young bootlegger.

July 1958 issue of *Motor Trend*, Loftin "stepped out, unharmed, and seemingly, unruffled" after the stunt. The article also contains a photo of a mechanic grinding on a reinforced and widened bumper installed for the scene. The stunt car allegedly could reach 140mph on the flats.

Loftin and Mitchum spent four weeks on location in Transylvania County, near Asheville, North Carolina, looking for places for the stunts. The production crew commandeered a local garage, where they stripped excess equipment from the stunt cars, and installed in its place such safety devices as braces made of welded steel pipes, which were put throughout the cars. They also installed "grab

Sheriff Andy Taylor takes a disapproving sniff at moonshiner Jubal Foster's latest distillation. Foster (played by Everett Sloane) burned down his own barn in Episode #46 of the "Andy Griffith Show." This item is trading card #255, one in a trio of a 111-card series that are the most popular Mayberry collectibles among the enthusiastic members of the 740-plus chapters (as of April 1993) of The Andy Griffith Show Rerun Watchers Club. *Copyright 1990, Mayberry Enterprises*

"Jubal, Jubal, Jubal, Ju-ball!"
— Barney Fife

The Andy Griffith Show

bars" in the cars, at seat level on the passenger's side. Loftin also wore double seatbelts (a precaution he judged necessary after a single belt broke during a critical phase of a stunt). Loftin's scenes took two weeks to film, and the stars stayed on location. One thrill occurred during the filming of a "deluxe turn-around" for the first time; the car "described an arc, turned over completely and came to rest on its wheels." When Loftin sailed into the bank of transformers at the fatal climax of the film,

Mitchum rushed forward to make sure he was OK, stepped into a hole, and broke a bone in his ankle.

Part of Mitchum's undeniable appeal is that he never seemed to be too impressed with himself, so it is perhaps understandable that his post-mortem on the stunt driving was cynical: "It did a great disservice to the industry, because, today, you can't film a baptism without a car crash."

Reflecting on *Thunder Road*, former ATF agent Charlie Weems observed, "There are lots of people in this area who think it really happened." He says that they seem to discuss the film as if it were a documentary. In reality, Weems said, the agents had some chases, but "we tried to avoid them if we could—they were dangerous." Furthermore, the high-speed chases usually didn't last that long.

In his article about the problems of directing a film, Mitchum described their search for cars. "As we sat in Hollywood, breathing smog, our representative, John E. Burch, combed the area to find some sixteen-year-old Mercury cars. These are hopped up by moonshiner transporters . . .

Jack Prince played moonshiner Rafe Hollister in several episodes of "The Andy Griffith Show." Prince's garb—overalls and long johns—was a polar opposite of his real personality. He was a hugely successful Las Vegas entertainer. This photo is from an episode titled "Rafe Hollister Sings." *The Andy Griffith Show Rerun Watchers Club Collection*

So could we find one or two? No. . . every time we found what we needed, we also found one of the local mountain boys had just bought it or outbid us!"

Author Alex Gabbard has made an exhaustive study of the film, and discusses some interesting background in his book, *Return to Thunder Road: The Story Behind the Legend*. He interviewed "a Tennessee official" who lived in the Knoxville area in the fifties and sixties, and who recalled that one of his relatives (who was about ten years older) was killed in a crash in Bearden, and that this crash was the origin of the film's final scene. He thought the wreck was in 1949 or 1950, on the Kingsville Pike. The driver had been heading for Knoxville, lost

control of the car, went down a steep bank, rolled, went through a fence at a power substation, and smashed into a transformer. He also told Gabbard that he had seen a photo of the wreck, showing the car on fire. Documentation of this wreck, however, had eluded Gabbard and other researchers.

Doolin's final ride was spectacularly unsuccessful; however, the popularity of the song and the film seem constant. The version of the song Mitchum later sang and made a hit, "The Ballad of Thunder Road," doesn't appear in the film. He recorded it for Capitol Records in 1958. Released in September, it climbed to #62 on the charts and spent eleven weeks in the top 100. The song was recorded by Tex Williams in February 1962, went to #65, and spent another ten weeks on the chart.

Several other films have featured liquor runners. Author Tom Wolfe's *Esquire* article about Junior Johnson was filmed in 1973 as *The Last American Hero*, starring Jeff Bridges as Junior, Art Lund as his moonshining father, with smaller parts by Valerie Perrine and Gary Busey. The film, according to one critic, was "moderately successful." Pop critic Leonard Maltin described it as the "unusual, engrossing saga of Junior Jackson [sic], North Carolinian backwoods moonshiner and racing fanatic, pitting his ability against the System."

Greased Lightning, starring Richard Pryor, Beau Bridges, Cleavon Little (along with guitar player Richie Havens and politician Julian Bond) told the life story of the first black NASCAR driver, Wendell Scott, who appeared as a stunt driver. One reference calls the 1977 film a "plodding, episodic bio," and a "waste of Pryor."

Jim Mitchum later made several youth-oriented films that raced straight into oblivion, including (in 1975) a role as a whiskey runner in *Moonrunners*. Waylon Jennings had a bit part. Maltin wrote that the film "sputters because of Mitchum's lethargic acting and the script's lack of credibility." This film was the precursor to the television series, "The Dukes of Hazzard," set in a county by that name in Kentucky. The popular series starred John Schneider as Bo and Tom Wopat as Luke. Waylon Jen-

nings was "The Balladeer." The comedy ran for 149 episodes from January 26, 1979, until February 8, 1985. The two stars left for a short time in 1982; in the show, their absence was explained by saying that they were racing their car, the *General Lee*, on the NASCAR circuit.

Other films in the genre include *The Moonshine War* (1970), which had a surprisingly top-notch cast (Richard Widmark, Alan Alda, and Patrick McGoohan) and was based on a script by Elmore Leonard. *Bootleggers* (1974), with Slim Pickens and a pre-"Charlie's Angels" Jaclyn Smith, concerned rival moonshining families in Arkansas in the 1930s, running their liquor into Memphis. *Moonshine County Express* (1977), with John Saxon, Susan Howard, and William Conrad, pits a murdered moonshiner's trio of daughters against the local moonshine mogul. Of all the films described, only this film earned more than two stars from Maltin (it got two-and-a-half).

Jackie Gleason played the role of federal Prohibition agent Izzy Einstein in a 1985 television film called *Izzy and Moe*. The film is significant as the final reunion of Gleason and Art Carney; however, in his biography of Gleason, entitled *The Great One*, Williams A. Henry III called it "an amiably airy nothing" and a "major aesthetic failure." A current film guide called it "colorful though episodic, and only marginally amusing."

As is the case with NASCAR drivers, some entertainers had real-life experience with moonshining or bootlegging. Junior Samples of "Hee Haw" once ran a still near Coal Mountain in Forsyth County, Georgia. And in the spring of 1992, an episode of "Cops" (instead of the usual and endless series of drug busts) showed police seizing a still in a suburban garage.

But in most cases, a majority of television moonshiners were fictional, and harmless at that. They made sporadic appearances on "The Andy Griffith Show," as might be expected in a show set in rural North Carolina. The one recurrent moonshiner was Rafe Hollister, played by Jack Prince, who had met Andy Griffith on Broadway in the play "Destry Rides Again," which had starred Griffith.

Prince's first appearance in "The Andy Griffith Show" was as moonshiner Ben Sewell in "Alcohol and Old Lace," episode

#17, on January 30, 1961. "It's still among the favorite episodes of Mayberry fans today—a masterpiece," wrote Jim Clark in *The Bullet*, official newsletter of The Andy Griffith Show Rerun Watchers Club. Prince also played moonshiner Luke Grainer in "The Inspector" (episode #26), and, in his fourth show, became Rafe Hollister (episode #33). According to *Aunt Bee's Mayberry*

Cookbook, co-authored by Clark and Ken Beck, Rafe considered himself an artist; his "preferred genre is the still life." Prince's last appearance was in 1963, when he left to pursue a singing career.

In episode #17, "Alcohol and Old Lace," Barney bragged to Sheriff Taylor that he had almost located a still at Hawk's Point:

A haggard Arthur Hunnicut, playing a character named Jess, checks the bead on a gallon of moonshine in the 1975 film *Moonrunners*. Film critic Leonard Maltin faults the film for a "lack of credibility," but this scene looks authentic. *American International/Ron Main Collection*

"I just came [snaps his fingers] that close to knocking it over," he said, because he saw Otis staggering down the road nearby, "weaving and singing and throwing kisses to the world." However, two apparently prim and proper sisters, Clarabelle and Jennifer Morrison, soon reported that they knew where it was—Council Flat. They had seen Ben Sewell "pouring and corking the bottles himself." Andy and Barney investigated, finding Ben at a reasonably realistic still (perhaps for photographic reasons, the coil went right into a funnel, instead of being in a barrel of water or a creek). Ben was surprised that they were going to arrest him because they were what he called "local law," not "federal law, revenuers." Andy told him that they were in a dry county, nevertheless.

The sisters next reported that Rube Sloan was operating a still at Furnace Crick. Then, having disposed of their competition, they raised the price of their moonshine to $4.00 a quart. Opie found the sisters' still in their hothouse; he later described it to Andy as a "flower making machine." At the show's conclusion, when Barney took the ax to it, a big spray hit Andy in the face three times in a row. He smiled and licked his lips. "Well, I guess it's all right to have a little taste, after all—it's National Still-Smashing Day."

A moonshiner also appeared in an episode called "The Haunted House" (epi-

sode #97) which was set at "the old Rimshaw Place." Spooky noises scared off Opie and his friend after they hit a baseball through a window. Town drunk Otis tried to convince Andy and Barney that the old house was really haunted; "Axes float in the air," he claimed, because old man Rimshaw allegedly killed his hired man with an ax. While investigating, Andy pretended to be scared, then hid. Otis and moonshiner "Big Jack" Anderson emerged, the former holding a bottle of dark liquid. "I'm going to be able to run that still downstairs for 20 years," Big Jack boasted. Andy scared them, however, by making an ax appear to float in the air. He then grabbed the ax and summoned Barney: "We got to bust up a still."

The June 7, 1993, episode of "The Untouchables" was called "Halsted Holler," synopsized in one television guide as follows: "A moonshiner angers Capone when he sells his superior whiskey in Chicago." The show included several scenes at the old family farm in Boone Hollow (always pronounced "Holler"), Kentucky.

Early in the episode, the moonshiners loaded white lightning into the back of a souped-up Ford pickup truck; "ain't no revenooers' car catch this thing," one of them bragged. It turned out that they didn't have to try to chase him: he ran into a roadblock where the law-enforcement agents just blasted away with guns, killing him.

The story used a common theme in the history of moonshining in America: that the folks who made illicit liquor only did it to keep from starving, or (in the case of the show) because the local bank was threatening to foreclose on the family homestead. "We just gotta keep the farm, Ma," one son said. Eliot Ness later described them as a "good family fallen on hard times."

Perhaps the prime cartoon visualization of the moonshiner is in Fred Lasswell's rendering of the character Snuffy Smith. Snuffy was a minor character in the strip "Barney Google and Snuffy Smith," created by Billy De Beck. Lasswell, born in Kennett, Missouri (in the general vicinity of the Kentucky boondocks where Snuffy Smith lived), worked on the strip as De Beck's assistant from 1933 until 1942. De Beck died that year, and Lasswell took over; he continues to draw the strip.

Chapter 12

Famous Places

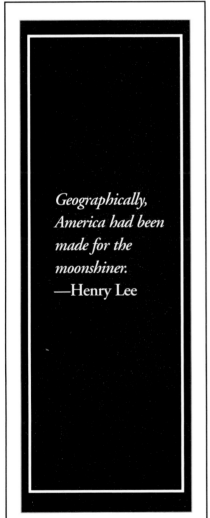

Geographically, America had been made for the moonshiner.
—Henry Lee

The operators of the passenger boat *Thistle* were caught with a riskier cargo during this liquor seizure in Skagway, Alaska, in 1879. Customs officers stand near barrels on the shore. *Library of Congress*

Our legal and economic systems, our politics, even our ethnic roots played roles in America's colossal history of illicit liquor. Fiercely independent whiskey-makers settled in rugged mountain strongholds and brooked little interference. Local temperance societies ensured a thriving business for moonshiners and bootleggers, who were duly rewarded for ingenuity and persistence. Entrepreneurs, more interested in making money than obeying laws, handled distribution and transportation. Remote areas—from Flori-

Pvt. Billy Smith sent this postcard from Fort McClellan, Alabama, to his folks in September 1944—comic relief from the grim reality of World War II.

da swamps to Appalachian forests—offered privacy; urban areas offered thirsty customers.

Arrayed against these powerful forces of tradition and opportunity have been a comparative handful of law-enforcement agents from the U.S. Customs Service and U.S. Border Patrol, the U.S. Coast Guard, state and local police, the federal Bureau of Alcohol, Tobacco and Firearms (and its earlier incarnations), various units of the Treasury Department, the Internal Revenue Service, and (while the Eighteenth Amendment was in effect) the Prohibition Bureau.

Their job, Lee explained, was "to penetrate the mountains where haughty hillbillies tolerated no furriners, to paddle through the Dismal Swamp and the Everglades, to seek out the malefactors who hid themselves in hundreds of river islands along the Mississippi and all the other great streams."

The task was daunting, to be sure. America's Atlantic, Pacific, and Gulf coasts combined to offer 12,000 miles of beach, cove, inlet, and estuary. Our land borders, north and south, offered another 3,700 miles that even the most amateurish smuggler stood a fair chance of penetrating. Appalachia, the traditional hotbed of moonshining, encompassed 195,000 square miles, stretching from lower New York state to northern Mississippi, and from mid-central Ohio to South Carolina. The foggy hollows of the Great Smokys, the Blue Ridge, the Cumberlands, the Ozarks of Missouri and Arkansas, and the Alleghenies were havens for generations of independent distillers.

During the best of times, the success of the revenuers was sporadic; during Prohibition, it was nonexistent. According to Andrew Sinclair, author of *Prohibition: The Era of Excess,* "Prohibition brought some prosperity to the backwoods. Sharecroppers, tenant farmers, fishermen of the bayous, dwellers on the mud banks of the Mississippi, all found the tending of stills or the sailing of rumrunners more profitable than the cultivation of overworked soil." Old habits die hard, and exorbitant federal taxes on liquor virtually guarantee the continued survival of the American moonshiner (just as modern Canada's tobacco taxes, which raise the cost of a pack to more than $7.00, guarantee a thriving business for cigarette smugglers).

Geographic patterns change, with the Appalachians ceding their dubious title to what ATF agents in the 1960s began calling

"While the old sow waits for the mash to be dumped, Pa is training the Boys in the ways of business," the caption on the back of this Arkansas postcard says. "Steve stands guard against free samplers and Revenoors." Hogs were not unknown around still sites, since they could help dispose of the residue evidence. Chickens, on the other hand, are not mentioned in moonshine's impressive historic record. The coiled copper "worm" snaking through the air is a typical feature of display stills, but is pointless unless submerged in cool water.

the "Moonshine Belt" (Oklahoma, Arkansas, Virginia, West Virginia, Tennessee, North and South Carolina, Georgia, Alabama, Mississippi, and Florida). In the mid-1970s, 90 percent of all illicit distilling was done in this section of the country. What doesn't change is the roll call of famous places in the annals of bootleg booze. The sentiments of the residents of these places run the gamut from embarrassment to resignation to pride. Some view it as a dismal chapter, best forgotten. Others see it more objectively. Among the former, according to an item in *Newsweek* on June 21, 1993, was West Virginia state senator Sondra Lucht, who expressed her outrage that her state was represented by an icon depicting an outhouse in a graphics software package. She called Jim Cooper, owner of the company that produced the program, to protest. She told a reporter, "I'd have been less offended if he'd used a jug of moonshine."

This chapter offers an introductory atlas of those annals, a historic map of the places that acquired a documented notoriety during the past two centuries.

Alabama

In Cleburne County during a revenuer crackdown in the late 1900s, when moonshiners realized that the government was serious, they offered to surrender in exchange for suspended sentences. Forty-three people turned themselves in, about three quarters of the county's population, including constables, ministers, and storekeepers.

George Griffith (a former federal judge and author of *Life and Adventures of Revenooer No. 1*) wrote vividly about the Paint Rock region in the northeast corner of the state. "Don't you ever go alone into Paint Rock during the daytime and don't go

at all at night, or you'll come out in a box," he recorded as a local warning to revenuers. Local officers refused to go in there at night; they heard dynamite signals whenever they went there. Griffith also cited the "rough and crooked 32 mile stretch (now Alabama 65) from Paint Rock, Alabama, to Huntland, Tennessee" as a main road for liquor transporters. In the 1920s and 1930s, Lick Skillet (on the west side of Putman Mountain) was a notorious hotbed, and Lauderdale County has been mentioned as particularly active in the moonshine business.

Florida

Florida's illicit-liquor history is particularly fertile. During Prohibition, government officials cited the problems in that state as "smuggling and a kind of Everglade distilling problem." In early 1928, the Coast Guard dispatched two destroyer divisions (twelve ships) to the east coast of Florida, in an effort to cut off the liquor flowing in from the Bahamas and Cuba. Bimini is fifty-eight miles from Miami Beach, and Havana just ninety miles from Key West. The maze of islands in the Florida Keys were ideal for smuggling, as were the beaches, small inlets, and estuaries north of Miami. To make matters worse, the Department of Commerce had installed a chain of flashing beacons for aircraft down the entire state. Inbound rumrunners merely had to take a fix on two of these beacons.

After Prohibition, the Big Bend region along the St. Mary's River on the Georgia-Florida border north of Jacksonville acquired a reputation among revenuers, who concentrated on Nassau, Baker, and Duvall counties. Activity here peaked in the 1940s, with moonshine sloshing down U.S. Highway 1 all the way to Miami.

Georgia

This state, with 116 dry counties and forty-three wet ones, is understandably in the first rank of moonshine bastions. Colorful names—Persimmon and Gum Log in the northeast, Tobacco Road near Augusta—punctuate any history of American moonshining.

Dawson County, fifty miles north of Atlanta, "was for years Georgia's undisputed corn whiskey capital, and during part of its history was the country's leader," Joseph Dabney wrote in *Mountain Spirits: A Chronicle of Corn Whiskey from King James' Ulster Plantation to America's Appalachians and the Moonshine Life.* In the early 1800s, its primary moonshine market was the settlement

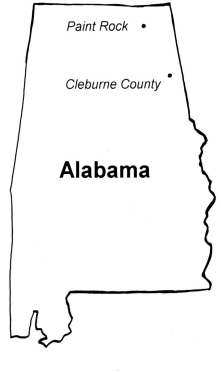

A rural still in the Florida pine barrens, 9 miles northwest of Glen St. Marys, Baker County, August 17, 1943. Note the pump by the large barrel at the right. This still doesn't seem to have a doubler, so the still feeds directly into the cooler barrel. These wooden barrels are larger than 50 gallons, and may have been used for olives. *Lacy Livesay photo file, ATF Reference Library*

here in Atlanta. I had thirty to thirty-five people in my class at school, and probably half of them had something to do with moonshine."

Other hot spots in Georgia were the counties of Lumpkin, Gilmer, and Pickens. By the early 1940s, these counties were sending an estimated one million gallons of whiskey a year into Atlanta, where the first mayor, Moses Formwalt, had been a well-know still-maker. Dabney pointed out that Atlanta "for decades has had the dubious title of the moonshine-consuming capital of the world." During the mid- and late-1950s, one historian figured that the annual influx had reached 1.5 million gallons. Jess Carr, speaking of the early 1970s, pointed out that "the city of Atlanta seems unable to

McDuffie County, Georgia, 1953–1954. Lawmen pause for a photograph on the site of a steam-fired still. The still was discovered in the Rousseau section of the county, north of Thompson. The boiler and cookers can be seen, as well a fire hose that was used to pump water from a nearby creek to the still. In the right foreground are wooden mash boxes. Back row, left to right: Boyce Norris, McDuffie County Sheriff Lynn J. Norris, and an unidentified revenue agent. Front row: revenue agent Charlie Tudor, and Robert Phillips. They appear to be in high spirits, but they haven't taken the ax to the heavy steel apparatus yet. *C. W. Herndon, courtesy Georgia Department of Archives and History*

of Terminus (later named Marthasville, then Atlanta).

"Dawsonville was one of the big pockets of moonshining, even back when I was a kid," Fred Goswick said. "After the war, the demand was so great, especially

The Pride of Dawsonville

Unfortunately, one of the true landmarks in the moonshine universe is defunct. It was the Moonshine Museum in Dawsonville, Georgia, opened by Fred Goswick in 1968. Goswick got the idea for the museum from an uncle who was a bondsman in Miami, a former site of massive sugar imports from Cuba. Goswick's uncle mentioned that he had heard of people who wanted to visit Dawsonville. "I wondered, 'What could they see?'" Fred recalled. After he had the idea for the museum, he explained, "Word got out, and people there liked the idea. I'd get up in the morning, and there'd be stuff for the museum laying there outside my house." He also had the parts of various stills here and there. He had to get a permit, and the still had to be set up so that it couldn't operate. "Informers would come in and try to buy barrels, or parts of stills," Goswick recalled. "But I knew they were informers, and I never would sell anything to them." He also said that federal agents were regular visitors, making sure that the stills were dry.

The museum had four stills set up, ranging from an old copper one to a big, modern, 3,000-gallon outfit. Goswick said they were assembled by Carl Phillips, a sixty-five-year-old former moonshiner who had started when he was nine, and who had spent a total of sixty-nine months in jail. "I'm not trying either to knock moonshining or glorify it," Goswick told a writer from the National Geographic Society in 1972. "I'm just trying to show what once was here."

The museum was later moved to a Georgia amusement park called Frontierland (which is no longer in operation), then sold to an operator in Gatlinburg, Tennessee, who died in December 1992; it has been closed down since then.

Tourists interested in an official moonshine site, however, can attend the Moonshine Festival in Dawson County, Georgia, forty-eight miles north of Atlanta in the foothills of the Appalachian Mountains. The festival is celebrated the last three Sundays in October. Why Dawsonville? Gold was discovered there in the 1820s. According to Goswick, moonshining was an alternative after the gold rush petered out in the early 1900s. A county history says moonshining "was a widely practiced undercover business well into the fifties, and longer for some. A by-product of the 'Moonshine Era' was some of the fastest cars and best drivers in the country, with Dawson County having many auto-racing greats, such as Gober Sosbee [who was fifteenth in the 1949 final point standings for the NASCAR Strictly Stock division], Bernard Long, Carleen Rouse and Bill Elliott."

The late, great Moonshine Museum as it stood in Dawsonville, Georgia, before its ill-fated odyssey. *Courtesy Fred Goswick*

This still was on display in front of the Rabun County Courthouse in Clayton, Georgia, during the early 1930s. When the sheriff seized a still, he displayed it here. Left to right: Luther Rickman, Sheriff Billy Page, Harley McCall, and Frank Rickman. *Courtesy Georgia Department of Archives and History*

eradicate the 'nip joints' which plague its alleys and back streets."

More modern estimates of the moonshine market in Atlanta are as low as a mere 8,000 gallons per week, a sixth of former levels. During and after Prohibition, law-enforcement officers in the city would seize fifty "whiskey cars" a month; in 1972, they got just seven in the whole year.

Illinois

Apart from famous gangsters in Chicago, Illinois' moonshine history is comparatively modest. The state's high point (or low point, depending on your perspective) was reached during Prohibition, when, in Chica-

Illinois

Chicago

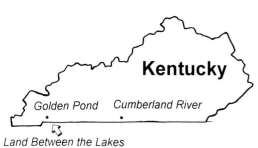

Kentucky

Golden Pond *Cumberland River*

Land Between the Lakes

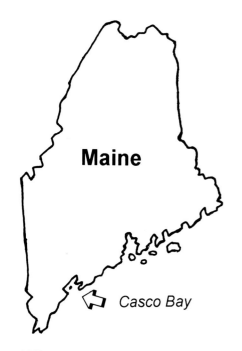

Maine

Casco Bay

This postcard was sent to Gloucester, Massachusetts, from Lexington, Kentucky, in March 1910. The still pictured is a large, well-established operation, though the purpose of the wooden box-like structures at right is unclear.

go, federal officials reported that they were getting "practically no cooperation from the police department."

Kentucky

Although producing illegal liquor is scarcely the sort of thing that most civic boosters and local historians brag about, Kentucky has earned its share of accolades. Recently, Esther Kellner wrote, "It is doubtful that the history of moonshine in any other state is as colorful as that of Kentucky."

One notorious spot, the seven-mile Coe Ridge south of the Cumberland River near the Kentucky-Tennessee border, was a place where "the legends grew, filled with frightening accounts of feuds, beatings, treachery, and murder." On "Big Six" Henderson's first raid there, his group seized seven stills, 4,000 gallons of mash, forty gallons of moonshine, and several moonshiners.

Another legendary area was Golden Pond in the Land Between the Lakes, between the Cumberland and Tennessee Rivers. In the 1930s and 1940s, this area had just 200 or 300 residents, yet, during

Prohibition, Golden Pond whiskey became famous around the country, establishing the Land Between the Lakes as "the moonshine center of the United States," according to Esther Kellner in *Moonshine: Its History and Folklore*. Airplanes arrived from New York and Chicago to make pickups, with as much as 5,000 gallons per day leaving the area. Some of the hollows had as many as fifteen operating stills. A major raid in February 1956 ended the area's spree. The town was moved to make way for the Land Between the Lakes National Outdoor Recreation Area, which features a moonshine display in the visitor center. After World War II, a legal distillery even named one of its products after Golden Pond.

Maine

Insular and maritime oriented, this long-time dry state offered in opportunity what it lacked in population during Prohibition, and figures in numerous accounts of smuggling. Casco Bay alone has more than 1,000 miles of coastline.

Michigan

Federal prohibition officials once reported that "the situation in Detroit is not very good . . . the retail end is wide open." The city, according to Andrew Sinclair, was "the busiest smuggling area" on the Canadian border, where "graft averaging two million dollars a week bought immunity for liquor traders."

New Jersey

New Jersey's place in the annals of illicit liquor is secure, at least on the fanciful maps that record such achievements: the area between Barnegat Bay, Cape May, and Greenwich has been known as Smugglers' Woods.

An anonymous but irate businessman wrote a letter to the Secretary of the Treasury in October 1923, complaining that Atlantic Highlands, "together with the adjoining borough of Highlands, is commonly referred to as a 'free port of entry' for the rum fleet." He also alleged that the Coast Guard was paid $3.00 per case, local police and Prohibition officers $1.00 per case, and another $1.00 per case to a gang of local hijackers for "protection." Having bribed every conceivable law-enforcement agency, it is unclear from whom they needed protection.

Henry Lee recorded a story about a fishing resort in south New Jersey ("within the headland of Sandy Hook") that lost most of its tourists because of the "rattle of night gunfire as rum runners fought off hijackers." But the local people were making so much money that it didn't matter—they even bought their own mother ship (a 3,000 ton freighter) and made a trip to France to stock up. It was promptly captured by the Coast Guard upon its return.

New York

As early as 1868, civilian revenuers and soldiers were pursuing moonshiners in New York—not in the boondocks of the state, but in New York City itself. "The prime target was Brooklyn's Democratic Irish of the waterfront district," a historian noted, describing massive raids employing hundreds of soldiers.

During Prohibition, Long Island hosted the largest and most persistent of all the Rum Rows up and down the Atlantic coast. Once, when the Coast Guard ship *Argus* anchored in Rockaway Bay, the crew encountered extremely hostile local citizens. One observer described their predicament, saying the Coast Guard vessel was "a floating island in the midst of enemy country, a target for bootleggers' bullets, and the abuse of the Long Island countryside."

In the early years of Prohibition, bootleggers found large markets and high prices in what local people called the North Country, including cities such as Glens Falls, Saratoga, and Albany, as well as New York City itself. Route 9 at Rouses Point in Clinton County on the Quebec-New York border was called Rum Trail. However, by 1923, Everest wrote, New York City was "being so well supplied with hard liquor by the 'Rum Row' of offshore boats that overland whiskey began to lose its biggest market."

North Carolina

Statistics on legally distilled liquor in this state were kept in the early 1800s. These tallies showed a statewide consumption of nearly 1.4 million gallons in 1810. An energetic and successful temperance movement caused some reduction, but, as Daniel Whitener pointed out in *Prohibition in North Carolina, 1715–1945*, "In any case, a million gallons, if consumed at home, would indicate that the supply was ample for a lot of intemperance." As has always been the traditional case, most of the illegal activities took place where temperance societies were most common. In the case of North Carolina, that meant the piedmont.

By the 1880s, Wilkes County was already "long famous for its blockaders." Several sources cite the South Mountains in Burke County as a "moonshiner enclave." Also, the Snider Settlement in Ashe County "was an enclave ruled by a band of outlaws."

Like so many dry or partly dry states, North Carolina has had an almost schizophrenic history of distilling and damning distilling. It had 733 licensed grain distilleries in 1895 and more than 1,300 licensed fruit distilleries. Nevertheless, the state voted itself officially dry in 1908.

Michigan

Detroit

New Jersey

Atlantic Highlands

Greenwich

Barnegat Bay

Cape May

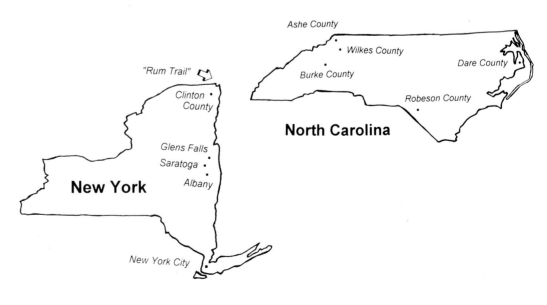

"Rum Trail"

Clinton County

Glens Falls

Saratoga

Albany

New York

New York City

Ashe County

Wilkes County

Dare County

Burke County

Robeson County

North Carolina

A customs agent inspects a reel of cable that was used in a unique underwater smuggling system set up under the Detroit River. The photo's original caption called it a "submarine liquor runway." A mile-long cable stretched just under the surface of the river from border to border. Motors pulled torpedo-shaped containers on the cable, delivering forty cases per hour to a small boathouse on the American side. The scheme was detected when customs inspectors noticed ripples on the water in the bright moonlight on a calm surface. December 26, 1931. *National Archives*

The result was predictable. In 1914, the state's commissioner of internal revenue said, "Bootlegging is principally carried on in States operating under local prohibition laws, and appears to be one of the hardest propositions that the revenue officers are called on to solve. . . As the various States vote 'dry' the operations of the bootlegger grow larger." Five years later, on the eve of Prohibition, this state official was more direct: "We have more illicit distilleries than any other State in the Union or any other portion of the earth; and the number is increasing."

Wilkes County's record of moonshine activity dates back to the mid-eighteenth century, but the white lightning action really picked up in the 1930s. Near the end of World War II, some young men from the area had auto tags that said, "The Moonshine Center of America." A famous article by Vance Packard, published in *American* magazine in 1950, estimated that 500,000 gallons of moonshine came out of Wilkes County in 1949. This report stirred up the ATF, which increased enforcement, sending in a team of thirteen agents who destroyed seventy-seven stills in the first month. According to a retired ATF agent, in the mid-1950s, the dozen agents assigned there meant that Wilkes County had more revenuers tracking moonshiners than any other place in America. One former transporter estimated that, during this heyday, a typical Wilkes County still could produce 600 gallons a week. A former moonshiner who still lives in the county recalled that revenuers once caught thirty or forty moonshiners a week.

The state has other entries in its moonshine resume. A 1935 seizure of 7,100 gallons in a house raid, Dabney wrote, was "the largest inland seizure of untaxed whiskey ever made in the United States."

In Dare County, moonshiners once set up as many as thirty steam distilleries, running off 50,000 gallons a week. The product received excellent reviews, Dabney observed, being "gently flavored by the juniper brown water of Mill Tail Creek." It was mainly retailed in Baltimore.

Robeson County, in the southeastern part of the state, also claimed the state crown. At one time, some estimates claimed that there were more stills in the county than anywhere in America. One former agent said, "We could go to the Lumber River and chop up ten to twelve stills on any afternoon."

During Prohibition, coastal bootlegging and moonshining on the Outer Banks of North Carolina centered at East Lake, on the mainland opposite Roanoke Island. Finally, in Nash County, next to Halifax, legendary revenuer Garland Bunting seized one of the largest stills that he ever found. This incident, as well as other experiences, so impressed Bunting that he took to calling it "Mash" County.

Ohio

This state's most prolific moonshiners have traditionally set up shop in Lawrence County on the Ohio River, in the southern tip of the state. They sold their product to steamboaters and river travelers, and in nearby railroad towns.

New Straitsville, in the Hocking Hills of central Ohio, celebrates an annual Moonshine Festival; logging and coal mining have always been the standard job producers in this area, with moonshining as "a sort of fallback occupation," one resident wrote.

In a recent magazine article, Danny Fulks wrote evocatively of the heyday of the roadhouse: "Through the years, roadhouses with their live bands, dance floors, and gravel parking lots provided a lively mixture of fun and trouble for Kentuckians, West Virginians, and southern Ohioans. Long gone from Route 7 in Lawrence County, Ohio, the Blue Moon, the Rome Beauty Inn, and the Hi-De-Ho remain in the dusty memories of the 1950s. Between sets played by local hillbilly pickers, patrons went outside to their cars to sip from jars of moonshine."

Pennsylvania

Southwest Pennsylvania was one of the new nation's centers of distilling in the late 1700s. In 1790, of the 2,500 known distilleries in the thirteen states, 570 were concentrated in the four counties around Pittsburgh.

During Prohibition, many distilleries turned to producing denatured alcohol, ostensibly for industrial purposes, but widely

According to the caption on the back of the North Carolina postcard, the photographer happened on this operating still and found a willing subject. "In making moonshine it is necessary to have cold water, and as you can see there is an oversupply here," the caption says. Note the rifle propped at lower right. The violator himself appears to be leaning on a stirring stick, used to agitate the mash.

Ohio

New Straitsville

Lawrence County

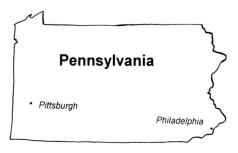

Pennsylvania

• *Pittsburgh*

Philadelphia

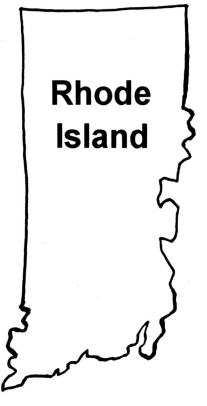

Rhode Island

The style of ceramic jugs shows the old and the new in moonshine containers. This is a traditional, handmade jug, whose shape is described by collectors as "ovoid." Collectors can locate the source of old jugs by the color of the glaze; prized examples bring hundreds of dollars.

This square-sided jug, although perhaps more familiar, is a newer, factory-made version. One advantage of the factory-made jug was that its square shoulders allowed it to be stacked.

suspected of being "diverted into illicit channels," a report said, because it could be re-distilled. After one month a federal crackdown in the Philadelphia district was credited with cutting this suspicious output from 1.7 million gallons at the denaturing plants to 500,000 gallons.

Philadelphia also got a black eye from federal prohibition-enforcement officials, who cited "not only a lack of active cooperation, but a very bad situation in the police department."

Rhode Island

Our smallest state made a big name for itself by being one of just two states to refuse to ratify the Eighteenth Amendment. State officials "blatantly disregarded"

Prohibition for the first three or four years, according to author Thomas Coffey.

South Carolina

One "old moonshiner stronghold" in this state possessed one of the more evocative names in this geographical rogues' gallery: the Dark Corner of the Glassy Mountains, north of Greenville (near Gowansville) in the northwestern part of the state. Other enclaves were Hogback Mountain and the Winding Stairs; notorious moonshiner Lewis Redmond operated there. Later, Joseph Dabney talked to a retired preacher who had been a sentry for moonshiners as a youth; he said that "there was a blockade distillery on every branch up there then." At age twelve, he used to drive a team of mules pulling a wagon full of moonshine into Greenville.

A place called Jugtown was southwest of the Dark Corner. Edward D. Sloan, Jr.,

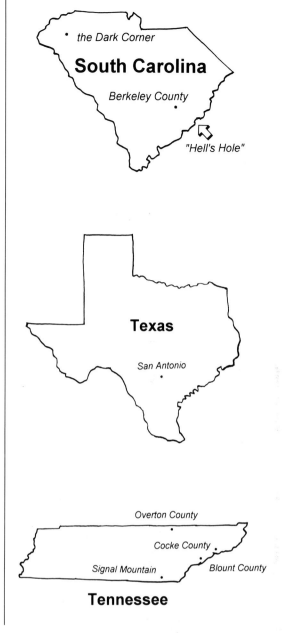

This still was on display at Hillbilly Village in Pigeon Forge, Tennessee. It was captured, the sign says, on Webb Mountain in the Great Smoky Mountains in May 1957. An unusual cooling barrel is at right; "Whiskey comes out here," the small signs points out at lower right.

president of the Greenville County Historical Society explained, "Many local potters made jugs for local and Tennessee distillers in the late 19th and early 20th centuries. About World War I, low-cost screw-top Mason jars drove these potters out of the functional jug business." Gary Thompson, a pottery collector in Greenville, South Carolina, has found references to a trio of Jugtowns in North Carolina (notably in Buncombe County), as well as in South Carolina and Georgia. Jugtowns developed where potters tended to concentrate, along the geologic "fall line" where clay deposits were.

Tennessee

One nineteenth-century enclave in eastern Tennessee was Chesnut Flats in Cades Cove, Blount County, which was "periodically inundated by outlaws of all descriptions who drank, gambled, whored, and shot each other to pass the time," according to a contemporary source quoted by Wilbur Miller in *Revenuers & Moonshiners: Enforcing Federal Liquor Law in the Mountain South, 1865–1900.*

A famous spot was Signal Mountain, outside Chattanooga, where moonshiners used to ship their product in wooden kegs inside wooden boxes marked "books." Greene County also earned mention in some accounts.

Cocke County is a revered name in moonshine circles, with illicit operations centered in Cosby, near the Great Smoky Mountains. Still-tenders there used dynamite blasts to warn of revenuers. They sent whiskey to Lexington, Kentucky; Asheville, North Carolina; and Johnson City, Tennessee. One night J. Carroll Cate, chief of Prohibition enforcement in the area, captured twenty-eight cars that were hauling liquor.

In more modern times, this part of the state was still up to its old tricks. "East Tennessee, especially Cocke County, was notorious for moonshining," former ATF agent

Charlie Weems wrote. "It wasn't so much the size of the distilleries as the proliferation of them. There was a still in every hollow and on almost every farm."

Newport was "the southern end of a bootlegging concern run out of Chicago," according to one source. Local people called the area "Little Chicago" because hoodlums would come down to vacation or hide out, and because a lot of local moonshine went up to that city.

Texas

Moonshining in Texas, as with many other nontraditional places, peaked during Prohibition. Particularly in the southern and midwestern part of the state, gangs set up intricate bootleg networks, coercing local farmers to operate stills for them.

Virginia

Although rarely cracking the list of the top five states in terms of still seizures, the Old Dominion's moonshiners perhaps earn credit for sheer persistence. During Prohibition, a nascent Rum Row appeared off the Virginia Capes; three Coast Guard cutters were on patrol off Norfolk at the end of May 1923.

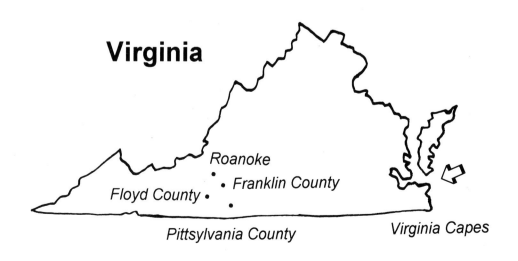

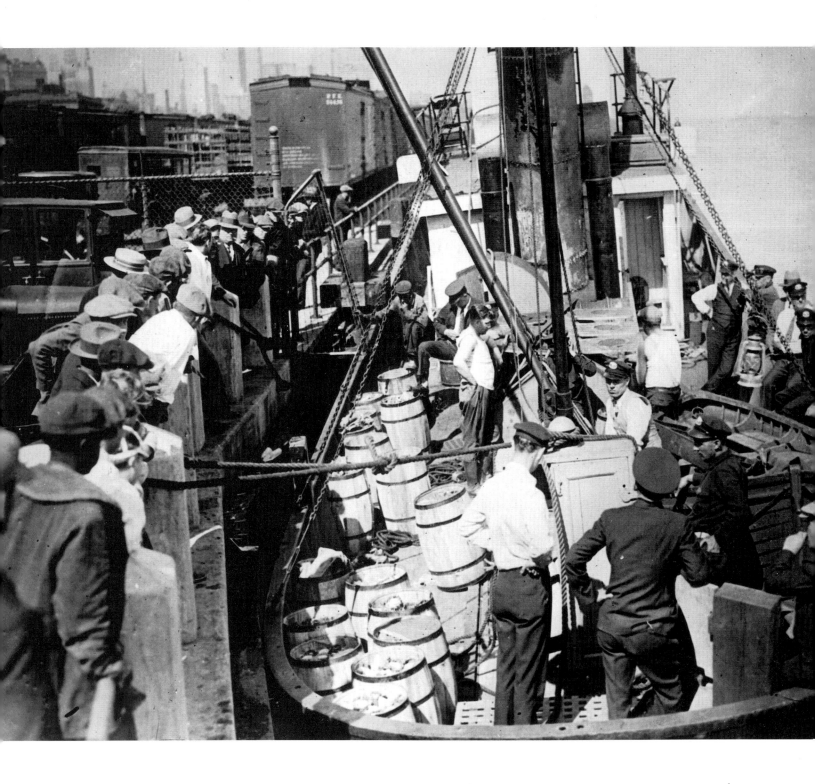

In Lufkin, Texas, authorities inventory a nautical bootlegger's vessel. There is no shortage of spectators, police, or barrels of liquor. This ship was operating in the Neches River (a large river at the eastern edge of Texas, which heads to the Gulf of Mexico through Beaumont). *National Archives*

In April 1935, Sherwood Anderson covered a legendary moonshine trial for *Liberty* magazine (published in the November issue). He asked, "What is the wettest section in the U.S.A., the place where, during prohibition and since, the most illicit liquor has been made? The extreme wet spot, per number of people, isn't in New York or Chicago. By the undisput-

ed evidence given at a recent trial in the United States Court at Roanoke, Virginia, the spot that fairly dripped illicit liquor, and kept right on dripping it after prohibition ended, is in the mountain country of southwestern Virginia—in Franklin County, Virginia."

The trial involved an elaborate bootlegging syndicate of merchants, car sales-

At the start of a rumrunning expedition, *Arethusa* loads up in Bermuda in 1924. Bermuda was one of several Caribbean centers of liquor production and transshipment. *Courtesy of the Mariners' Museum, Newport News, Virginia*

men, "liquor financiers," sheriffs and deputies, and state and federal officials. According to testimony, 70,448 pounds of the yeast used in distilling had been sold in the county in the previous four years, enough for millions of runs of moonshine. Single families in the county were credited with using 5,000 pounds of sugar per month. Other suspicious purchases for the four-year period, according to government statisticians during the trial, included nearly 34 million pounds of sugar, 13 million pounds of cornmeal, and 600,000 5-gallon cans. These colossal totals, Anderson wrote, "would account for some 3,501,115 gallons of moon liquor pouring down out of this mountain county, being rushed at night in

fast cars into the coal-mining regions of West Virginia, to the big Virginia towns along the valley, to Roanoke, Lynchburg, Norfolk, and on into Eastern cities."

Thirty-five years later, the moonshine business in that area was still perking along. In 1970, an ATF agent quoted in a Roanoke newspaper said, "In the past five years we have seen a gradual decline in the manufacturing of moonshine. But we still have a problem as can be seen in last week's raid in Franklin County." This raid netted eighteen stills capable of putting out 4,500 gallons per week.

An article in the *Roanoke Times & World News*, published on March 9, 1993, and datelined Chatham, covered "the largest illegal whiskey operation ever discovered in Virginia," which had been raided on January 6. The illegal distillery was a "36-pot— or 28,200-gallon—still." Agents found 28,800 gallons of fermenting mash, "abandoned and slowly turning rancid." Paul Henson was later arrested; he lived in a house several hundred yards from the still, and agents found a farm truck registered to him with empty sugar bags in the back.

Agents had had the still under surveillance from December 24 to January 6, but couldn't identify Henson as one of the two or three people seen going in and out of the site; they had last seen someone at the site on December 29. Six weeks later, a Pittsylvania county grand jury failed to indict Henson.

On May 1, 1993, the *Roanoke Times & World News* covered a raid in Floyd County that was "perhaps the largest ever in that county." This raid, at a still found along the Blue Ridge Parkway near the town of Floyd, uncovered a dozen 800-gallon pots inside a barn-like building, capable of producing 200–240 gallons of whiskey. On April 19, 1993, the newspaper ran an article entitled, "Shine on: Franklin County's still the champ." Since the Pittsylvania county raid, a staff writer wrote, "There has been a lot of tongue-in-cheek discussion about Franklin County losing its title: 'Moonshine Capital of the World.'" The recent seizure of a thirty-six-pot still was 50 percent larger than a twenty-four-pot still seized in the Endicott section of Franklin County in 1974. Howev-

West Virginia

Logan County

er, in terms of numbers, "Franklin County's title is secure," the article said.

Statistics for recent fiscal years prove that Franklin and Pittsylvania counties dominate the state's moonshine scene. For fiscal year 1989, compared to the total for the rest of state, these two counties led in still seizures nineteen-to-four (and in numbers of pots seized, ninety-nine-to-eleven). They had double or triple the number of still seizures compared to the rest of the state for the previous two fiscal years, as well. Not only that, but from July 1992 through February 1993, both counties had already eclipsed any of these three years, apart or combined. Franklin County had had seventy-five pots seized, higher than the seventy it had during fiscal 1991, and more stills. Pittsylvania County had already yielded fifty-three pots, just three less than the previous three years combined.

West Virginia

"The blockader's paradise was undoubtedly West Virginia," wrote one historian, talking about the late nineteenth century: convictions for moonshining exceeded 50 percent only twice from 1870–1877, and only three times from 1882 to 1900.

A resident of Logan County once uttered the classic statement of the traditional southern moonshiner: "Up in this holler, we make our own laws."

Foreign Countries

Especially during Prohibition, even the best efforts of American moonshiners and bootleggers were insufficient to slake the national hankering for a stiff jolt. Several other countries, large and small, allies and neutrals, all played a role in the spirited supply and demand.

The Central American nation of Belize, for example, supplied the Gulf Coast. Nassau was a major point of transshipment: 50,000 quarts of liquor passed through Nassau en route to the United States in 1917. By 1922, that amount was up to 10 million quarts.

Bimini, according to Harold Waters in *Smugglers of Spirits,* was "a bustling depot of Canadian whiskey intended for Florida and rum from the West Indies." The island was the main supply base for Florida.

Canada, where a majority of the citizens always thought that Prohibition was a pointless and futile law to begin with, blithely continued to export whiskey directly to the U.S., in spite of furious protests from American officials that our neighbor should help us enforce the law. In 1925, Canada cleared 1.1 million gallons of whiskey and 3.9 million gallons of malt liquors for export to America. The country finally succumbed to pressure from American politicians and agreed to stop issuing clearances for shipments of whiskey to American ports. Did Canadian distillers and brewers suffer as a result? Hardly— their output increased. Between 1925 and 1929, Canadian exports of whiskey to the West Indies doubled, and tripled to British Honduras, where it was simply forwarded on to its actual destination, the United States.

In Cuba, Havana was a major supply base for American rumrunners.

France got into the act in a couple of ways. Its distillers and vintners sent shiploads of liquor from Europe to the various Rum Rows off the American coast. A French possession, the Miquelon Islands, eight miles south of Newfoundland, became a continental powerhouse in the liquor business as well. During Prohibition, one historian noted, "rum had almost replaced cod as the reason for St. Pierre's existence." More than 1 million cases were stored there, with Scotch selling for $8.00 per case, bourbon and rye for $7.00, and gin for $6.00.

St. Pierre is the name of both a town and the smallest island of the group, which includes two larger neighbors, Miquelon and Langlade (formerly called "Little Miquelon"). In the early 1920s, small-town St. Pierre became a "bustling trans-shipment centre," according to a newspaper account. "Every available building was turned over to the distillers' agents," and 100,000 cases arrived every month. French-speaking islanders refer to Prohibition as the time of *la fraude* ("the smuggle").

The Rise and Fall of Rum Row

The most interesting place in the liquor smuggling business never appeared on maps, and during Prohibition it assumed almost mythical proportions: Rum Row. It wasn't so much one place as many, and it waxed, waned, anchored, and vanished in response to weather, Coast Guard action, and conditions ashore.

The first rum ship anchored off Long Island in May 1921, according to one account. The smuggling fleet reached as many as 100 ships at one time. Soon, Scott Corbett wrote in *The Sea Fox: The Adventures of Cape Cod's Most Colorful Rumrunner,* "A dozen miles off the tip of Cape Cod [lay] an impressive segment of the last great sailing fleet ever assembled off the coast of America . . . A more raffish and villainous fleet had not been brought together since the days of Jean Lafitte . . . Rum Row, it was called, and the Eighteenth Amendment had brought it into being. Anchored in a long line, the rum fleet was like an armada drawn up in battle array and firing its broadsides of bottles at a thirsty America."

In 1924, author Jess Carr reported, "as many as 336 rum ships were known to be bringing in contraband beverages. Specially equipped—syndicate-owned or freelance—fishing boats operated from port to the anchored ships lying at the fringes of territorial waters. Some were equipped with special high-powered motors for speed."

Adm. Alfred C. Richmond, who retired as commandant of the Coast Guard, explained that Rum Row ships brought liquor "much like a farmer would bring produce to market." Customers "would shop from ship to ship to get the product or the price they wanted." In the early years, before the Coast Guard mounted a dedicated strategy of harassment, Rum Row was a sort of community, with regular deliveries of supplies and newspapers from shore, happy hours, and dancing on the main deck of the larger vessels. Entertainers and hookers would visit, constituting an added attraction for customers and crew members alike. Ship chandlers made rounds, taking orders for such necessaries as fuel and paint. Some rumrunners advertised their cargoes and prices with large, bright signs.

Waters noted that "sightseeing boats, loaded down with curious tourists, made the rounds of the fleet during the summer months, shouting good wishes and salutations at rummy crews." An old excursion steamer anchored off New Jersey served as a floating nightclub. On behalf of outraged moralists ashore, a fishing schooner re-

Another photo from Bill McCoy's scrapbook, this one captioned, "Where we loaded at Halifax, N.S. from Furness Withy Dock from distillers Corporation Seagrams." *Courtesy of the Mariners' Museum, Newport News, Virginia*

named the *Beacon of Hope* was converted to a "Gospel Barge," manned with evangelists and sailing a "Repent Sinners" banner. In the early days, the rumrunners would tolerate the visits as a diversion. Once the Coast Guard crackdown started and things were getting serious, the skipper once tried going alongside and bellowing sermons from a makeshift pulpit on the pilothouse. The first rumrunner turned a fire hose on him and washed him out of his pulpit.

The various Rum Rows along the Atlantic seaboard were all close to major ports and big cities. According to Waters, "The most extensive of them stretched from the Delaware Capes in the south to Montauk Point, Long Island, in the north." (Long Island Sound, one writer noted, "had a smuggling tradition dating back to early Colonial times.") Another historian put the greatest concentration of rumrunners off the New Jersey Highlands, handy to the port of New York.

In June 1923, the Norfolk *Ledger-Dispatch* published an editorial called "The Rum Runners," in which the writer observed that it had proven impossible to "bottle up" the entrance to the Chesapeake Bay and the inlets on the ocean side of the eastern shore. Partly for that reason, New Jersey rumrunners appeared to have relocated off the Virginia Capes. A June 2 news item that year reported that rumrunners were indeed using Pamlico Sound at the top of the

North Carolina coast; the Coast Guard had dispatched two cutters to the area, with a third stationed between Cape Henry and Pamlico Sound, along with a tug between Cape Henry and Cape Charles, and two smaller boats in the harbor, stopping and inspecting all launches and yachts. The rum fleet was reported to be lying twenty miles off the coast. "The market afforded by the populous districts of tidewater Virginia, and the unobstructed passage to Baltimore and Washington, is the Eldorado which has lured many of the rum craft from their station off New York to this vicinity," the article continued. "A successful passage of the Virginia Capes opens up to rum smugglers a populous section full of rich possibilities."

Farther south, the Coast Guard also patrolled the Straits of Florida in the Gulf of Mexico, particularly the Dry Tortugas, historically frequented by smugglers of all types.

Rum Row underwent many changes during the 1920s. When Manny Zora, the "Sea Fox," first started his career as a smuggler, Corbett noted that "there were still a great many independent rum ships out on Rum Row, ships not tied in with any of the big syndicates. On these ships liquor was sold over the side to all comers." Gradually, organized criminal syndicates, ruthless and efficient, drove the freelance speculators and adventurers out of the trade.

In some cases, fortunes were made, as the experience of Bill McCoy indicates. Others, such as the owners of the ship on which Alastair Moray was supercargo, found slim pickings and near disaster. Most historians agree that by 1925, conditions and prospects on Rum Row had changed profoundly when compared to the festival atmosphere of the early years. "After the first four years of easy profits and quick sales, bitter competition, murders by hijackers, harassment by the Coast Guard, and long months at sea with too much liquor on board reduced the ships on Rum Row to a desolate line of vessels which barely paid their way," Andrew Sinclair wrote.

The original three-mile limit was easy to beat. As international treaties extended it to an average of about twelve miles (or one hour's sailing distance from shore), rumrunners found it much more difficult. As Corbett wrote, toward the end of Prohibition, "the local rum fleet had been pushed out and out until it was a good eighteen miles offshore. Conditions had changed considerably from the days when no more than a six-mile round trip was involved." Rendezvous was harder to arrange, anchoring was more difficult, and the Coast Guard had faster ships and more room to chase the contact boats. Concentrated Coast Guard blockades dispersed the larger rumrunners along the Atlantic coast to less patrolled areas. According to one historian, by the end of 1925, "Rum Row in the original sense had simply ceased to exist."

Prohibition forces at the time would have liked to believe these statements, but the historical record is unclear. Rumrunning continued throughout Prohibition, at least on a smaller scale. What to make of the assertion, then, made by the Coast Guard commander at New London, Connecticut, that in the early summer of 1930 (five years after the so-called "victory" over Rum Row) there were still 150 rumrunners between Montauk Point, Long Island, and Maine?

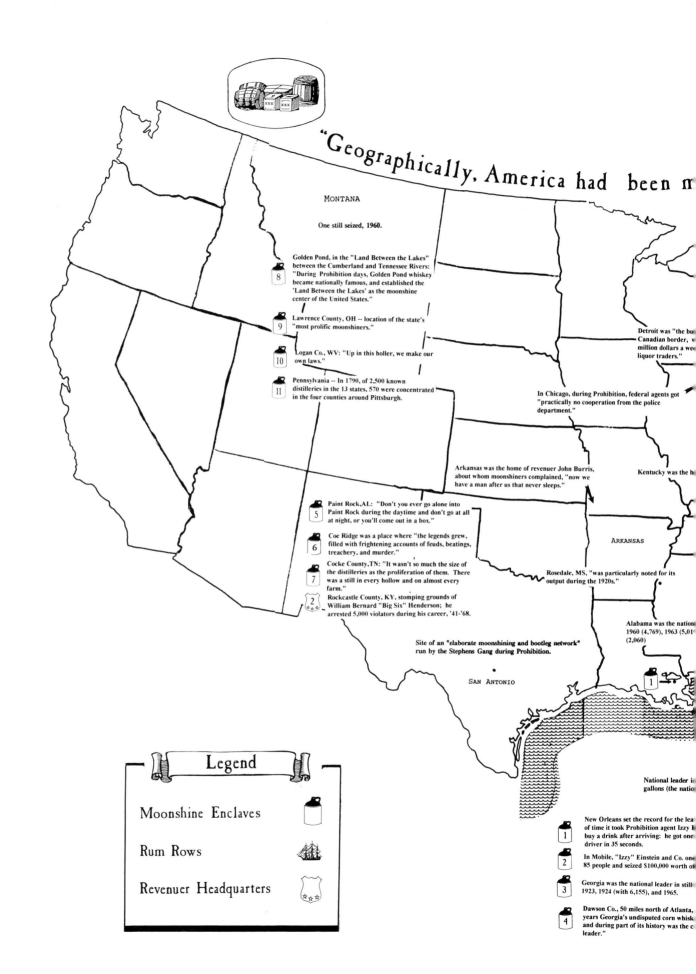

MONTANA

One still seized, 1960.

8 Golden Pond, in the "Land Between the Lakes" between the Cumberland and Tennessee Rivers: "During Prohibition days, Golden Pond whiskey became nationally famous, and established the 'Land Between the Lakes' as the moonshine center of the United States."

9 Lawrence County, OH -- location of the state's "most prolific moonshiners."

10 Logan Co., WV: "Up in this holler, we make our own laws."

11 Pennsylvania -- In 1790, of 2,500 known distilleries in the 13 states, 570 were concentrated in the four counties around Pittsburgh.

Detroit was "the bu Canadian border, v million dollars a wee liquor traders."

In Chicago, during Prohibition, federal agents got "practically no cooperation from the police department."

Arkansas was the home of revenuer John Burris, about whom moonshiners complained, "now we have a man after us that never sleeps."

Kentucky was the h

ARKANSAS

5 Paint Rock,AL: "Don't you ever go alone into Paint Rock during the daytime and don't go at all at night, or you'll come out in a box."

6 Coe Ridge was a place where "the legends grew, filled with frightening accounts of feuds, beatings, treachery, and murder."

7 Cocke County,TN: "It wasn't so much the size of the distilleries as the proliferation of them. There was a still in every hollow and on almost every farm."

2 Rockcastle County, KY, stomping grounds of William Bernard "Big Six" Henderson; he arrested 5,000 violators during his career, '41-'68.

Rosedale, MS, "was particularly noted for its output during the 1920s."

Alabama was the nation 1960 (4,769), 1963 (5,01 (2,060)

Site of an "elaborate moonshining and bootleg network" run by the Stephens Gang during Prohibition.

SAN ANTONIO

1

National leader i gallons (the natio

1 New Orleans set the record for the lea of time it took Prohibition agent Izzy l buy a drink after arriving: he got one driver in 35 seconds.

2 In Mobile, "Izzy" Einstein and Co. one 85 people and seized $100,000 worth o

3 Georgia was the national leader in still 1923, 1924 (with 6,155), and 1965.

4 Dawson Co., 50 miles north of Atlanta, years Georgia's undisputed corn whisk and during part of its history was the c leader."

Legend

Moonshine Enclaves

Rum Rows

Revenuer Headquarters

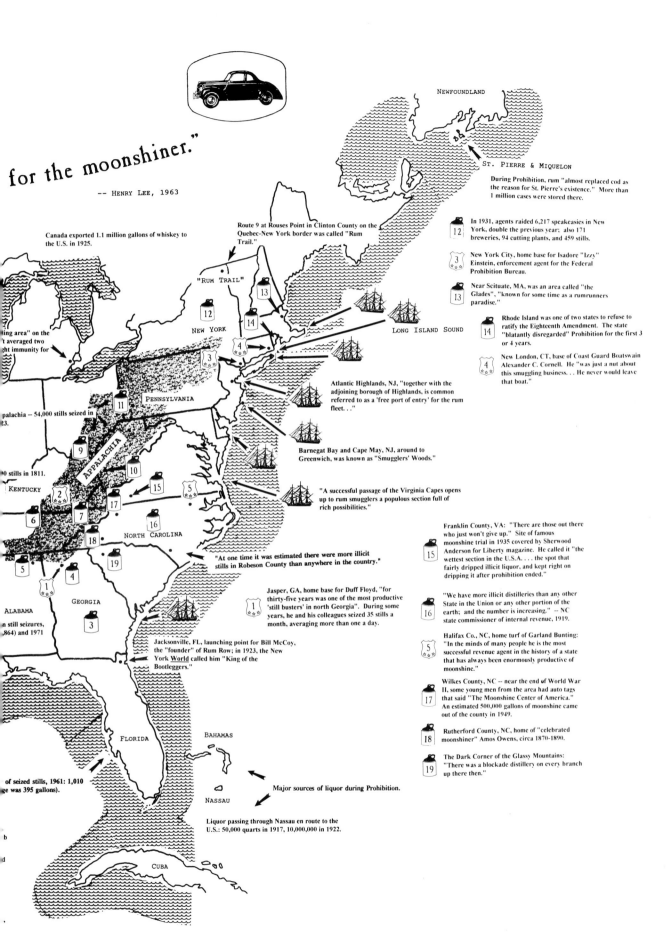

for the moonshiner."

-- HENRY LEE, 1963

NEWFOUNDLAND

ST. PIERRE & MIQUELON

During Prohibition, rum "almost replaced cod as the reason for St. Pierre's existence." More than 1 million cases were stored there.

Canada exported 1.1 million gallons of whiskey to the U.S. in 1925.

Route 9 at Rouses Point in Clinton County on the Quebec-New York border was called "Rum Trail."

"RUM TRAIL"

12

NEW YORK

14

13

4

3

11

PENNSYLVANIA

LONG ISLAND SOUND

In 1931, agents raided 6,217 speakeasies in New York, double the previous year; also 171 breweries, 94 cutting plants, and 459 stills.

New York City, home base for Isadore "Izzy" Einstein, enforcement agent for the Federal Prohibition Bureau.

Near Scituate, MA, was an area called "the Glades", "known for some time as a rumrunners paradise."

Rhode Island was one of two states to refuse to ratify the Eighteenth Amendment. The state "blatantly disregarded" Prohibition for the first 3 or 4 years.

New London, CT, base of Coast Guard Boatswain Alexander C. Cornell. He "was just a nut about this smuggling business. . . He never would leave that boat."

Atlantic Highlands, NJ, "together with the adjoining borough of Highlands, is common referred to as a 'free port of entry' for the rum fleet. . ."

Barnegat Bay and Cape May, NJ, around to Greenwich, was known as "Smugglers' Woods."

"A successful passage of the Virginia Capes opens up to rum smugglers a populous section full of rich possibilities."

ing area" on the
t averaged two
ght immunity for

palachia -- 54,000 stills seized in
23.

APPALACHIA

9

10

15

5

KENTUCKY

0 stills in 1811.

2

17

16

6

7

NORTH CAROLINA

18

5

19

4

ALABAMA

n still seizures,
864) and 1971

GEORGIA

3

"At one time it was estimated there were more illicit stills in Robeson County than anywhere in the country."

Jasper, GA, home base for Duff Floyd, "for thirty-five years was one of the most productive 'still busters' in north Georgia". During some years, he and his colleagues seized 35 stills a month, averaging more than one a day.

Jacksonville, FL, launching point for Bill McCoy, the "founder" of Rum Row; in 1923, the New York World called him "King of the Bootleggers."

Franklin County, VA: "There are those out there who just won't give up." Site of famous moonshine trial in 1935 covered by Sherwood Anderson for Liberty magazine. He called it "the wettest section in the U.S.A. . . . the spot that fairly dripped illicit liquor, and kept right on dripping it after prohibition ended."

"We have more illicit distilleries than any other State in the Union or any other portion of the earth; and the number is increasing." -- NC state commissioner of internal revenue, 1919.

Halifax Co., NC, home turf of Garland Bunting: "In the minds of many people he is the most successful revenue agent in the history of a state that has always been enormously productive of moonshine."

Wilkes County, NC -- near the end of World War II, some young men from the area had auto tags that said "The Moonshine Center of America." An estimated 500,000 gallons of moonshine came out of the county in 1949.

Rutherford County, NC, home of "celebrated moonshiner" Amos Owens, circa 1870-1890.

The Dark Corner of the Glassy Mountains: "There was a blockade distillery on every branch up there then."

FLORIDA

BAHAMAS

of seized stills, 1961: 1,010
ge was 395 gallons).

NASSAU

Major sources of liquor during Prohibition.

Liquor passing through Nassau en route to the U.S.: 50,000 quarts in 1917, 10,000,000 in 1922.

CUBA

Glossary

The classic, old-time moonshiner, clad in overalls. The barrel at center is a "doubler" or "thump keg." Note the tin cup hanging on the condensing barrel at right, no doubt for sampling the fresh product, and the ceramic jugs, which date this operation as from the pre-Mason jar era. The original photo is uncaptioned. *Library of Congress*

Like the customers that rumrunners, bootleggers, and moonshiners worked so hard to satisfy, the American vocabulary itself seemed to go on a bender during Prohibition. Perhaps times of high adventure or social stress, such as military combat or frontier life, tend to germinate colorful phrases and expressions. If so, the subjects of this book are perfect candidates.

Some of the terms below derive from the eighteenth and nineteenth centuries. Many of them come from Prohibition, the same fecund, erratic period studied by Edmund Wilson in 1927, when he compiled a list of 155 words and phrases meaning "drunk." The following glossary, which I assembled from multiple primary and secondary resources in the course of my own research, clearly reflects the fears, fantasies, and foes of a peculiar subculture. It is fun to read both on its own and as an index of the times.

aging: Academician John Chommie, with a touch of rare sarcasm, calls this "that period of time it takes to get the moonshine to the consumer."

bargain days: Courtroom tactic developed to cope with the backlog of liquor cases in federal courts during Prohibition. Prosecutors traded low fines and short sentences for quick pleas of "guilty." Nine of every ten convictions under the Volstead Act were obtained in this manner; partly as a result, only one case in three resulted in jail time, and fines averaged just $100–$150.

bell tree: Tree where a customer could ring an attached bell, leave money, and return shortly to collect a cup of moonshine.

black pottin': Type of still in which a single vessel serves as both the mash box and the still; spillage and scum, both inside and out, become black, as does the distillate itself during later runs.

blind tiger: Place where you could buy illegal whiskey (see "speakeasy"). The term was much in use in North Carolina at the end of the nineteenth century, during temperance campaigns to close down saloons and to increase the severity of sentences for those convicted of breaking liquor laws.

body heat: In making moonshine, the temperature (90 to 100 degrees Fahrenheit) to which the mash must cool so that the yeast can be added.

booster: Chemical substance, usually urea, added to the mash to speed fermentation. Can contain dead yeast cells, magnesium sulfate, potassium chloride, and calcium phosphate. Also known as a "kicker" or a "tickler."

bootleg bonnet: Black felt hat, prominent in cartoons of moonshiners, used to strain whiskey.

bootlegger: This flexible term has been applied to people who make, carry, or sell illegal liquor, and even to people who merely adulterate brand-name liquor with cheap booze; also called "blind-pigger." Evangelist Billy Sunday defined the term in this way: "a symptom of three diseases on the body politic—a traitorous, vile citizen who sells the liquor, a traitorous, vile citizen who buys it, and a spineless official who winks at the proceedings." The term remains in use.

booze ballet: Sarcastic term for what smugglers did to try to elude the Coast Guard boats that were trailing them. They would darken the ship abruptly and change course, sometimes right across the bow of the trailer. The destroyer *Davis* collided with and sank a rumrunner named *Shubenacadia* when it tried this ploy.

built time: Time spent in the penitentiary for making or hauling moonshine.

bumper joint: Illegal saloon in a big city (usually in a ghetto) that sells moonshine; also known as a "shine house."

bush-bond: Humorous term for when a bootlegger had to abandon his car and flee through the woods.

Cape Horn rainwater: Sailor slang for rum in colonial times; someone who had drunk too much was said to be "carrying too much sail," "flying the ensign," or "listing to starboard."

Carry Nation's Navy: The Coast Guard during Prohibition.

Clark's No. 20 telegraph line: ATF investigator Jack Kearins' term for the fine black thread that some moonshiners strung around their stills so that they could tell if anyone had been there.

cobweb: 1930's slang in Virginia for a smalltime, backwoods moonshiner.

coffin varnish: See "rotgut."

Cold Water Brigade: Name of a temperance group; another group was called the Children of Drunkards.

column still: One of the two types of stills. This type, used by legal distilleries, was invented by Robert Stein in 1826 and provides continuous distillation. It has by far the largest capacity, but also requires more skilled labor, and is much more expensive and complex to build.

convoying: Using an extra car to accompany a load of moonshine, in order to act as a lookout. If the liquor was in a truck, for example, the convoy car would pass the truck to check the highway ahead for roadblocks, then drop back to check behind for trailing cars.

cooling barrel: Traditionally, a barrel of water in which the condenser was submerged.

crashing the pavement: When a police officer was strictly enforcing the law in a particular area of town.

dead line: Newspaper slang from the 1920s for the three-mile limit.

deadwagon: Car driven by revenuers, and ridden in by arrested moonshiners.

deal man: Person whose business it was to sell liquor and help haul it.

deluxe turnaround: A bootlegger's tour de force, it involved throwing the car into a skid, applying the emergency brake lightly, spinning the steering wheel, and flooring the accelerator; also called a "bootleg turn." National Association for Stock Car Automobile Racing (NASCAR) driver Curtis Turner allegedly once did a deluxe turnaround for a West Coast journalist in the middle of a Los Angeles freeway, and then did another for the state trooper who pulled him over.

doubled and twisted: According to author Joseph Dabney, this term "refers to the fact that doubled whiskey makes a final twist when it leaves the end of the condenser."

doubler: Second still, which helped remove residue from the distillate and also raised its alcohol content.

draggers: Slang for small fisherman's boats, from the fact that they dragged nets. Author Everett Allen also uses this term for the boats that ferried liquor ashore, boats that he says "never went fishing," recalling that their quarter bitts were brand new, whereas the bitts on a working vessel were worn.

dropped over the wall: Coast Guard slang for "thrown overboard," the fate of many rumrunners at the hands of seagoing hijackers, or vice versa.

fix: To bribe; to "fix a bull" meant to pay off a cop.

flusher: An agent who slips into a still, "grabs one or more" violators, and "shoots signals to designate the direction those trying to escape are taking," as George Griffith, a former federal judge, explained.

four-stacker: Slang for the Navy destroyers reconditioned and used by the Coast Guard when they stepped up their war against the rumrunners.

la fraude: On St. Pierre, "the French remember 1922 to 1933 as the time of *la fraude* ('the smuggle')," a newspaper article said.

frog eyes: If you shake fresh moonshine, it produces bubbles, called the "bead." The bead indicates the proof of the liquor by how much of the bubble is out of the liquid. According to author Esther Kellner, "frog eyes" is a term for "big, loose, collapsing bubbles," which meant "the whiskey was weak and inferior." Also called "rabbit eyes."

Gospel Barge: Nickname for a fishing schooner (named the *Beacon of Hope*) that was manned with evangelists and that visited Rum Row in the early days, hoping to convert the sinners.

go-through men: People who hijacked liquor at sea.

granny fees: Bribes paid by bootleggers to local authorities in small towns. The places where these fees were paid were called "grease spots" or "toll bridges."

groundhog: A still that has a wood top and bottom, and metal sides; it is buried and heated from the sides only.

ham: Six bottles of illegal liquor packaged in a burlap sack stuffed with straw. One source described this packaging containing six bottles as a "pyramid padded with straw or corrugated cardboard," also referred to as a "sack" or a "burlock."

hatchet man: The revenuer whose job it was to smash up a still, in the days before dynamite became the destructive agent of choice.

headache producer: Journalist slang in the 1920s for liquor.

headache stick: The pipe that runs into the doubler.

hell-kettles: Temperance society term (circa late 1800s) for a distillery, especially distilleries located outside of town, which were prohibited by some of the restrictive state laws enacted before statewide prohibition.

hootchmobile: A rumrunner's car, auctioned by authorities after it was confiscated; also "boozemobile," "beermobile," and "toddy wagon."

hoss eyes: The highest proof moonshine.

hulled out: A bootlegger's car with the braces removed between the rear seat and trunk, to enlarge the capacity of the trunk.

keg men: Middlemen who picked up moonshine from local moonshiners who worked as subcontractors for wealthy gangsters, investors, or organizers.

kingpin: Term for a well-known or successful transporter.

knee-walker: Descriptive term for what you embark on when you drink too much moonshine.

knock off: To hijack.

known-still seizure: Seizure that nets the operators at the site.

loafing rooms: Recruiting sites in New England fishing towns for rumrunners who were looking for workers. The rooms were sometimes located in the back rooms of grocery stores or in shacks on the wharves; out-of-work men hung out there, swapping news and getting illegal drinks.

lush: Rumrunner slang for booze.

mash hounds: Alcoholics who discovered stills and drank directly from them.

mashing-in: Using some of the mash from a previous batch as a source of yeast to start a new batch of mash. Also called "yeasting back," "slopping back," or "backing up."

meal mammy: Fermented mash. North Carolina revenuer Garland Bunting told author Alec Wilkinson that the name comes from the fact that "after it's processed it's so strong it'll make you fight your mammy." Also called "still beer" or "meal beer."

milk route: Slang for delivering liquor, usually in smaller amounts.

moonshine: This term appears in eighteenth-century British dictionaries, meaning someone who made and smuggled liquor into England from France and Holland. "As early as 1796, white brandy smuggled on the coasts of Kent and Sussex, and gin smuggled in the north of Yorkshire, were known as 'moonshine,'" Esther Kellner writes. Note that this old meaning doesn't refer to making the liquor, just transporting it (an eighteenth century euphemism for smuggling was "fair trade"). Another old meaning of "moonshine" was "airy fabrication or empty talk," a common result of consuming the liquor. Modern dictionaries say that the term is usually attributed to a simple joining of the root words.

Moonshine Belt: Term used in the anti-moonshine annual reports published by Licensed Beverage Industries, Inc., referring to Oklahoma, Arkansas, Virginia, West Virginia, Tennessee, North and South Carolina, Georgia, Alabama, Mississippi, and Florida. As the 1971 report pointed out, still seizures in this region averaged 14.9 per 100,000 population; outside the Moonshine Belt, seizures were just 0.09 per 100,000 (less than 1 percent, in other terms).

moonshiner: Often used to mean the maker of illegal liquor, as opposed to the "runner" (who transported it, also called a "blockader" or "transporter").

needle: To add a one-ounce vial of alcohol to a bottle of near-beer, producing a beer that is roughly 8 percent alcohol.

owlers: What British excise offices called rumrunners in New England during colonial times.

piss pot: A smalltime still, ignored by federal agents who were after bigger operators.

porthole business: Buying small amounts of illegal liquor ship to ship.

pots: Individual units of distilleries, generally (in modern times) holding 800 gallons From the term "black pot stills."

pot still: The smallest, simplest, and most common type of still, usually run once a week and producing between fifty and several hundred gallons; also called a "turnip bottom." Several types of pot stills have been described by ATF: steamer, copper pot, metal pot, groundhog, Alabama type, submarine (wood top and sides, metal bottom, set over furnace), and jimbuck (fire built in a metal flue inside a wooden box or barrel).

pot-column stills: Hybrid of the two basic types of stills; variants include the "St. Louis" and the "mushroom."

puking: When steam and solid matter arrive in the doubler while the still is operating, they signal a stage of the operation; however, when an operating still boils over and sends too much solid matter into the pipes, doubler, or worm, it can be disastrous, spoiling the whiskey.

pull the copper: To quickly disassemble a still after hearing a warning that revenuers were coming.

pulled: Seized or destroyed; used when talking about a still.

puller: A small, speedy boat used by rumrunners to transport illegal liquor from the "mother ships" anchored out beyond the nautical limit of Coast Guard enforcement. Also called "contact boats," "go-through jobs," and "the sunset fleet."

pumice: A fruit-based mash used for making moonshine brandy. Crushed apples, for example, would be used for making apple brandy. It was also called "pummie."

quill: Straw used for sampling the finished mash (also called "still beer"), which, Dabney wrote, many moonshiners consider a tasty drink.

racket: Physical disturbance created by enforcement of liquor laws, circa 1880s. In a description of an 1881 still seizure, the word was defined as "a difficulty" in "moonshine parlance."

rat houses: Turn-of-the-century log cabins in Appalachia, next to the road, which had a small opening through which you could insert a container and buy moonshine.

red dog: Ground rye meal, an ingredient of moonshine.

red liquor: In some accounts, "red liquor" means spirits, usually whiskey, bought legally but sold illegally. On the other hand, "white liquor" is made illegally. Dabney defines "white" whiskey as "distilled but unaged." According to Kellner, "red liquor" was also an early name for legal bourbon.

rotgut: A common term for bad moonshine or adulterated liquor; also called "coffin varnish" or "embalming fluid."

rummies: Coast Guard nickname for rumrunners.

Rum Row: Nickname for the areas at sea (just outside the distance where the Coast Guard could enforce the law) where rumrunner ships would congregate awaiting the smaller boats that smuggled the liquor ashore. Rum Rows existed along the Atlantic seaboard, near the major ports and big urban centers; the largest was off the New Jersey Highlands, handy to the port of New York. The original three-mile limit was easy to beat; it was later extended to twelve miles or one hour's sailing distance from shore.

run, running: These terms appear in descriptions of stills (where you "run" off a batch of moonshine), and in transporting. Police and ATF agents use the term to mean "chasing," often called "running 'em."

running cold: A bootlegger who carried a cargo of water to keep his car from at-

tracting attention by riding too high; by exchanging the water for moonshine, you were "running wet."

sandpounders: Coast Guard members stationed ashore near areas of dangerous navigation or frequent shipwreck; they made frequent beach patrols.

scout: A Coast Guard boat, usually a destroyer, that kept track of the identity and location of rumrunners. Or Coast Guard craft that followed the rumrunners; these boats were called "trailers."

scratch feed: Hog or chicken feed, used in moonshining because it is cheaper than cornmeal.

shock houses: Rotgut-serving speakeasies in the New York slums, sometimes selling wood alcohol, which, as Henry Lee described them in *How Dry We Were*, "sent their shabby patrons reeling into the streets where they collapsed, blinded, paralyzed and often dead."

silver cloud: Nickname for stills made during World War II from galvanized sheet metal or barn roofing, when other, higher-quality metals were scarce. These stills posed a serious health hazard because edges were soldered (which leached toxic lead into the distillate) rather than welded or riveted. Also called "blue kettle" or "gray ghost."

singlin's: First distillate that begins to run from the still. Also called "low wines" (when this liquid is run through the still again, called "doubling," it becomes "high wines").

six-bitter: Seventy-five-foot Coast Guard cutter, the "mainstay" of the picketing fleet ("two bits" is old slang for a quarter, twenty-five cents).

slop: Leftover grain from the first run of whiskey. When more ingredients are added to it, it is called "slopping back."

snowballs: Bubbles produced as the mash is fermenting.

sneak car: A beat-up old car, also called a "slip by"; the bootlegger's alternative to an expensive, customized hot rod.

speakeasy: Perhaps the most common Prohibition era term for an illegal bar; also called an "oasis."

squatting and scooting: Description of what a loaded liquor car does.

standing on its head: Appearance of an unloaded car equipped with extra springs for carrying moonshine (also called "tiptoeing"). A load of moonshine would "level" it.

stash house boys: Still hands who tend the

storage aspect of the operation.

steam plant: A huge still, some rivaling legal distilleries, capable of producing thousands of gallons. Also called "factory stills"; they have been known to ship from North Carolina and Georgia to the major cities of the Northeast.

still: Derives from the word "distill." There are two basic kinds of stills: the traditional small, family-type still was often called a "copper boiler" (using wood, coal, or coke to apply flame directly to the mash). The newer, larger stills are called "steamers" (no direct flame is applied to the mash; the steam is piped in).

still cutters: Revenue agents who specialize in demolishing stills. When a still has been "cut," it has been seized and destroyed.

still jigger: Vehicle like a dune buggy, used by moonshiners in the Big Bend region along the St. Mary's River on the Georgia-Florida border north of Jacksonville. They run it on trails made by pigs, hunters, or timber crews.

still rations: Rural convenience-store diet, favored by moonshiners, revenuers, and construction workers alike: canned pork and beans, Vienna sausages, Saltines, and soft drinks.

submarine: Device used by nautical bootleggers on Lake Champlain; it held the contraband liquor and was towed on a rope behind the smuggler's boat. If they were caught, they cut the rope and the submarine would sink. They could then return, find the floating rope, and retrieve the load.

submarine still: A large, professional pot still, capable of holding as much as a thousand gallons of mash, sometimes used in tandem. They were developed to meet the skyrocketing demand for moonshine during Prohibition.

suitcase brigade: Train passengers who filled their luggage with illegal liquor, usually traveling down from Canada to the U.S.

sunset fleet: Coast Guard's foes during Prohibition: small, speedy, or disguised boats that carried liquor from the large ships on Rum Row to shore. See "contact boats" and "pullers."

tailin's: Last of the run from a still, of a higher alcohol percentage. Also called "backin's" or "faints."

ten sack: Measurement of the capacity of a still. Weems wrote that a "ten sack ground hog" was a 1,000 gallons, groundhog-style still.

test boat: Undercover boat operated by the Coast Guard to make liquor purchases. If successful, the Coast Guard could cite several apparent infractions of the law. They could then seize the boat from which they had bought the liquor.

thump keg: Nickname for the "doubler," located between the still and the worm, which accomplished the second distillation. The steam from the still made a thumping noise as it arrived. Some moonshiners didn't like the device because they thought the sound would attract revenuers.

tote and tell man: A minor bootlegger who moved to the city, and used his trips home to load up on moonshine, which he took back to sell in the city, circa 1930–1970.

trap: Where moonshine would be hidden in a house: under floorboards or trapdoors under carpets, in walls behind mirrors or pictures, behind sliding doors in cabinets.

trip boys: The people who deliver moonshine. Also called "trippers," and (in the mountains of the South) "ridge runners."

wet goods importer: How New York newspapers referred to rumrunning mobsters such as Charles "Vannie" Higgins (he called himself a "lobster fisherman").

whammy: A six-inch-wide strip of steel with spikes in it, like the one that caused Luke Doolin's fatal crash at the conclusion of the film *Thunder Road*. These devices were actually used.

Revenue agents display at least two copper stills they have confiscated; the worms decorate the front fenders. For some reason, they have disassembled the stills carefully, instead of chopping them up. Perhaps they could sell the scrap copper and keep the profit. Left to right: Thomas S. Tyson, Thomas Brown, and Enoch Oliver. Emanuel County, Georgia, 1920s. *Courtesy Georgia Department of Archives and History*

whisky fire: Supreme hazard for rumrunners in wooden ships loaded with liquor.

white lightning: In some accounts, as late as the nineteenth century some Americans believed that there were two kinds of lightning, one white, the other red or bluish red. A fire started by the former allegedly couldn't be put out, which suggests the initial sensation produced by a gulp of moonshine whiskey.

whopping the cap: Tapping the cap of a still with a stick in order to judge if the pressure is building or reducing.

wildcatter: Another name for a moonshiner, circa 1920–1960.

worm: The coil that runs from the mash container and acts as a condenser during distillation.

Year of the Big Thirst: Nickname for the Prohibition era.

Bibliography

Books

Allen, Everett S. *The Black Ships: Rumrunners of Prohibition*, Boston: Little, Brown and Co., 1965.

Atkinson, George, Frew and Campbell. *After the Moonshiners: By One of the Raiders*, Wheeling, W. Va.: Steam Book and Job Printers, 1881.

Baker, Charles H. *Around the World with Jigger, Beaker and Flask* (Vol. II of *The Gentleman's Companion*), Crown Publishers, 1956.

Beck, Ken and Jim Clark. *Aunt Bee's Mayberry Cookbook*, Nashville, Tenn.: Rutledge Hill Press, 1991.

Benyo, Richard. *Superspeedway: The Story of NASCAR Grand National Racing*, New York: Mason/Charter, 1977.

Butterworth, W. E. *The High Wind: The Story of NASCAR Racing*, New York: Grosset & Dunlap, 1971.

Carr, Jess. *The Second Oldest Profession: An Informal History of Moonshining in America*, Englewood Cliffs, N.J.: Prentice-Hall, Inc., 1972.

Carter, Joseph. *Damn the Allegators*, Tabor City, N.C.: Atlantic Publishing Co., 1989.

Chapin, Kim. *Fast as White Lightning: The Story of Stock Car Racing*, New York: Dial Press, 1981.

Chommie, John C. *The Internal Revenue Service*, New York: Praeger Publishers, Inc., 1970.

Coffey, Thomas. *The Long Thirst—Prohibition in America, 1920–1933*, New York: W.W. Norton & Co., Inc., 1975.

Corbett, Scott. *The Sea Fox: The Adventures of Cape Cod's Most Colorful Rumrunner*, New York: Thomas Y. Crowell Co., 1956.

Crider, Curtis. *The Road to Daytona*, Ormond Beach, Fla.: self-published, 1987.

Dabney, Joseph Earl. *Mountain Spirits: A Chronicle of Corn Whiskey from King James' Ulster Plantation to America's Appalachians and the Moonshine Life*, New York: Charles Scribner's Sons,1974.

Everest, Allan S. *Rum Across the Border*, Syracuse, N.Y.: Syracuse University Press, 1978.

Fielden, Greg. *Forty Years of Stock Car Racing: The Beginning 1949—1958*, Pinehurst, N.C.: Galfield Press, 1988.

Fisher, Ronald M. *The Appalachian Trail*, National Geographic Society, Washington, DC, 1972.

Fisher, Irving. *Prohibition at Its Worst*, New York: The Macmillan Co., 1926.

Gabbard, Alex. *Return to Thunder Road: The Story Behind the Legend*, Lenoir City, Tenn.: Gabbard Publications, 1992.

Girdler, Allan. *Stock Car Racers*, Osceola, Wis.: Motorbooks International, 1988.

Griffith, George P. *Life and Adventures of Revenooer No. 1*, Birmingham, Ala.: Gander Publishers, 1975.

Henry, Williams A. III. *The Great One*, Doubleday, 1992.

Herter, George Leonard. *Moonshiners Bible*, Wauseca, Minn., 1976.

Kearins, Jack. *Yankee Revenooer*, Durham, N.C.: Moore Publishing Co., 1969.

Kellner, Esther. *Moonshine: Its History and Folklore*, Indianapolis: The Bobbs-Merrill Co., 1971.

Lee, Henry. *How Dry We Were: Prohibition Revisited*, Englewood Cliffs, N.J.: Prentice-Hall, Inc., 1963.

Libby, Bill. *Heroes of Stock Car Racing*, New York: Random House, Inc., 1975.

Marill, Alvin H. *Robert Mitchum on the Screen*, South Brunswick and New York: A.S. Barnes and Co., 1978.

McCarthy Todd and Charles Flynn (eds.). *Kings of the Bs: Working Within the Hollywood System*, New York: E.P. Dutton & Co., Inc.,1975.

McMullen, W. George. *Twenty-Eight Years a "T-Man,"* self-published, 1986.

Merz, Charles. *The Dry Decade*, Doubleday, Doran and Co., 1930.

Miller, Wilbur. *Revenuers & Moonshiners: Enforcing Federal Liquor Law in the Mountain South, 1865–1900*, Chapel Hill, N.C.: University of North Carolina Press, 1991.

Moray, Alastair. *The Diary of a Rum-Runner*, New York: Houghton Mifflin Co., 1929.

Pack, A. J. and Kenneth Mason. *Nelson's Blood*, Homewell, Havant, Hampshire, England, 1982.

Roberts, Jerry. *Robert Mitchum, a Bio-Bibliography*, Westport, Conn.: Greenwood Press, 1992.

Schmeckebier, Laurence. *The Bureau of Prohibition, Its History, Activities and Organization*, Service Monographs of the U.S. Government No. 57, The Brookings Institution, Washington, DC, 1929.

Sinclair, Andrew. *Prohibition: The Era of Excess*, Boston: Little, Brown and Co., 1962.

Stick, David. *The Outer Banks of North Carolina*, Chapel Hill, N.C.: University of North Carolina Press, 1958.

Travis, Kenneth L. *"Buck" Davis and Northwest Florida Moonshine Whiskey*, unpublished manuscript, April 1963.

Waters, Harold. *Smugglers of Spirits: Prohibition and the Coast Guard Patrol*, New York: Hastings House, Publishers, 1971.

Weems, Charles. *A Breed Apart*, Tabor City, N.C.: Atlantic Printing, 1992.

Whitener, Daniel J. *Prohibition in North Carolina, 1715–1945*, Chapel Hill, N.C.: University of North Carolina Press, 1945.

Wilkerson, Tichi and Marcia Borie. *The Holly-*

wood Reporter: The Golden Years, New York: Arlington House, Inc., 1984.

Wilkinson, Alec. *Moonshine: A Life in Pursuit of White Liquor*, New York: Alfred A. Knopf, Inc., 1985.

Wilkinson, Sylvia. *Dirt Tracks to Glory: The Early Days of Stock Car Racing as Told by the Participants,* Chapel Hill, N.C.: Algonquin Books,1983.

Magazine and Newspaper Articles

Barbiaux, Clarey. "Thunder on the Road," *Motor Trend,* July 1958.

Bunting, Garland as told to Jane Sanderson. "Wisdom by the Gallon," *People Weekly,* March 31, 1986.

Calver, John. "Rum Running in the Good Old Days," *Newfoundland Lifestyle,* undated.

Canney, Donald L. "Rum War: The U.S. Coast Guard and Prohibition," The Coast Guard Commandant's Bulletin Bicentennial Series, undated.

Christopher, Rita. "That Good Ol' Mountain Dew," *Maclean's,* March 3, 1980.

Clark, Jim (ed.). *The Bullet,* official newsletter of The Andy Griffith Show Rerun Watchers Club, Vol. 8, Issue 3, April 30, 1993.

Durward, John. "The Portland Rum Runners," *Portland* magazine, 1984.

Fetterman, John. "The People of Cumberland Gap," *National Geographic,* November 1971.

Fulks, Danny. "Moonshine Reflections," *Timeline,* Ohio Historical Society, June/July 1990.

Gabbard, Alex. "Return to Thunder Road," *Down Memory Lane,* May 1992.

Hadley-Garcia, George. "Mitchum!," *Hollywood Studio Magazine,* March 1983.

Hopkins, Harold. "Blue Language and the Jakewalk Blues," *FDA Consumer,* June 1980.

"Illicit Distilling," *Investigator Basic Training Publication No. 1490,* Alcohol and Tobacco Tax-Enforcement Division, Internal Revenue Service, February 1966.

Kobler, John. "King of the Moonshiners," *Saturday Evening Post,* August 2, 1958.

Loh, Jules. "Big Six Henderson," reprinted in *The Word* by Rene J. Cappon, New York: Associated Press, 1982.

"Marion County Moonshiner," Associated Press, *Atlanta Journal,* May 26, 1977.

Mooney, Brenda. "Moonshine Squeeze," *Atlanta Constitution* (Associated Press), October 5, 1975.

"Moonshine—Misery for Sale," pamphlet, 23rd Annual Report of Licensed Beverage Industries, Inc., 1971.

Raver-Lampman, Greg. "A Short Time in a Very Hard Place," *Virginian-Pilot,* Norfolk, VA, June 3, 1990.

"Rumrunner—Enemy No. 1," *Daily News,* St. John's, Newfoundland, July 1965.

Salter, Charles. "Chasin' Moonshiners Wasn't Like Thunder Road," *Atlanta Journal,* June 28, 1977.

Sibley, Celestine. "Moonshiner Gives Judge No Promises," *Atlanta Constitution,* June 22, 1977.

Starman, Ray. "Arthur Ripley," *Films in Review,* March 1987.

Swan, Neil. "Moonshiners at Work Here—Brewing Gasohol, Legally," *Atlanta Journal,* November 30, 1978.

"The Coast Guard vs. Smugglers, 1920s Style," Naval History magazine, oral histories from Adm. Alfred C. Richmond, USCG (Ret.) and Adm. Edwin J. Roland, USCG (Ret.), Summer 1988.

"The Early Years," *Naval Aviation News,* May/June 1983.

Thompson, Richard. "Thunder Road: Maudit—'The Devil Got Him First'," 1969, *December,* No. 11.

Thornton, Mark. "Prohibition's Failure: Lessons for Today," *USA Today,* March 1992.

Tucker, Cynthia. "Moonshine Goes Suburban," *Atlanta Journal,* December 1977.

Virginian-Pilot and *Norfolk Landmark:* Issues include 1/4/21, 4/23/21, 5/1/23, 5/30/23, 6/2/23, 6/3/23, 6/4/23, 6/5/23, 12/10/24, 2/23/25, 2/26/25, 3/2/25, 3/4/25, 3/21/25; 5/1-5/4, 1926; 6/9/36. The series of articles about the woman moonshiner ran in the Norfolk *Virginian-Pilot* beginning on December 9, 1924. Issues of the Norfolk *Ledger-Dispatch:* 6/2/23, 6/4/23, 12/9/24, 12/11/24, 5/5/25, 5/3/26.

Weisburger, Bernard. "Reflections on a Dry Season," *American Heritage,* May/June 1990.

"Seeking a Real Tax Revolt," *American Heritage,* May/June 1991.

Zierler, Amy. "St. Pierre: *C'est si bon," Atlantic Insight,* July 1981.

Movies and Video

"Main Attractions," P.O. Box 4923, Chatsworth, CA 91313-4923.

Index